# GREEN'S GUIDE TO

# ENVIRONMENTAL LAW

# IN SCOTLAND

GREEN'S GUIDE TO

# ENVIRONMENTAL LAW

IN SCOTLAND

Edited by Colin T. Reid
*Senior lecturer in law*
*University of Dundee*

W. GREEN/Sweet & Maxwell
EDINBURGH
1992

First published 1992

ISBN 0 414 01022 1


A catalogue record for this book
is available from the British Library


Typeset by LBJ Enterprises Ltd.
of Aldermaston and Chilcompton
Printed in Great Britain by
Butler and Tanner Ltd.,
Frome, Somerset

# PREFACE

Environmental Law is becoming increasingly important for many aspects of legal and commercial life. However, the law is also becoming more complex, and the mass of detailed regulations which face anyone trying to find the law is both confusing and off-putting. There appeared to be a need for a book which would introduce people to the subject and present an overall picture of the most important areas of environmental control. This book is an attempt to meet that need. Its aim is as stated in the title: to offer a Guide to Environmental Law in Scotland.

The contributors were each asked to provide, in their own way, a short introduction to their topic, to offer a sketch-map presenting the general outline and structure of the law and pointing to where more information could be found. We have not attempted to provide a comprehensive statement of the law, nor to provide a critical assessment of it, but rather to present an introduction for those who are not familiar with the areas of law covered. We hope that it will provide a starting point for legal practitioners and a useful guide for all those who need to understand something of the range of legal measures designed to regulate our impact on the environment.

Environmental Law is developing rapidly at present, with new legislation emerging every year. This has had two consequences for the presentation of this book. First, a considerable amount of significant legislation was due to come into force during and shortly after the writing and production of the book, e.g. it has been announced that several parts of the Environmental Protection Act 1990 will be coming into force during 1992 and early 1993. In such circumstances it is virtually impossible (and not necessarily particularly helpful) to state the law as at one particular date, which would inevitably have to be a considerable time prior to publication, thereby guaranteeing that the book was out of date when it was bought. In view of the general aim of the book, we thought it better to look forward rather than back, and throughout the book it has generally been assumed that the recent legislation has been or will be brought

v

*Preface*

into force as scheduled, so that we can present a guide to the law as it is developing, rather than as it was in the past.

Secondly, the mass of recent legislation has resulted in many amendments to older statutes and regulations, sometimes changes of major importance, but frequently mere consequential amendments arising from the changing names of public bodies or from amendments to the law in related fields. Listing every amendment to every piece of legislation mentioned in this book would fill pages by itself (some have been amended almost a dozen times, with no fundamental alterations), and again bearing in mind the aim of this book, as a general rule we have mentioned specifically only those amendments of particular significance. In all cases the statutory references should be read as references to the relevant provisions as amended.

As editor, I must express my sincere gratitude to all of the contributors who, despite their many other commitments, so willingly embarked on the task of providing their chapters within a fairly short timescale. Several may have missed the first deadline I gave them, but every contribution was in my hands in time for the real deadline which had been arranged with the publishers. I must also thank the families, secretaries and colleagues who may have assisted in meeting the deadlines, or suffered as a result of them. My thanks also go to Fiona Walker for her assistance with the references.

I must also express my thanks to the various staff at Green's for their work in producing the book. Mention should perhaps also be made of the indirect role played by Green's in its conception, as I first proposed the idea in detail and discussed it with potential contributors at the reception to mark the opening of their Alva Street offices (at an early stage in the evening!).

Colin T. Reid
5 February, 1992


At proof stage is has proved possible to include some more recent developments, but the intervening months have only added to the uncertainty on several issues, *e.g.* the future of the registers of potentially contaminated land (chapter 4).

CTR
8 June, 1992

# CONTENTS

## 1. Introduction                                                1
Colin T. Reid,
*Senior Lecturer in Law, University of Dundee*

## 2. Air                                                        16
Jennifer M. Fletcher,
*Solicitor*

## 3. Water Pollution                                            38
Francis Lyall,
*Professor of Public Law, University of Aberdeen*

## 4. Waste                                                      58
Paul Q. Watchman,
*Freshfields; Visiting Professor of Land Economy, University of Aberdeen; formerly Partner and Head of Environmental Law, Brodies,W.S.*

## 5. Integrated Pollution Control                               80
J. Michael G. Blair,
*Environmental Partner, Thorntons, W.S.*

Contents

# Table of Cases

# Table of Cases

# Table of Cases

xi

# Table of Cases

# Table of Statutes

# Table of Statutes

# Table of Statutes

# Table of Statutes

# Table of Statutes

# Table of Statutes

# Table of Statutory Instruments

## Table of Statutory Instruments

# Table of Statutory Instruments

# Table of Statutory Instruments

# Table of European Legislation

# Table of European Legislation

# 1. Introduction

Although environmental law is thought of as being a new subject, the **1.1.1** law in Scotland has long been concerned with such matters. Looking simply at legislation from the Scottish Parliament, the main concern at first was with the preservation of natural resources for exploitation by the community (or often by certain privileged members of the community), *e.g.* there are many provisions concerned with protecting the king's forests[1] and regulating the taking of game,[2] including a partial moratorium on hunting at a time when a shortage of game had developed.[3] Protecting people and their property from the risks of the natural world was another aim, *e.g.* in laws encouraging the destruction of birds viewed as agricultural pests[4] and prohibiting the pulling of vegetation on sand dunes to prevent erosion causing harm to inhabited areas.[5] Other laws fit more closely the modern conception of environmental law, *e.g.* prohibitions on water pollution resulting from the washing of green lint in lochs and streams[6] and regulations on where and how offensive and hazardous trades could operate in Edinburgh.[7]

However, other than the game laws, these provisions have left little **1.1.2** trace in the modern law, which is essentially a response to the problems of the industrial age. The law of nuisance developed at the end of the eighteenth century[8] and during the nineteenth century there was considerable legislative intervention to protect the living and working conditions of the population: the Factories Acts from 1833, the Nuisances Removal and Diseases Prevention Act 1848 and its successors, the Alkali Acts from 1863, and the Public Health (Scotland) Act 1897, parts of which remain in force. During the twentieth century the authorities responsible for administering such provisions have been transformed, and environmental regulation has increased dramatically in scope and detail. The Clean Air Acts of 1956 and 1968 and the Control of Pollution Act 1974 established frameworks for a broad range of controls, supported by volumes of delegated legislation, while the Environmental Protection Act 1990 marks the start of a new chapter in our environmental law.

**1.1.3** Recent developments in the law reveal a number of trends. First, the international scale of modern environmental problems has meant that our law is increasingly influenced by developments at a European and global level. Pollution does not stop at national frontiers, and states have become increasingly aware of the need for concerted action to ensure that the environment is adequately protected, the willingness to co-operate being enhanced by the realisation that differing environmental standards could considerably distort the international marketplace. Thus although the law continues to be structured and enforced within a national framework, the substantive rules contained in the law are increasingly the product of international agreement at some level, whether detailed European legislation or the broad declarations from global conferences.

**1.1.4** A second trend has been towards integration of the legal approaches to environmental matters. Just as it has been realised that national environments cannot be treated separately, it has been realised that it is also impossible to isolate the various elements of the environment and to deal with each separately. The traditional approach had been to deal with air pollution separately from water pollution and from waste disposal, but the need for a more integrated approach has been realised, to ensure that pollution is not merely transferred from one medium to another and that the best environmental option can be chosen. This is reflected in various recent changes to the law, *e.g.* Integrated Pollution Control under the Environmental Protection Act 1990, whereby all of the environmental consequences of a process are considered at once,[9] and environmental assessment in the planning system, where all aspects of the environmental impact of a proposed development are considered.[10] Likewise, the duty of care in relation to waste ensures that those producing and handling waste must think about all stages in its processing "from the cradle to the grave,"[11] and the growing use of environmental auditing[12] aims to encourage industrial concerns to assess all of the consequences of their activities.

**1.1.5** The desire for an integrated approach is also reflected by the reduction in the number of authorities with responsibilities for environmental matters. Scottish Natural Heritage has been created as a single body concerned with nature conservation, landscape preservation, amenity and recreation in the countryside, merging the functions previously split between the Nature Conservancy Council for Scotland and the Countryside Commission for Scotland.[13]

More significantly, proposals have been announced for the cre- **1.1.6** ation of a single Scottish Environment Protection Agency to take over the environmental responsibilities of local authorities, the river purification boards and Her Majesty's Industrial Pollution Inspectorate (HMIPI).[14] It is proposed that a non-departmental public body should be created, operating at arm's length from the government and providing a single expert agency to operate environmental controls in Scotland. This body would be able to take a fully integrated approach to its tasks and would be free from the potential conflicts of interest which arise from the range of functions carried out by local authorities. The new body is to be organised on a regional and area basis, building on the existing structure of the river purification boards, and regional advisory committees may be established to advise it in its work. The new agency would take over all the tasks of the river purification authorities[15] and HMIPI[16] and assume responsibility from local authorities in their capacities as waste regulation authorities[17] and as the operators of local authority air pollution control,[18] although some responsibility for air pollution, *e.g.* in relation to smoke control, may remain with local authorities. It is thought that April 1995 is the earliest that the new body could come into operation.

A third trend has been to increase the potential for public involve- **1.1.7** ment in environmental regulation. One of the features of the past reliance on regulatory authorities has been the very limited opportunities for members of the public to become involved in matters of environmental control. In the absence of legal title deriving from some direct consequences for individual health or property rights, it has not been possible for individuals to take action to enforce environmental standards, or even discover the basic information on which assessments of the health of the environment and the level of pollution could be made. Everything was left to the wide discretion of the regulatory bodies.

Now, largely prompted by European developments,[19] much more **1.1.8** information is available through public registers which are a feature of many of the new regulatory schemes,[20] and through the availability of environmental assessment statements for certain new developments.[21] The availability of this information allows the public to discover the state of the environment and the causes of harm to it,

3

enabling those concerned to apply pressure much more effectively on the government and the regulatory bodies. Whether the citizen armed with such information may also be able to take legal action against the regulators or polluters in order to enforce compliance with the prescribed standards has not yet been fully explored in Scotland, but the Scots tradition on title and interest may be more generous in this respect than that in England and Wales where environmental claims have foundered on this point.[22] In the United States, action by citizens to ensure that environmental requirements are met are a major feature of this area of the law, and some European proposals have also indicated a willingness to allow citizens to play a major role.[23]

## LEGAL APPROACHES

**1.2.1**  A variety of methods is used in the regulation of man's impact on the environment. The law of delict, especially nuisance, still has a role to play in imposing liability for harm caused to other people and their property.[24] The common law is, however, limited, primarily because it is only a pursuer whose legal rights have been damaged who can raise an action. This means firstly that the law cannot be activated by some forms of environmental harm (*e.g.* chemical pollution killing wild animals, since these are not the subject of any property rights) or can be activated only when the harm reaches a fairly serious level at which property rights are affected (*e.g.* there is no general legal right to insist on wholly clean air or a clean environment, the only right of action being to protect one's health and the value and quiet enjoyment of one's property).

**1.2.2**  The second limitation of the common law arises from the limited class of pursuers. There must be a pursuer whose rights have been affected willing to raise the action. If activity on a piece of land is causing severe environmental damage, but only to the same proprietor's land, there is no possibility of third parties intervening, and in many situations the personal or economic relationship between the potential pursuers and the defender may be such that legal action is unlikely. On the other hand, the protection of an aggrieved neighbour's private rights may be allowed to stand in the way of works which may inevitably cause some nuisance, but are very much in the public interest. The common law is also not very good at ensuring that appropriate preventive steps are taken. It may be possible to obtain an interdict where there is a clear risk of harm being caused, but something more is needed to ensure that proper safeguards are taken at all stages of the construction and operation of potentially polluting plant, etc.

There is thus a need for legal intervention in the public interest. This **1.2.3** can take several forms. Perhaps the most common is to create some form of administrative regulatory system. Before an activity can lawfully be carried out, official permission is required from a regulatory agency. Within the broad framework set by legislation, the agency will have considerable discretion in deciding whether and on what conditions permission should be granted, and in the event of a breach of control, in deciding what sanction, if any, should be applied. This model allows for a flexible system of control, taking account of all the local and particular factors affecting individual sites.

In terms of determining the standards to be applied, again there is **1.2.4** a range of possibilities. In the past the British tendency has been for the flexible approach which flows from a requirement that any factory or the like adopt the "best practicable means" to avoid pollution, allowing the environmental context and other considerations, including the costs of reducing pollution, to be taken into account, rather than insisting on fixed and measurable limits. This flexible approach has now been refined into the concept of Best Available Techniques not Entailing Excessive Cost (BATNEEC), which will entail a greater commitment to achieving the minimum environmental harm, but still leaves some room for flexibility.[25]

The alternative of establishing fixed limits can be applied in various **1.2.5** ways. Quality standards can be set for the river or local atmosphere into which emissions are being made, limits can be set for emissions from particular sites, standards can be prescribed for particular processes, or for particular products. Each of these will influence in different ways the conduct of the processes likely to cause pollution, but will provide objective tests against which performance can be tested.

**Enforcement**

A common feature of the legislation in this area is the attention **1.2.6** given to the enforcement of the law. Whether or not a special inspectorate is established, the authorities responsible for each regime are given powers of entry, search and seizure to ensure that they are not thwarted by unco-operative operators. The law usually includes offences of strict liability, and where this is modified by the existence of defences, the onus is commonly on the accused to establish that the exculpatory features do in fact exist. Such an approach encourages those concerned to take the utmost care to avoid breaches of the law, whilst relieving the enforcement authorities of the often impossible task of proving exactly how and through whose fault a particular polluting incident occurred.

**1.2.7** The reliance on strict liability does, however, allow a considerable element of discretion to the authorities. Every infraction of the law, however minor or blameless, could result in a prosecution, but the authorities do not seek to prosecute in every case, often relying on persuasion and co-operation rather than the strict enforcement of sanctions to ensure future compliance with the law. The reluctance to prosecute stems from a variety of reasons, including the costs in terms of time and labour in preparing cases for the courts (e.g. in gathering proof to the legal standard), the problems of persuading the busy prosecution authorities to devote their energies to cases which may be seen as marginal to their main work, and the limited results achieved—penalties in the past have tended to be low, leaving the stigma of conviction as the only real penalty.[26]

**1.2.8** Recent developments suggest that the position may be changing. In England and Wales the National Rivers Authority has expressly adopted a policy of being more active in mounting prosecutions. In some cases heavy fines have been imposed by the courts, *e.g.* the fine of £1 million imposed in February 1990 for oil pollution of the Mersey,[27] and recent legislation such as the Environmental Protection Act 1990 provides substantial maximum penalties for many offences, including terms of imprisonment. Moreover there is the increased possibility of personal liability for directors, managers and other senior officers of companies through whose neglect the company commits an offence.[28]

ECONOMIC FACTORS

**1.3.1** Environmental controls inevitably entail costs for industry, both compliance costs and the fees charged by the regulatory authorities.[29] As environmental controls become stricter, and as liability in various forms comes to be imposed for harm that is caused, these costs become more significant, prompting a close examination of how materials are used and disposed of; already the disposal of waste has been transformed into a major element in the cost of many processes, not something which can simply be ignored. However, there is also the possibility of using economic or pricing mechanisms more directly as a means of achieving environmental goals. Examples in the present law include the lower duty levied on lead-free petrol[30] and the use of management agreements,[31] whereby sums are paid to landowners in return for their agreement to manage their land in ways which do not achieve the maximum economic return but are beneficial to nature conservation.

Much attention is paid to the Polluter Pays Principle as the basis for **1.3.2** considering the economic aspects of environmental law. However, although the principle is fully accepted by the British and European authorities, it is often far from clear exactly what it should mean in practice. It can be seen as limited to ensuring that the person responsible for a pollution incident should pay the compensation and clean-up costs arising directly from the incident, it can be seen as requiring the recovery of all the costs of regulation and environmental control from those whose activities require control, or it can be seen as requiring that those responsible for pollution contribute in some way for the total detriment suffered by the community. Moreover, there may be difficulty in identifying the most appropriate "polluter" in the long and complex chain from the provider of raw materials to the ultimate consumer of a product or disposer of waste.

Ambitious schemes can be considered to play a more major role in **1.3.3** environmental controls. Rather than imposing limits on emissions, taxes could be levied on the amount of pollution emitted. In addition to providing an economic incentive for reducing pollution, such a scheme might encourage industry to minimise emissions, not merely to reduce them to meet the prevailing legal standard. Tradeable pollution permits could be introduced, the total volume of emissions in one area being set and then divided between polluters, who could then sell any of their unused quota to other concerns. The perceived advantage of this approach is that the burden of meeting the desired standard is divided between the polluters in an economically efficient way, not imposing a uniform standard, but allowing each concern to choose its response according to the practicality of cleaning up its own processes. Other possibilities include the introduction of a carbon tax, a tax charged on fuels according to the amount of carbon dioxide produced in their use.

**1.3.4** Such radical innovations would probably be feasible only in conjunction with some form of regulatory scheme, and their effects are difficult to predict; if the financial incentives are set too low, the impact may be minimal, if too high, there may be a disruptive effect on industry and unforeseen and inequitable consequences for groups unable to adjust their conduct. It is likely, though, that there will continue to be interest in developing economic means of influencing our impact on the environment, both as incentives for "good" conduct and to penalise those causing unacceptable pollution.[32]

## AUTHORITIES

**1.4.1** The administration of environmental matters in Scotland involves a wide range of governmental bodies. Increasingly, the major initiatives come from the European Community, which in this field has been able to benefit from the varied experiences of the Member States on environmental matters. There may be years of argument and many fundamental amendments before proposals made by the European Commission are accepted and take any legal form, but anyone wishing to look to the future of environmental law in this country must examine what is being discussed in Brussels. The importance of the Community may increase further if the proposed European Environment Agency develops monitoring powers of any significance.[33]

**1.4.2** In this country, central government becomes involved in many ways. The details of the law are directly in the hands of the government as so much of the law in this area is to be found in delegated legislation, with the Acts of Parliament offering merely a framework within which the detailed legal regime is constructed. Here, though, the freedom of action for the government may be limited, as the Scottish or British rules must comply with, and frequently must implement directly, the rules decided at the European Community level, the extent of the European influence being hidden by the fact that the rules take the form of domestic legislation.

**1.4.3** As well as determining the general rules, central government can become involved in particular issues as individual cases may be referred to the Secretary of State and his staff, either where there is a requirement for official consent or approval, or where there is an appeal from the decisions of other bodies.[34] The importance of central government is increased by the number of indirect controls at its disposal, such as its influence over the membership (and often funding) of public bodies such as river purification boards and Scottish Natural Heritage. Such issues generally fall under the ambit of the Scottish Office Environment Department, but on many matters there must be close liaison with the Department of the Environment south of the border, while the influence of other branches of the Scottish Office (especially the Scottish Office Agriculture and Fisheries Department) and other departments (*e.g.* the Treasury) must also be remembered.

Local government is also heavily involved. Sewerage and water **1.4.4** supply are in the hands of regional councils, the control of waste, aspects of air pollution and (in most areas) the detailed working of the planning system in the hands of district councils. Public health also falls within the remit of local government, and the authorities' wide powers in relation to recreation and amenity may also be exercised with a view to environmental considerations. Within the islands areas, the councils combine these roles with responsibility for river purification.[35]

A number of other public bodies are also involved. The river **1.4.5** purification boards are responsible for ensuring the quality of water in mainland Scotland, Scottish Natural Heritage has the main responsibility for nature conservation and countryside matters, while Her Majesty's Industrial Pollution Inspectorate carries out much of the detailed work of pollution control. Such bodies are created and regulated by statute, and although they enjoy considerable independence from government, their ultimate dependence on the public purse can restrict their freedom of action.

Obviously the activities of many other bodies can also affect the **1.4.6** environment, and increasingly regard for environmental consequences is being included within the general aims and functions of public bodies. Thus the Forestry Commission must endeavour to seek a reasonable balance between the promotion of commercial forestry and the conservation of nature and of natural beauty,[36] and Scottish Enterprise is required to have regard to the desirability of safeguarding the environment.[37] Only in the most blatant instance of environmental factors being wholly ignored it is likely that any court would hold a body in breach of such vague obligations, but their presence does ensure that public bodies must at least give some

*Introduction*

consideration to the environmental impact of their action and listen to arguments from those expressing environmental concern.

**1.4.7** Mention should also be made of the important role played by a large number of non-governmental organisations. In relation to the protection of the countryside and of wildlife, much practical work is carried out by charitable bodies such as the National Trust for Scotland[38] and the Royal Society for the Protection of Birds. The role of these and other bodies in conserving aspects of our natural heritage and in drawing attention to environmental issues has been of great importance, especially in the decades before environmental matters became a matter of significant official concern.

OTHER TOPICS

**1.5.1** The topics covered in this book are those which play the most obvious part in regulating our environment, but by no means exhaust those which may be relevant. Many other areas of law are concerned with environmental matters, and some of the more significant are noted below. However, it is important to stress that wherever one attempts to draw the boundary, environmental law cannot exist as an isolated area of law, set apart in a compartment on its own. All kinds of human activity can affect the environment for good or ill, therefore all forms of law may be relevant to environmental issues. For example, the present rural landscape has been affected more by the laws on landownership and financial support for agriculture and forestry than by any other legal or administrative factor. Perhaps competition law and product labelling should be included as important environmental tools, since they are vital to the increasing power of "green consumerism" in shaping industry in line with the public's environmental concern (or lack of it). A good environmental lawyer must be prepared to make use of all aspects of the law which might be relevant to the task in hand.

**Hazardous Substances**

**1.5.2** The control of hazardous substances falls between environmental law and the law on health and safety, and is generally under the supervision of the Health and Safety Executive. The risks posed by the transport, storage and use of such material have led to a broad

10

range of legal controls, aiming to protect the working environment of those involved with the materials and the environment in general. There are controls on the transport of hazardous substances by road, air and sea,[39] and the relevant authorities must be notified of installations using and storing such substances.[40] More detailed controls over the importation and use of certain materials exist, and there are rules designed to secure the monitoring of their usage and to protect those working with hazardous materials from harmful exposure.[41]

The Secretary of State has a general power to prohibit or restrict **1.5.3** the importation, use, supply or storage of any substance or article where necessary in order to prevent pollution of the environment or harm to the health of humans, animals or plants.[42] Wide powers exist to make emergency orders to prohibit or restrict the distribution of food which may have become contaminated at any stage in the food chain.[43] More generally, the basic obligations under the Health and Safety at Work Act 1974 to protect employees and others from dangers to their health should also achieve a degree of environmental protection.[44]

Legislation also exists to require "hazardous substances consent" **1.5.4** for the keeping of certain substances, but has not yet been brought into force.[45] The provisions would require the grant of consent from the planning authority before more than the prescribed quantities of the hazardous substances to be specified in regulations were kept on, over or under land. The procedures for granting consents and for enforcement would be similar to those for obtaining planning permission. On application within six months of the coming into force of the provisions, consent will be deemed to be given for all existing accumulations of hazardous substances, unless the authority decides to refuse consent or to impose restrictive conditions, in which case compensation is payable.

**Radioactive Substances**

The particular hazards of radioactive substances have produced a **1.5.5** further set of legal controls. The Nuclear Installations Act 1965 requires that all sites using significant quantities of radioactive material be licensed, imposes a duty to prevent injury or damage to property and provides a statutory right to compensation for injury caused, with an extended limitation period of 30 years to take account of the particular nature of radiation-related illnesses. The Radioactive Substances Act 1960 lays down a registration scheme for the use and storage of radioactive material, while any disposal or accumulation of radioactive waste requires an authorisation from the Secretary of State. There are also regulations controlling the transport of such material.[46] The domestic rules are closely linked to those drawn up by Euratom (the European Atomic Energy Community) and the International Commission on Radiological Protection.

**Pesticides**

**1.5.6** The sale and use of pesticides are strictly controlled under Part III of the Food and Environment Protection Act 1985 and regulations made under it. Before a pesticide can be advertised, sold, supplied, stored or used, it must gain ministerial approval, which will be granted subject to conditions, including a duty to take all reasonable precautions to safeguard the environment,[47] and limits are set for the permissible levels of pesticide residues in food.[48] The use of other chemicals for similar purposes is also controlled in some circumstances.[49]

**Genetically Modified Organisms**

**1.5.7** A new area of environmental law which is likely to become of increasing importance as the technology develops and its applications are expanded is the control of genetically modified organisms, widely defined to include the products of all forms of genetic engineering other than traditional breeding techniques. Under Part VI of the Environmental Protection Act 1990, any person importing, releasing, acquiring or marketing genetically modified organisms must carry out an assessment of the risks to the environment and to human health, and must employ the Best Available Techniques not Entailing Excessive Cost[50] in order to avoid or minimise the risks. The Secretary of State may require notice of the risk assessments and may impose a requirement for consent to be obtained before certain activities are carried out.

*Further Reading*

S. Ball and S. Bell: *Environmental Law* (London, 1991, Blackstone Press).

## Further Reading

J.F. Garner: *Garner's Environmental Law* (formerly *Control of Pollution Encyclopaedia*) (London, 1976, Butterworths).

D. Hughes: *Environmental Law* (2nd ed., London, 1992, Butterworths).

F. Lyall: *Air, Noise Water and Waste* (Glasgow, 1982, Planning Exchange).

S. Tromans: *The Environmental Protection Act 1990* (London, 1991, Sweet & Maxwell).

*Stair Memorial Encyclopaedia of the Laws of Scotland*, "Environment" (vol. 9), "Fisheries," "Game" (vol. 11), "Nuisance" (vol. 14), "Public Health" (vol. 19), "Town and Country Planning" (vol. 23), "Water and Water Rights," "Water Supply" (vol. 25) (Edinburgh, 1987–, Butterworths/Law Society of Scotland).

*This Common Inheritance*: Britain's Environmental Strategy (HMSO), Cm. 1200 (1990).

### NOTES

1 *e.g.* APS II 343 c.9 (1535), III 560 c.35 (1592), IV 67 c.20 (1594), and *Leges Forestarum*; see generally John M. Gilbert, *Hunting and Hunting Reserves in Mediaeval Scotland* (Edinburgh, 1979, John Donald).

2 *e.g.* APS I 576 (1400), II 52 c.36 (1457), II 107 c.15 (1474), II 483 c.3 (1551).

3 APS II 486 c.15 (1551).

4 APS II 51 c.32 (1457).

5 APS IX 452 c.54 (1695).

6 APS IV 287 c.12 (1606).

7 APS IV 632 c.29 (1621).

8 N. Whitty, "Nuisance," paras. 2007–2016, vol. 14, *Stair Memorial Encyclopaedia*.

9 See Chap. 5.

10 See paras. 6.4.17 *et seq.*

11 See paras. 4.5.1 *et seq.*

12 Not yet a legal requirement, but being discussed within the European Community.

13 See para. 9.1.3.

14 *Improving Scotland's Environment: The Way Ahead*, Scottish Office Consultation Paper, Jan. 1992.

15 See Chap. 3.

16 See paras. 2.2.1 *et seq.*

17 See Chap. 4.

[18] See Chap. 2.
[19] See para. 11.5.22.
[20] See, *e.g.* paras. 4.4.1 *et seq.*, 5.4.3.
[21] See para. 6.4.17.
[22] *R. v. Secretary of State for the Environment, ex p. Rose Theatre Trust Co.* [1990] 1 Q.B. 504, *R. v. Poole B.C., ex p. Beebee* [1991] J.P.L. 643.
[23] See, *e.g.* the initial draft of the proposed Directive on Civil Liability for Waste O.J. 89/C 251/3; see para. 8.3.4.
[24] See Chap. 8.
[25] See paras. 2.5.1 *et seq.*, 5.4.12 *et seq.*
[26] J. Rowan-Robinson, P. Watchman and C. Barker, *Crime and Regulation* (Edinburgh, 1990, T. & T. Clark).
[27] *National Rivers Authority v. Shell UK Ltd.* [1990] Water Law 40.
[28] Environmental Protection Act 1990, s.157.
[29] The fees for authorisations under Integrated Pollution Control and licences for handling and disposing of waste are supposed to be set so as to ensure that the schemes are self-financing.
[30] Hydrocarbon Oil Duties Act 1979, s.13A.
[31] See para. 9.3.2.
[32] See generally: Economic Instruments for Environmental Protection, Annex A to *This Common Inheritance* (Cm. 1200 (1990)); D. Pearce, A. Markandaya and E.B. Barbier: *Blueprint for a Green Economy* (London, 1989, Earthscan).
[33] Council Regulation (EEC) 1210/90; see generally Chap. 11.
[34] See, *e.g.* paras. 4.3.47 *et seq.*
[35] See para. 3.5.4.
[36] Forestry Act 1969, s.1(3A) (added by Wildlife and Countryside (Amendment) Act 1985, s.4).
[37] Enterprise and New Towns (Scotland) Act 1990, s.4(4).
[38] The Trust enjoys some special legal status under a series of private Acts of Parliament.
[39] *e.g.* Dangerous Substances (Conveyance by Road in Road Tankers and Tank Containers) Regulations 1981 (S.I. 1981 No. 1059); Air Navigation (Dangerous Goods) Regulations 1985 (S.I. 1985 No. 1939); Merchant Shipping (Dangerous Goods and Marine Pollutants) Regulations 1990 (S.I. 1990 No. 2605).
[40] Notification of Installations Handling Hazardous Substances Regulations 1982 (S.I. 1982 No. 1357); Control of Industrial Major Hazards Regulations 1984 (S.I. 1984 No. 1902).
[41] Control of Substances Hazardous to Health Regulations 1988 (S.I. 1988 No. 1657).
[42] Environmental Protection Act 1990, s.140.
[43] Food and Environment Protection Act 1985, Part I (as amended by Food Safety Act 1990, s.15).

*Notes*

44 Health and Safety at Work Act 1974, ss.2–6.
45 Town and Country Planning (Scotland) Act 1972, ss.56A–O, 97B (added by Housing and Planning Act 1986, ss.35, 36); see (1986) 18 S.P.L.P. 47, (1987) 20 S.P.L.P. 11.
46 *e.g.* Radioactive Substances (Carriage by Road) (Great Britain) Regulations 1974 (S.I. 1974 No. 1735); the power to make such regulations is now contained in the Radioactive Material (Road Transport) Act 1991.
47 Control of Pesticides Regulations 1986 (S.I. 1986 No. 1357).
48 Pesticides (Maximum Residue Levels in Food) Regulations 1988 (S.I. 1988 No. 1378).
49 *e.g.* Control of Pollution (Anti-fouling Paints) Regulations 1987 (S.I. 1987 No. 783).
50 See para. 2.5.4.

# 2. Air

**2.1.1** Any discussion or dissertation on the legislation concerning Air as a medium of the environment[1] is a discussion of the legislation for control of air pollution. The industrial revolution of the late eighteenth and nineteenth centuries and the urbanisation created by the new industries of that revolution intensified atmospheric pollution[2] with its attendant hazards to human health. The atmosphere was polluted both by industry and by smoke from domestic fires. The Public Health (Scotland) Act 1897 started some control of air pollution but the main problem of restricting industrial air pollution caused by smoke and other injurious substances emitted from factory chimneys was provided for in the first of the Alkali Acts,[3] which were later consolidated in the Alkali Etc. Works Regulation Act 1906.[4] Smoke from domestic fires and combustion processes was variously dealt with[5] within enactments which however failed to prevent the winter "smogs" which afflicted most large British cities. After a particularly bad smog in London in December 1952[6] the Beaver Committee[7] was set up by the Government of the day to examine air pollution, its causes and effects and the legislation controlling such pollution. The Beaver Committee's recommendations, in particular that of the creation of smoke control areas, were implemented in the Clean Air Acts of 1956 and 1968.

**2.1.2** The Health and Safety at Work, Etc. Act 1974, gave power to the Secretary of State to make regulations to replace the provisions of and regulations made under the Alkali Acts to control the emissions of nauseous or offensive substances to the atmosphere.[8] The Clean Air Acts are concerned with the emission into the air not only of dark smoke, from a domestic or industrial chimney or otherwise, but also of grit and dust from combustion processes. The division between the Clean Air Acts and the Alkali Acts was not one between domestic emissions and industrial emissions but a division of responsibility

16

between those bodies with responsibility for controlling emissions. Her Majesty's Industrial Pollution Inspectorate[9] was made responsible for nauseous and offensive emissions from industrial processes under the Alkali Act of 1906 while the islands or district council has responsibility for the control of smoke, grit and dust from combustion processes under the Public Health (Scotland) Act 1897 (s.12) and the Clean Air Acts.[10]

The Alkali Act of 1906 and the Clean Air Acts of 1956 and 1968 **2.1.3** were United Kingdom legislation to deal with United Kingdom pollution of United Kingdom air. In the post-war period of the twentieth century, air pollution has become a global problem requiring international co-operation. Atmospheric pollution crosses borders borne by winds which are not signatories to international border treaties. The "acid rain" controversy is a case in point where Germany and Scandinavia aver that emissions of sulphur dioxide from United Kingdom power stations are responsible for the damage to their forests. The other international anxieties of the twentieth century concern the "greenhouse effect" and the hole in the ozone layer. The former is the scientific debate as to whether increasing levels of carbon dioxide emissions from the combustion of fossil fuels could lead to higher global temperatures or could alternatively lead to global cooling as the sun's heat does not penetrate the cloud of pollutants. The hole in the ozone layer is thought to be caused by chlorofluorocarbons and as the hole in the ozone layer is enlarged, ultraviolet radiation is increased and thereby the incidence of human skin cancer. The Stockholm Conference[11] and the Heads of Government of the European Community declaration in 1972[12] helped to determine United Kingdom policy on pollution control leading to the Control of Pollution Act 1974.

**European Community Legislation**

The United Kingdom as a member of the European Community has **2.1.4** to comply with EC Legislation.[13] The European Community has had four Environment Action Programmes since 1973, the fourth (1987–1992) setting out its objectives in relation to air pollution as:
  (a) to identify pollutants and their sources;
  (b) to determine the most appropriate focus for control—the pollutants themselves or their source;
  (c) to set and implement EC-wide objectives for substantial emission reductions in order to combat acid deposition and forest die-back;

(d) in the longer term, to reduce ambient air concentrations of pollutants to levels acceptable for sensitive ecosystems.

**2.1.5**    E.C. Directives on air pollution fall broadly into four categories.

(a) Air Quality: directives have set limit values for the concentrations of sulphur dioxide and smoke,[14] lead[15] and nitrogen dioxide.[16]

(b) Emissions from Industrial Plants: Member States are required to ensure that certain industrial[17] and large combustion[18] plants operate only under authorisations which impose pollution controls.

(c) Emissions from Motor Vehicles: A number of directives lay down construction requirements for motor vehicles in order to limit the emissions which they produce.[19]

(d) Product Requirements for Gas Oil and Petrol: The sulphur content of gas oil[20] and the lead content of petrol[21] are controlled.[22]

**2.1.6**    However, continuing public awareness and concern for the environment and the United Kingdom Government's obligations to comply with the European Community's legislation on environmental protection resulted in the Environment Protection Act 1990 (EPA). The 1990 Act marks a radical change in the Government's pollution control policy[23] introducing the system of Integrated Pollution Control for the environmental media of air, land and water.

REGULATORY BODIES WITH RESPONSIBILITY FOR CONTROL OF POLLUTION OF THE AIR

**2.2.1**    The Alkali Act 1863 set up an inspectorate known as the H.M. Alkali Inspectorate and provided for the appointment of an inspector of alkali works with such number of sub-inspectors as was deemed necessary. In December 1971 the name was changed to H.M. Industrial Pollution Inspectorate for Scotland which more truly reflected the responsibilities of the inspectorate for as the years progressed the alkali aspect of the inspectorate diminished and the "etc." part of the short title of the 1906 Act became more and more important. In England and Wales these functions were carried out by H.M. Inspectorate of Pollution.[24] There is frequent co-operation to ensure that relevant legislation is uniformly applied. Liaison with the Health and Safety Executive is mainly through the Chief Inspector of Pollution.

The islands and district councils have responsibility for the control **2.2.2** of the emission of smoke from chimneys (industrial or domestic) under the Clean Air Acts and for the control of smoke, grit and dust from combustion processes and prescribed gases.[25]

The Environmental Protection Act 1990 introduced the system of **2.2.3** Integrated Pollution Control (IPC) for the environmental media of air, land and water.[26] The Alkali Act of 1906 is now virtually totally repealed but H.M. Industrial Pollution Inspectorate (HMIPI)[27] is still retained as the body to administer IPC and has responsibility for air pollution by what were formerly emissions governed by the Alkali Acts. The Secretary of State appoints the Chief Inspector and inspectors for IPC control of prescribed processes.[28] The Clean Air Acts have been extended to include prescribed gases and local authority responsibility for air pollution is retained and extended and responsibility for pollution of air is now divided between HMIPI and LAAPC that is, Local Authority Air Pollution Control.[29] While HMIPI still has responsibility for preventing or minimising pollution of any environmental medium, that is, water and land as well as air (s.4(2)), LAAPC is responsible only for preventing or minimising pollution of the air (s.4(3)). A local authority may appoint inspectors under whatever title it decides to implement the provisions of EPA in relation to prescribed processes subject to LAAPC (s.16(6)). Recent proposals to create a Scottish Environment Protection Agency would transfer all responsibility to the new agency.[30]

Inspectors under EPA have wide powers of entry to and examina- **2.2.4** tion of premises; powers to take samples, photographs and measurements; powers of testing and of requiring the production of documents (s.17). The inspector, however, cannot compel the production of a document which a person could withhold on an order for production of documents in an action in the Court of Session.

CONTROL OF AIR POLLUTION— IPC AND LAAPC

## Prescribed Processes

Under the Environmental Protection Act 1990 responsibility for the **2.3.1** control of pollution of the air in Scotland is now divided between HMIPI and Local Authority Air Pollution Control (LAAPC). Both authorities will have processes and substances prescribed for their control with the attendant requirement on operators to apply for authorisation to carry on a prescribed process.[31] Pollution of the air by smoke is controlled by local authorities under the Clean Air Acts. Section 2 of EPA empowers the Secretary of State by regulations to prescribe those processes for which authorisation is required and in the description of a process to designate whether it is for HMIPI or local authority control. If it is designated for HMIPI control, this will cover the release of substances to all three media. Designation to local authority control will of course only cover releases into the air. The regulations may describe the process either by the method of the process, the area where it is carried on or the operation of the process.

**2.3.2**  Regulations[32] made under the Act divide industry into main groups:
  (a)  production of fuel and power industry;
  (b)  metal industry;
  (c)  mineral industry;
  (d)  chemical industry;
  (e)  waste disposal industry; and
  (f)  other industries.

The industries are then divided as to process, e.g. the fuel and power industry is divided into:
  (i)  gasification and associated processes;
  (ii)  carbonisation and associated processes;
  (iii)  combustion processes;
  (iv)  petroleum processes;

and each of these classifications are further subdivided into Part A and Part B processes.

**2.3.3**  Part A processes are then subject to control under IPC and Part B are subject to LAAPC. There will obviously be debate as to whether a particular industrial process or plant is subject to IPC or LAAPC. In the case of a prescribed process carried on by means of a mobile plant the local authority which has control of that process will be the one where the person carrying on the process has his principal place of business, otherwise it is the local authority where the prescribed process is carried on (s.4(3)).

**2.3.4**  The exception to the regulations is any process which does not result in the release into the air of any prescribed substances or does release a prescribed substance but in such trivial amounts as cannot result in any harm (reg. 4). The responsibility for proving that the amounts released are trivial will rest with the person carrying on the process. However, authorisation is still required under EPA if there is an offensive smell outside the premises where the process is being carried on. Other exceptions are historical industrial museums or processes for educational purposes under s.135(1) of the Education (Scotland) Act 1980, private dwellings and propulsion engines for aircraft, ships or vehicles. The process will not be considered to fall into Part B processes unless it releases more than trivial amounts.

**2.3.5** Schedule 2 to the Regulations gives guidance in the form of rules for the interpretation of Schedule 1. Paragraphs 4 and 5 of that Schedule deal with the difficulty of a process falling into a Part A and Part B description. Paragraph 4 prescribes that where a process falls within two or more descriptions the process shall be regarded as falling only within the description which fits it most aptly but if the description includes both Part A and Part B, Part A rules and no regard has to be had to Part B. In other words, IPC takes precedence over LAAPC. Where processes fall within two or more descriptions under either Part A or Part B and are carried on by the same person at the same location those processes are to be treated as a single process.

## Prescribed Substances

**2.3.6** Section 12 of EPA also provides for specific substances to be prescribed in regulations[33] whereby any release of a prescribed substance is subject to the requirement for an authorisation under the Act. As with prescribed processes, where a substance is prescribed for releases into the air it will be designated for IPC or LAAPC. It is possible that where a substance is prescribed for all three media, substances could be prescribed for central control for releases to water and land but for local control for releases to air. Schedule 4 to the Regulations describes those substances whose release into the air is controlled under the Act and where an authorisation is required. The prescribed substances whose release into air is subject to control and requires an authorisation under ss.6 and 7 are those contained in the EC Air Directive.[34] Guidance will be issued from the Scottish Office in conjunction with the Department of the Environment to inspectors at HMIPI and to local authorities for the various classes of process.[35]

EMISSIONS, LIMITS AND QUALITY OBJECTIVES

**2.4.1** Section 3 of EPA provides the Secretary of State with power to make regulations to establish standards, objectives or requirements in relation to particular prescribed processes or particular substances. The regulations may prescribe standard limits for the concentrations, the amount of any substance, or the amount in any period of any substance which may be released, or they may prescribe a requirement for the measurement of releases. The Secretary of State may make plans for establishing limits for the total amount or the total amount in any period or area within the United Kingdom. The regulations may allocate quotas to persons carrying on processes in respect of which any such limit is established, establish progressive improvement in the quality objectives and the quality standards. Notice will be given in the *Edinburgh Gazette* of these plans.[36] The objective of the plans is a uniformity of approach to the United Kingdom as a whole although s.3(3) rather dilutes this uniformity in providing that the regulations may make a different provision in relation to different cases and for different processes, persons or localities. With the increase of EC powers concerning transboundary environmental pollution the plans will reflect EC emission limits and quality objectives.

**2.4.2**   It is possible under section 3 for a system of tradeable emission permits to be created whereby permits can be traded among companies; such a system already exists in the United States. Where permits are issued under powers contained in regulations, such permits can be traded: that is, where a company has a permit for a certain level of emission and it has not used all its permitted allowance, the surplus can be sold. It is thought that in the EC tradeable emissions permits are most likely to be introduced for sulphur oxide, oxides of nitrogen and volatile organic compounds as an extension of the Large Combustion Plant Directive.[37]

**"Best Practicable Means" BATNEEC and BPEO**

**2.5.1**   Since the nineteenth century control of pollution has been determined by the phrase "best practicable means" rather than by a system of fixed standards contained in statutes. The disadvantage of the latter system is that as techniques and technical knowledge advance such standards quickly become obsolete. Prior to EPA the owner of an alkali works had to use the "best practicable means" to prevent the escape of nauseous or offensive gases into the atmosphere.[38] "Best practicable means" was defined in the Alkali etc. Works Regulation Act 1906 and had reference not only to the provision and efficient maintenance of appliances for preventing an escape, but also to the manner in which appliances are used and to the proper supervision by the owner of any operation where such appliances are involved (s.27).

The Clean Air Act of 1956 defines "practicable" as being reason-**2.5.2** ably practicable having regard to local conditions and circumstances and to the financial implications and the current state of technical knowledge, while "practicable means" means the provision and maintenance of plant and the proper use thereof (s.34). HM Industrial Pollution Inspectorate has been the body responsible for interpreting the term "best practicable means."

Section 72 of the Control of Pollution Act 1974 defines "best **2.5.3** practicable means" in the part of the Act dealing with noise pollution. "Practicable" means reasonably practicable having regard among other things to local conditions and circumstances, to the current state of technical knowledge, and to the financial implications. It goes on to state that the means to be employed include the design, installation, maintenance and manner and periods of operation of plant and machinery and the design, construction and maintenance of buildings and acoustic structures. Regard must also be had to any relevant provision of a code of practice. This definition would seem to have regard to local conditions: in other words, that a level of pollution may be tolerated in one area where the receiving environment is less likely to be affected than in another area.[39] The definitions in the Clean Air Act of 1956 and the Control of Pollution Act 1974 have regard to the question of the financial cost of pollution control.

The European Community has used the term "best technical **2.5.4** means available."[40] This terminology has now been translated into United Kingdom legislation in the Environmental Protection Act 1990 in the provisions for authorisations to be granted for the carrying on of a prescribed process (s.7). In the granting of an authorisation by the enforcing authority the objectives will be that the prescribed process will be carried on using the best available techniques not entailing excessive cost (BATNEEC) for preventing the release of substances into the air, and where that is not practicable by such means, for reducing the release of such substances to a minimum and for rendering harmless any such substances which are so released and to render harmless any other substances which might cause harm if released into the air. The objective contained in the Alkali Etc. Works Regulation Act 1906 and earlier legislation for either preventing release or rendering releases harmless where prevention is not practicable is therefore preserved in the case of prescribed substances. Thus those considering an authorisation would identify those techniques which do not involve excessive costs and which can be used to prevent the release of a prescribed substance and then whether or not it is practicable to prevent any release using those techniques. If a substance is not prescribed the question is whether the substance might cause harm if released, and if so BATNEEC has to be considered with regard to rendering it harmless; but it may not be necessary to actually prevent the substance being released.

**2.5.5**   If a process is one designated for central control not local control and is likely to involve the release of substances into more than one environmental medium, the objectives must include that of ensuring that BATNEEC will be used for minimising the pollution which may be caused to the environment taken as a whole, having regard to the best practicable environmental option (BPEO) available in respect of the substances which may be released. BPEO is not defined in the Act but there is a definition in the Royal Commission on Environmental Pollution[41] which stated: "a BPEO is the outcome of a systematic consultative and decision-making procedure which emphasises the protection and conservation of the environment across land, air and water. The BPEO procedure establishes, for a given set of objectives, the option that provides the most benefit or least damage to the environment as a whole at an acceptable cost in the long term as well as in the short term." Section 7(7) would therefore appear to require the identification of the substances that may be released, deciding what is the BPEO in relation to such substances and, having regard to the BPEO so identified, to use the BATNEEC which will minimise the pollution which may be caused to the environment as a whole—*i.e.* to minimise pollution by the application of BATNEEC having regard to BPEO. Enforcing authorities must have regard to any guidance issued by the Secretary of State as to the application of BATNEEC and BPEO (s.7(11)).

**Liability for Air Pollution**

The Environmental Protection Act 1990 provides that "no person **2.6.1** shall carry on a prescribed process . . . except under an authorisation granted by the enforcing authority and, in accordance with the conditions to which it is subject" (s.6(1)). All authorisations are subject to a condition that BATNEEC be used to prevent or minimise the release of prescribed substances and to render harmless any other substances which are released (s.7(4)). Breach of these provisions is a criminal offence (s.23(1)), and the onus is on the accused to establish that there was no better technique which did not entail excessive cost available other than the technique which he actually used (s.25). Otherwise the offence carries strict liability and there is no defence of ignorance of the fact that the condition was being contravened. The offence may occur whether or not it was committed only intermittently.[42]

STATUTORY NUISANCES

The Public Health (Scotland) Act 1897 provides for certain statutory **2.7.1** nuisances,[43] that is, circumstances which constitute a "nuisance" or are "injurious or dangerous to health" or "offensive." Section 16 of the Clean Air Act 1956 provides that smoke which is a nuisance to a neighbourhood is a nuisance liable to be dealt with under the 1897 Act.[44] The Environmental Protection Act 1990 has extended the definition of nuisances in s.16 of the 1897 Act to include not only certain smoke from dwellings but also fumes, gases or vapours which are injurious or dangerous to health and also any dust caused by trade, business, manufacture or process.[45]

SMOKE AND THE CLEAN AIR ACTS

**1. The Control of Smoke Pollution of Air**

As stated before, air pollution policy in the United Kingdom is **2.8.1** divided into areas of control, that is, those emissions which are controlled by HMIPI and those emissions which are subject to local authority control. The Environmental Protection Act 1990 provides for local authority control of certain industrial emissions. It however does not affect local authority control under the Clean Air Acts of 1956 and 1968. These acts were concerned with "smoke" which includes soot, ash, grit and gritty particles emitted in smoke and includes visible non-carbonaceous vapours such as water and solid particles.[46] Section 85 of EPA extends the Clean Air Acts to include prescribed gases.[47]

**2.8.2** As mentioned earlier, the great London "smog" of December 1952 which lasted an impenetrable five days alerted the government of the day to the fact that much of the atmospheric pollution at that time came not only from industry but also from the burning of coal in domestic grates. The Clean Air Act 1956 introduced a system of smoke control which with smoke-control areas and the change to other means of domestic heating reduced significantly the emission of smoke into the air. The local authorities, that is, the islands or district councils,[48] have the responsibility of control of "dark smoke." Smoke which is not dark smoke is controlled either by a Smoke Control Order[49] or by the smoke nuisance provisions of the 1956 Act.

*Control of Dark Smoke*

**2.8.3** Local authorities have power to control the emission of "dark smoke" which is smoke that is "as dark or darker than shade 2 on the Ringelmann Chart."[50] Section 1 of the Clean Air Act 1956 prohibits the emissions of dark smoke from a chimney[51] of any building on any day[52] and from railway engines[53] and vessels[54] within territorial waters and from chimneys serving furnaces of boilers in industrial plants on land.[55] The Clean Air Act 1968 extended the prohibition to include the emission of dark smoke from industrial or trade premises whether or not the emission is from a chimney.[56] Where material is burned on industrial trade premises and the circumstances are such that there is likely to be an emission of dark smoke it will be presumed that there has been an emission of dark smoke unless the occupier or person in charge of the burning can show no dark smoke was emitted. Where an emission of dark smoke occurs the occupier of the building or premise is guilty of an offence. Similarly if the owner of a railway engine fails to use any practical means to minimise the emission of smoke from the engine he is also guilty of an offence. There are certain statutory defences to a charge under either the 1956 or 1968 Act.

*Statutory Defences to a Charge for Emitting Dark Smoke*

Where the offence is one of emitting dark smoke from a chimney, **2.8.4**
the occupier of the building containing the emitting grate has certain
statutory defences which he must prove to escape liability under the
Act. He must prove:
  (a) that the contravention was due solely to lighting up a cold
      furnace and that all practicable steps had been taken to
      prevent or minimise the emission;
  (b) that it was solely due to the failure of some furnace or
      apparatus used with the furnace and that the failure could
      not reasonably have been foreseen or if foreseen could not
      have been reasonably provided against or prevented or
      action taken until after the failure occurred;
  (c) if it was due solely to the use of unsuitable fuel, that this was
      because suitable fuel was unobtainable and that the least
      unsuitable fuel available was used and again that all practi-
      cal steps had been taken to prevent or minimise the emis-
      sion; or
  (d) that the emission was caused by a combination of two or
      more of the causes specified in (a) to (c) above and that the
      requisite preventive or mitigating action was taken. "Practica-
      ble" is defined in section 34(1) of the 1956 Act as being
      practicable having regard to local conditions, financial
      implications and the current state of technical knowledge.[57]
      There are regulations which give permitted periods during
      which it is allowable to emit dark smoke from domestic
      chimneys.[58]
The owner of a locomotive engine has the defence that he used **2.8.5**
any practicable means available for minimising the emission of
smoke from his engine's chimney. Again in this context, practicable
means reasonably practicable having regard to local conditions,
circumstances, financial implications and the current state of technical knowledge.
Where the occupier of industrial or trade premises has been **2.8.6**
charged with emitting dark smoke, it is a statutory defence that the
emission was inadvertent and that all practicable steps had been
taken to prevent or minimise the emission.[59]

*Air*

## 2. Furnaces

*Smoke from Furnaces*

**2.8.7** Any new furnace installed either in a building or in a boiler or industrial plant attached to a building must be capable of being operated continuously without emitting smoke, otherwise an offence is committed by the person installing the furnace.[60] Any new furnace to be installed must have prior consent from the local authority.[61] Building regulations consent is not sufficient and consent to the installation does not imply consent to the emission of dark smoke. Failure to obtain prior local authority consent to the installation is an offence.

*Grit and Dust from Furnaces*

**2.8.8** Power is given under the 1968 Act for regulations to be made prescribing limits for the emission of grit and dust from non-domestic furnaces (s.2(2)).[62] The occupier of a building which has a furnace which burns solid, liquid or gaseous matter and whose chimney is emitting grit and dust in excess of prescribed limits is guilty of an offence (s.2.(2)). The occupier, to avoid a charge under this provision, must prove that he used the "best practicable means" to minimise the emission.[63] Where no limits have been prescribed for a particular type of chimney or furnace the onus is on the authority to prove that the occupier failed to avail himself of any practicable means. Note the different standards between the two offences, and the more stringent standard for prescribed limits. Occupiers may be required to measure emissions of grit, dust and fumes.[64]

*Arrestment Equipment on Furnaces*

**2.8.9** Section 6 of the Clean Air Act 1956[65] requires all new furnaces which burn pulverised fuel or which burn solid fuel at the rate of one ton per hour or more to be fitted with approved equipment for arresting grit and dust. Approval of equipment is by the local authority, reasons for refusal must be given in writing and an appeal from an adverse decision lies to the Secretary of State within 28 days of notification of the decision. The Clean Air Act 1968 extended the provision to cover non-domestic furnaces burning solid, liquid or gaseous matters at a rate of 100 lbs or more an hour (s.6(1)). Any occupier using a non-domestic furnace not equipped with approved arresting equipment is guilty of an offence. The Secretary of State has power under the Clean Air Act 1968 to make regulations exempting prescribed furnaces[66] from the requirement to have arrestment equipment fitted to new furnaces. Regulations exempt mobile furnaces for purposes relating to construction, research or agriculture or certain furnaces used for the incineration of refuse. Furnaces may also be exempted if a local authority is satisfied that any emission of grit and dust is not prejudicial to health or a nuisance. Appeal against refusal to allow an exemption may be made to the Secretary of State. It is an offence to use for another purpose a furnace exempted from the need to have arresting equipment for one purpose.

## 3. Control of Chimney Heights

When a local authority[67] has submitted to it, plans for a new building, **2.8.10** other than a shop, office or residence, and the buildings show a proposed chimney to carry smoke, grit, dust or gases from the building the authority must refuse a building warrant[68] if the height of the chimney is insufficient to prevent so far as practicable the emission of smoke, grit, dust or gases which would be prejudicial to health or a nuisance.[69] Apart from shops, offices and residences this provision does not apply to an extension to an electricity generating station,[70] but it has been extended to apply to chimneys serving furnaces,[71] and using an unapproved furnace chimney is an offence.[72] The local authority in considering an application must have regard to the location of nearby buildings, levels of neighbouring ground and other relevant matters. Appeal lies to the Secretary of State within 28 days of receipt of a refusal of a warrant.[73] The local authority must give reasons for the refusal and must give an indication of the lowest chimney height that it would permit. The dispersal of pollutant away from the area of production by the means of high chimneys has served Britain well but not her neighbours. Prevailing winds carry the pollutants away from Britain but with increasing international concern with sulphur dioxide emissions more attention will be paid in the future to diminishing the emissions rather than simply dispersing them.

## 4. Smoke Control Orders and Smoke Control Areas

The introduction of smoke control areas or smokeless zones by the **2.8.11** Clean Air Act 1956 was the biggest factor in clearing the air in British cities. While a certain diminution of pollution could have been expected from the change to central heating, the 1956 Act certainly accelerated the process. A local authority may make an order declaring the whole or part of its district to be a smoke control area,[74] where it is an offence for smoke (not only dark smoke) to be emitted from a chimney of a building (s.11(2)). The occupier of a building has a defence that the emission was not caused by the use of an unauthorised fuel.[75] Different provisions for different parts of the control area of specified buildings or specified fireplaces can be contained in the smoke control order.[76] The Secretary of State may exempt certain fireplaces from the control order.[77] The Secretary of State has powers to require an authority to submit proposals for a smoke control order.

**2.8.12**   Prior to making a smoke control order a local authority must publish a notice in the *Edinburgh Gazette* and for at least two successive weeks in a newspaper which circulates in the area to be affected by the order. Objections to the order must be in writing and be considered by the local authority. An order should come into force six months after it is made.

**2.8.13**   Grants of 70 per cent may be made by the local authority towards the cost of adapting fireplaces in private houses and in cases of hardship it can increase the amount to up to 100 per cent in order that the fireplace can be adapted for use of smokeless fuels.[78] It is an offence not only to burn solid fuel other than smokeless fuel in a smoke control area but also to acquire or sell solid fuel other than an authorised fuel for use in a fireplace in a building or for use in a boiler or industrial plant or for delivery to premises where there is a boiler or industrial plant. The retailer charged with selling an unauthorised fuel has a defence if he can show that he believed and had reasonable grounds for believing that the fuel would be used within the limits of an exemption from control.

### 5. Straw and Stubble Burning

**2.8.14**   A problem which has given rise to considerable public concern in recent years is the burning of stubble or other crop residues by farmers after the harvesting of their crops. The smoke produced by stubble burning has been considered by the public at large as a nuisance and as a potential hazard to traffic when the smoke crosses motorways and other roads. Control of straw and stubble burning has been by voluntary codes and local authority bye-laws. However, it has been thought that these methods have been unable to control the problem and legislation was introduced in the Environmental Protection Act 1990 whereby the Secretary of State has power to make regulations to prohibit or restrict the burning of straw stubble or any other crop residue on agricultural land[79] and he may provide exemptions which will apply in all or in only specified areas or to specified crop residues or in specified circumstances. Where stubble burning is restricted the Regulations may impose requirements to be followed before or after the burning. Regulations may also create offences, but no offence is to be made punishable other than on summary conviction and the fine shall not exceed level five on the standard scale.[80] It is envisaged that some exemptions may be permanent for certain crop residues and some exemptions will be temporary and apply in particular circumstances. The provisions of the Act envisage the repeal of the local bye-laws.[81] A general prohibition will apply from the 1993 harvest onwards. The target date for this section coming into force is March 1993.

VEHICLE EMISSIONS

## Introduction

While writing this paragraph in 1991, 35 years after the passing of **2.9.1** the Clean Air Act 1956, London has again had a "smog" due to a climatic condition of freezing air holding pollution in the atmosphere, not on this occasion smoke from domestic fires but nitrates and oxides, carbon monoxides, hydrocarbons and particulates which contain lead, all emissions coming from motor vehicles. Pollution from vehicles is a pollution which, as a result of her membership of the European Community, the United Kingdom has introduced legislation to control. Air pollution from vehicles is regulated by specifying the composition of fuel and by specifying the construction of the vehicle.

## Sulphur Content of Gas Oil

European Community Directives have been made to set a limit on **2.9.2** the sulphur content of gas oil; gas oil is used for domestic heating, in diesel engine motor vehicles, and in some Member States of the

Community it is also used for cooking. Directive 75/716[82] allows only two grades of gas oil to be sold as from October 1, 1976. Type A (having a lower sulphur content) would be restricted to 0.5 per cent from October 1, 1976 and further reduced to 0.3 per cent from October 1, 1980. Type B gas oil (with a higher permitted content of sulphur) can be used only in certain permitted zones designated by each Member State. Directive 87/219[83] largely replaced directive 75/716 so that by January 1, 1989 there was no distinction between Types A and B and the sulphur content was not to exceed 0.3 per cent. The Secretary of State has power under the Control of Pollution Act 1974[84] to make regulations limiting the sulphur content of liquid fuels after consultation with representatives of the oil fuel industry, users and experts in pollution.

**2.9.3**   The United Kingdom definition of zones for the use of Type A and Type B gas oil was possibly not that envisaged by the Commission when it drafted the Directive. The United Kingdom decided that as the only problems arose at roadsides, Type A gas oil could be used throughout the United Kingdom and that roads would be the only areas designated for the use of Type A gas only,[85] with Type B being permitted on all other parts of the United Kingdom.[86]

**2.9.4**   EEC legislation has set limits on the lead content of petrol to reduce air pollution by lead and also to prevent barriers to trade of petrol.[87] The maximum permitted lead content of petrol sold within the Community is 0.40 g/l—that is, 40 gms per litre and the lower limit not less than 0.15 g/l or 15 gms per litre. As stated before, s.75 of the Control of Pollution Act 1974 gives the Secretary of State power to make regulations.[88] The 1979 regulations[89] permitted the sale from January 1, 1986 of unleaded petrol. In March 1987 the Budget established a tax differential in favour of unleaded petrol.[90] The price of unleaded petrol has reduced in relation to the price of leaded petrol in successive years.

**Construction of Motor Vehicles**

**2.9.5**   A number of directives have been made to limit air pollution by specifying the type and construction of the vehicle itself rather than the fuel that it uses to drive itself.[91] Directive 70/220 set limits for the emissions of carbon monoxide and unburnt hydrocarbons from petrol engine vehicles with the exception of agricultural tractors and public works vehicles. Directive 74/290 1974 further reduces the limits and

*Notes*

Directive 77/102 added limits for nitrogen oxides and the limits for all three pollutants were further reduced in 1978 and 1983. Directive 88/76 reduced the emission limit values further and changed the categories for deciding on emissions from vehicle weight to the engine capacity and requires that new vehicles must run on unleaded petrol. In the United Kingdom regulations were made first under the Road Traffic Act of 1972 by the Motor Vehicles (Construction and Use) Regulations 1973.[92] These were followed by various regulations. The construction and use regulations now require vehicles with petrol engines first used on or after April 1, 1991 to be designed and constructed to run on unleaded petrol. If such a vehicle is altered or adjusted to run on leaded petrol and is incapable of running on unleaded petrol this is an offence.[93] The responsibility for implementing the regulations lies with the Local Weights and Measures Authority.

*Further Reading*

D. Hughes: *Environmental Law* (2nd ed., London, 1986, Butterworths).
F. Lyall: *Air, Noise, Water and Waste* (Glasgow, 1982, Planning Exchange).
S. Tromans: *The Environmental Protection Act 1990* (London, 1991, Sweet & Maxwell).
Royal Commission on Environmental Pollution—"Air Pollution Control: An Integrated Approach," 5th Report, Cmnd. 6371 (1976).
Royal Commission on Environmental Pollution—"Lead in the Environment," 9th Report, Cmnd. 8852 (1983).
Royal Commission on Environmental Pollution—"Tackling Pollution: Experience and Prospects," 10th Report, Cmnd. 9149 (1984).

NOTES

[1] The definition of "environment" in s.1 of the Environmental Protection Act 1990 (EPA) contains the reference to the media of air, water and land and the medium of air includes the air within buildings and the air within other natural or man-made structures above or below ground.
[2] The Control of Pollution Act 1974 refers to both atmospheric pollution and air pollution. EPA drops the reference to "the atmosphere" but includes a broader definition of "air" (see note 1).

³ Alkali Act 1863.

⁴ Now repealed by EPA.

⁵ See the Smoke Nuisance (Scotland) Acts 1857 and 1865, the Public Health (Scotland) Act 1897, s.16(9)(10) (all repealed) and various Burgh Police and Local Acts.

⁶ It was estimated that the London smog of 1952 accounted for 4,000 deaths from bronchitis and other respiratory diseases.

⁷ Committee of Air Pollution Interim Report (Cmd. 9011 (1953)) and Final Report (Cmd. 9322 (1954)).

⁸ The Health and Safety (Emissions into the Atmosphere) Regulations 1983 (S.I. 1983 No. 943) extensively repealed the Alkali Etc. Works Regulation Act 1906, now repealed totally by EPA.

⁹ See para. 2.2.1 below.

¹⁰ The Clean Air Act 1956 ss.29(1), 34(1). The Clean Air Act 1968 is now amended to include prescribed gases by virtue of EPA, s.85.

¹¹ Report of the United Nations Conference on the Human Environment, Stockholm 5th/16th June 1972 (United Nations, New York 1973 (A/CONF 48/14 Rev.1)).

¹² Communiqué issued by the Heads of State and of Government of the Enlarged Community at their meeting in Paris on October 19/20, 1972 (Cmnd. 5109).

¹³ See generally Chap. 11, especially paras. 11.5.8 *et seq.*

¹⁴ Directive 80/979/EEC.

¹⁵ Directive 82/884/EEC.

¹⁶ Directive 85/203/EEC.

¹⁷ Directive 84/360/EEC.

¹⁸ Directive 88/609/EEC.

¹⁹ See para. 2.9.5.

²⁰ Directives 75/716/EEC and 87/219/EEC.

²¹ Directives 78/611/EEC, 85/210/EEC and 87/416/EEC.

²² See paras. 2.9.2.–2.9.4.

²³ "Whatever the arguments about the Bill it will surely provide us with the basic framework for much of our pollution control in Britain well into the next century": Mr. C. Patten, then Secretary of State for the Environment, *Hansard*, H.C. Vol. 165, col. 32, 15th January 1990.

²⁴ H.M. Inspectorate of Pollution is attached to the Department of the Environment.

²⁵ Clean Air Act 1946 ss.29(1), 34(1); Clean Air Act 1968, s.13(1) amended by EPA, s.162(2), Sched.16, Pt.1.

²⁶ See Chap. 5.

²⁷ In England and Wales IPC is administered by Her Majesty's Inspectorate of Pollution (HMIP).

²⁸ EPA, s.17.

²⁹ "Local Authority" is an islands or district council (EPA, s.4(11)).

[30] See para. 1.1.6.

[31] For an exposition of the procedure for an application for an authorisation, see chapter 5.

[32] Environmental Protection (Prescribed Processes and Substances) Regulations 1991 (S.I. 1991 No. 472).

[33] The Environmental Protection (Prescribed Processes and Substances) Regulations 1991, Schedule 4.

[34] Directive on the combating of air pollution from industrial plants 84/360. See para. 11.5.13.

[35] To date, certified guidance notes for local authority, air pollution controls have been published for prescribed processes. Hansard written answer, Vol. 196, col. 280, 18th October 1991.

[36] A national plan has been made regarding reductions of emissions of sulphur dioxide and oxides of nitrogen from existing large combustion plants in the UK for 1990 to the year 2003 and for sulphur dioxide emissions for the years 1990 to 1998 and emissions of oxides of nitrogen from power stations, refineries and other industry. It came into force on 20th December 1990.

[37] Large Combustion Plant Directive 88/609. Large Combustion Plant (Control of Emissions) (Scotland) Regulations 1991, S.I. No. 562.

[38] Alkali Etc. Works Regulation Act 1906, s.2(1) (now repealed).

[39] Royal Commission on Environmental Pollution Fifth Report, "Air Pollution Control—An Integrated Approach" (Cmnd. 6371 (1975)).

[40] Large Combustion Plants Directive 84/360/EEC and the Dangerous Substances Directive 76/464/EEC

[41] Royal Commission on Environmental Pollution, Twelfth Report (Cm. 310 (1987)).

[42] *Hodgetts* v. *Chiltern District Council* [1983] 2 A.C. 120.

[43] Public Health (Scotland) Act 1897, Pt.II; see generally paras. 8.3.7 *et seq.*

[44] Clean Air Act 1956, s.16(1) (amended by the Control of Smoke Pollution Act 1989, s.1).

[45] EPA, s.83(2).

[46] Clean Air Act 1956, s.34(1), applied by the Clean Air Act 1968, s.13(1).

[47] Clean Air Act 1968, s.7A.

[48] Clean Air Act 1956, ss.29(1), 34(1).

[49] See paras. 2.8.11 et seq.

[50] Named after Professor Ringelmann who devised the chart.

[51] "Chimney" includes the structures or openings of any kind through which smoke, grit, dust or fumes may be emitted and includes flues whether part of the building or separated (Clean Air Act 1956, s.34(1)).

[52] "Day" means a twenty-four hour period beginning at midnight (Clean Air Act 1956, s.34(1)).

[53] Clean Air Act 1956, s.19(1); however, the 1956 Act does not apply to smoke, dust or grit from such engines: s.19(3).

⁵⁴ Clean Air Act 1956, s.20(1).

⁵⁵ Clean Air Act 1956, s.1(4).

⁵⁶ Clean Air Act 1968, s.1(1), (1A), as amended by the Control of Smoke Pollution Act 1989, s.2; this section does not affect any emission of dark smoke to which the Clean Air Act 1956, s.1 applies (1968 Act, s.1(2)).

⁵⁷ See paras. 2.5.1 et seq.

⁵⁸ Dark Smoke (Permitted Periods) (Scotland) Regulations 1958, S.I. 1958 No. 1933.

⁵⁹ Clean Air Act 1968, s.1(1) and (4); there are also certain exemptions set out in regulations for the emission of dark smoke and the burning of certain materials (Clean Air (Emission of Dark Smoke) (Exemption) (Scotland) Regulations 1969 (S.I. 1969 No. 1389)).

⁶⁰ Clean Air Act 1956, s.3(1).

⁶¹ Clean Air Act 1956, s.3.

⁶² Domestic furnaces are those used for heated boilers with a maximum heating capacity of less than 55,000 bt units per hour (Clean Air Act (Emission of Grit and Dust from Furnaces) (Scotland) Regulations 1971 (S.I. 1971 No. 625); Clean Air Act 1968, s.2(5)).

⁶³ Clean Air Act 1968, s.2(3).

⁶⁴ Clean Air (Measurement of Grit and Dust from Furnaces) (Scotland) Regulations 1971, S.I. 1971 No. 626.

⁶⁵ As amended by Clean Air Act 1968, s.14(2).

⁶⁶ Clean Air Act 1968, s.4(1).

⁶⁷ Islands or district council, or regional council in Highland, Borders and Dumfries and Galloway.

⁶⁸ Under the Building (Scotland) Act 1959, s.6.

⁶⁹ Clean Air Act 1956, s.10(1).

⁷⁰ Clean Air Act 1956, s.10(4), Clean Air Act 1968, s.6(10) (both as amended by Energy Act 1983, Sched. 3).

⁷¹ Clean Air Act 1968, s.6(12).

⁷² Ibid., s.6.

⁷³ Clean Air Act 1956, s.10(3), Clean Air Act 1968, s.6(7)–(9).

⁷⁴ Clean Air Act 1956, s.11(1).

⁷⁵ "Authorised fuel" is a fuel authorised under regulations for the purposes of the Act (s.34(1)): Smoke Control Areas (Authorised Fuels) (Scotland) Order 1982 No. 449 as amended and revoked and replaced by the Smoke Control Areas (Authorised Fuels) Regulations 1991 (S.I. 1991 No. 1282) with effect from 1st July 1991 (further amended by S.I. 1992 No. 72). Fuel manufactured before that date which was authorised by the earlier regulations may be used notwithstanding their revocation.

⁷⁶ "Fireplace" includes any furnace, grate or stove whether open or closed (s.34(1)).

⁷⁷ Smoke Control Areas (Exempted Fireplaces) (Scotland) Orders 1982, S.I. 1982 No. 448 amended by S.I. 1983 No. 1573; S.I. 1984 No. 1865; S.I.

## Notes

1985 No. 315; S.I. 1987 No. 383; S.I. 1989 No. 888 and Smoke Control Areas (Exempted Fireplaces) Order 1990 (S.I. 1990 No. 345); Smoke Control Areas (Exempted Fireplaces) (No. 2) Order 1990 (S.I. 1990 No. 2457).

[78] Clean Air Act 1956, s.12.

[79] "Agricultural land" has the same meaning as in the Agriculture (Scotland) Act 1948.

[80] EPA, s.152.

[81] Ibid., s.152(4).

[82] Directive 75/716/EEC—Approximation of the laws of the Member States relating to the sulphur content of certain liquid fuels.

[83] 87/219/EEC (amending Directive 75/716/EEC).

[84] Control of Pollution Act 1974, ss.75–77.

[85] With the exception of Orkney and Shetland because of their low volume of motor traffic.

[86] Oil Fuel (Sulphur Content of Gas Oil) Regulations 1976 (S.I. 1976 No. 78), revoked and replaced by Oil Fuel (Sulphur Content of Gas Oil) Regulations 1990 (S.I. 1990 No. 1096); Motor Fuel (Sulphur Content of Gas Oil) Regulations 1976 (S.I. 1976 No. 89), amended by Motor Fuel (Sulphur Content of Gas Oil) Regulations 1990 (S.I. 1990 No. 1097).

[87] Directives 78/611/EEC, 85/210/EEC, 87/416/EEC.

[88] Motor Fuel (Lead Content of Petrol) Regulations 1976 (S.I. 1976 No. 1866); Motor Fuel (Lead Content of Petrol) (Amendment) Regulations 1979 (S.I. 1979 No. 1); Motor Fuel (Lead Content of Petrol) Regulations 1981 (S.I. 1981 No. 1523); Motor Fuel (Lead Content of Petrol) Regulations 1985 (S.I. 1985 No. 1728); Motor Fuel (Lead Content of Petrol) Regulations 1989 (S.I. 1989 No. 547).

[89] See note 1.

[90] Finance Act 1987, s.1, adding s.13A to Hydrocarbon Oil Duties Act 1979.

[91] Directives 70/220/EEC, 74/290/EEC, 77/102/EEC, 78/665/EEC, 83/351/EEC, 88/76/EEC, and 88/436/EEC.

[92] S.I. 1973 No. 24.

[93] All the earlier regulations were replaced by the Road Vehicles (Construction and Use) Regulations 1986, S.I. 1986, No. 1078 which has been amended to introduce more stringent limits on exhaust emission. Following that there have been further Construction and Use and Type Approval Regulations to implement the directives, e.g. S.I. 1988, No. 1522; S.I. 1988, No. 1523; S.I. 1988, No. 1524 and S.I. 1988, No. 1669; S.I. 1991 No. 2681; S.I. 1991 No. 2830.

# 3. Water Pollution

INTRODUCTION

**3.1.1** Water is of fundamental importance to life. The problems of its use and equitable regulation have, therefore, accumulated a considerable body of law.[1] In former centuries the common law was the principal mode through which water was dealt with. The Victorians recognised that the public interest required a more general approach to such questions. Statutory bodies, controls and procedures began to be introduced. The present statutory system, traceable in its principle to prior decades, dates from after the Second World War. In addition there is now a body of law emanating from the European Communities as to water quality standards, which interacts with the domestic arrangements. We will note this last element immediately after the discussion of the common law and before turning to the statutory system.

**3.1.2** As indicated elsewhere in this volume, steps have been announced to bring many of the environmental functions presently entrusted to local government agencies into a central environmental protection agency.[2] Precisely how this will affect the institutions dealt with below is unclear at the time of writing. The law will probably remain unchanged, with some change in the agencies responsible for its enforcement. Note also Chapter 5, Integrated Pollution Control.

## COMMON LAW

**3.2.1** Since water is so important, it comes as no surprise to find a considerable body of common law involved with questions of water. In particular the developing law of nuisance contains many "water" cases.[3] Of these, an important statement of general principle remains that of Lord Justice-Clerk Inglis in his charge to the jury in *Duke of Buccleuch* v. *Alexander Cowan and Sons*.[4] His statement can be

38

summarised for our purposes: (1) the separate proprietors of a watercourse may use a stream as they choose, but must send the water down to lower proprietors undiminished in quantity and unimpaired in quality; (2) since streams have (variable) self-cleansing properties, there can be no absolute standard of quality at common law, so minor impairment of quality by use of the stream for such natural purposes as washing, drinking or watering of cattle, is not actionable. However (3) the addition of unnecessary and artificial pollutants to a water system is actionable. In such an action (4) a complainer must show that a defender has polluted a stream so as to be a nuisance to him according to the normal concepts of nuisance. Later cases on nuisance establish that by acquiescence an individual may lose the right to complain about a given level of pollution, though not to object to an increased level.[5] A polluter cannot acquire an unfettered "right" to pollute by prescription.

**3.2.2** Other common law rules regarding landownership and the ownership and use of streams, lochs and stagna can play a role in questions of pollution, notably those relating to the alteration of a watercourse. Particular difficulties arise when an artificial watercourse is involved: that is, one which is completely artificial, or where a natural watercourse has been substantially altered in the past. Here much depends upon the law relating to servitudes (and in some cases to statutory provisions as to land-drainage).[6]

**3.2.3** Although it is still competent to proceed by action of nuisance in appropriate cases, the common law is not an entirely satisfactory method of dealing with questions of water pollution. An action will normally be raised only after the pollution has happened. Although a pre-emptive action is occasionally competent, they are rare. There is no duty imposed on anyone to raise a common law action. In effect only riparians have the right to take action, proof can be difficult, to bring a case is expensive and can be uncertain as to its outcome. It is very unlikely that someone with the necessary standing to bring an action will get legal aid, since in most cases he will need to be a landowner. Accordingly to bring an action will be worrying as well as time and energy-consuming. There can also be other reasons why an individual may not wish to invoke the law. In Victorian times many streams and rivers were grossly polluted, but landowners were not willing to take action because they were shareholders or the proprietors of the manufacturing industries causing the pollution. Finally, the "public interest" has little role in the older private law remedies. Other solutions are required.

**3.3.1** Before we turn to the detail of the statutory arrangements dealing with water pollution, the impact of European Community directives must be acknowledged. The statutory provisions are adapted to implement international obligations, not only those from the EEC, and contain powers to modify regulations, orders, consents, permissions and authorisations to reflect any changes in these obligations.

**3.3.2** One particular matter must, however, be specially noted. A problem or restriction of both common and statutory law in the past has been the question of standing—whether an individual (or pressure group) had the technical legal interest (as opposed to altruistic concern) to intervene in an environmental matter. Some of the language of European Community directives may allow that problem to be avoided. Depending on its terms a directive may make it possible for citizens to take action to require statutory authorities to implement their obligations under the directive without the citizens having to show a legal interest in the previous technical sense.

STATUTORY ARRANGEMENTS

**3.4.1** Statutory measures to deal with water pollution fall into four major divisions: river purification (now including parts of the sea), sewerage, questions of water supply, and a general category of miscellaneous provisions.

**3.4.2** We have seen that the raising of a common law action is optional; although a person may have a good case on the facts there is no requirement on him to go to court. An essential step in the statutory arrangements was the placing of a duty on local authorities to take matters up. The duty is now laid on the Secretary of State for Scotland who is required by s.1 of the Rivers (Prevention of Pollution) (Scotland) Act 1951 to promote the cleanliness of the rivers and other inland waters and the tidal waters of Scotland. This duty still subsists and undergirds government action in these matters. The duty has, however, been further elaborated to include matters particularly of water quality and conservation under s.1 of the Water (Scotland) Act 1980, as indicated below.

**3.4.3** These duties are fulfilled through a variety of agencies which have interlocking responsibilities, powers and duties in the field of the environment.

## Agencies

All the different agencies now active within environmental control **3.4.4**
have some responsibilities either directly or indirectly affecting questions of water pollution. Planning procedures must take pollution,
sewerage and water supply questions into account. Waste disposal
authorities must have regard to the effect of their activities on water,
as must other authorities with licensing and authorising powers in
environmental matters (see below, Lawful Entry of Matter and of
Pollutants).

RIVER PURIFICATION

River purification deals with virtually all waters within Scotland as well **3.5.1**
as parts of the sea off the Scottish coast as after described.

By the Rivers (Prevention of Pollution) (Scotland) Act 1951 respon- **3.5.2**
sibility for river and waters was taken from the then local government
authorities and given to separately constituted river purification
authorities. These deal with complete water systems within their areas
on a "source to sea" basis. The totality of a water catchment area
can therefore be dealt with by one authority irrespective of the way
local government boundaries fall across the catchment area. The
1951 Act was extended by a similarly-titled Act of 1963, and
subsequently amended by Part II of the Control of Pollution Act 1974
(known affectionately as "COPA") and the Water Act 1989. The
Environmental Protection Act 1990 and the Natural Heritage (Scotland) Act 1991 further amended the basic system and extended the
powers of river purification authorities. In what follows it is assumed
that all this legislation has fully come into force.[8]

The main water pollution provisions are contained in Part II of the **3.5.3**
Control of Pollution Act 1974, but unwary readers should be warned
that s.169 of and Schedule 23 to the Water Act 1989 substitutes new
ss.31–42, 46–51 and 53–56 of that Part.

### River Purification Authorities

Major actors in the control of water pollution in Scotland are the **3.5.4**
river purification authorities. Mainland Scotland is divided into seven
river purification areas, each with a river purification board, while the

islands councils act as river purification authorities within their own areas. River purification boards are established by order of the Secretary of State acting under ss.135 and 135A of the Local Government (Scotland) Act 1973.[9] By s.135 of the 1973 Act, each board may have a membership of up to three times the number of districts wholly or partly within its area. One-third of each board is appointed by regional councils and one-third by districts within its area, the remainder being appointed by the Secretary to represent agricultural, fishery, industrial and any other relevant interests in the area. However, by s.135A the Secretary has been given powers to vary the size of any board, and in particular to change the proportions of its composition to one-quarter each for regional and district councils and one-half for Secretary of State appointees. It is likely that this power will be used to reduce the size of boards.

**Controlled Waters**

**3.5.5**    The areas of jurisdiction of each board or islands council acting as a river purification authority were set in each of the orders originally constituting each, but the areas have been extended by later statute and order. The jurisdiction now extends to what are called "controlled waters." These, defined by s.30A of the Control of Pollution Act 1974,[10] consist of all naturally occurring inland waters (i.e. landward of the territorial sea) which form any sort of watercourse and include underground waters, lochs and ponds,[11] and certain reservoirs which are treated as lochs or ponds,[12] together with, in appropriate cases, freshwater coastal waters, the territorial sea up to three nautical miles from its baselines, and areas of the territorial sea beyond that limit if added by order of the Secretary of State.[13]

**Water Quality of Streams, etc.[14]**

**3.5.6**    By s.30B of the Control of Pollution Act 1974,[15] the Secretary of State has power to prescribe a system for the classification of waters in Scotland both generally as to their purpose, and specifically as to the substances and their concentrations to be present or absent in designated waters, and as to other characteristics. Regulations have been issued as to the classification of waters for supply after treatment as drinking waters by water supply authorities, and to the presences of certain dangerous substances.[16] By s.30C the Secretary may serve a notice on a river purification authority specifying the quality objectives for any waters under its jurisdiction. Such a notice may be reviewed after five years, or earlier at the request of an authority. By s.30D it is the duty of the Secretary and river purification authorities to ensure that the water quality objectives are met. Each authority maintains a register of quality objectives for its area, and this is open to the public (s.41(1)(*a*), COPA).

By s.54 of the Control of Pollution Act the Secretary of State may **3.5.7** give general or specific directions to each river purification authority as to the carrying out of its functions. In particular these directions may be used to implement international and EEC obligations. Similar powers are given in respect of Part I (Integrated Pollution Control) of the Environmental Protection Act 1990 by s.156 of that Act. Powers therefore exist to conform to the changing requirements of the EEC and international environmental agreements in force for the United Kingdom.

**Mechanisms for Attaining Water Quality**

The major controlling mechanism on water pollution is a general **3.5.8** prohibition on the entry of matter or pollutants into a water system except with the consent of the relevant river purification authority or other appropriate regulatory authority. Breach of that prohibition invites a criminal sanction. In addition authorities engaged in the supply of water have statutory powers to secure that their water sources are kept free from pollution.

An offence is committed only where a person is found guilty of **3.5.9** causing or knowingly permitting the unlawful entry of matter or of poisonous, noxious or polluting matter (s.31(1), COPA). In the past, construing similar language, "causing" has been interpreted in a simple commonsense way: had something been done the result of which was the entry of matter or pollution? Knowledge or intention is therefore not required to establish causation.[17]

**Lawful Entry of Matter and of Pollutants**

The entry of matter or of pollutants (including effluent)[18] into **3.5.10** controlled waters is dealt with under s.31 of the Control of Pollution Act. Such an entry is not unlawful if it conforms to the terms of a consent given by a river purification authority, and this covers both the case of the occasional entry, and that of a continuing discharge of trade or sewage effluent—on which, see the special section on Continuing Discharges, below.

**3.5.11**   Apart from that case, an entry is not unlawful if it complies with the requirements and procedures under the Environmental Protection Act 1990 (notably the terms of an authorisation under Part I (Integrated Pollution Control) or a waste management licence under Part II (Waste on Land).[19] Nor does the 1974 Act make it unlawful for a water authority to make a temporary discharge for the purpose of construction works under s.33 of the Water (Scotland) Act 1980 (s.31(2)(*b*)(i), COPA). A discharge licensed under Part II of the Food and Environment Protection Act 1985 is not caught by the 1974 Act (s.31(2)(*b*)(iii), COPA), nor is one sanctioned by a local Act or statutory order conferring power to discharge effluent (s.31(2)(*b*)(ii), COPA). An entry is also permitted in an emergency to avoid danger to life or health provided that the person making it takes all reasonably practicable steps to minimise the entry and its effects, and notifies the local river purification authority as soon as possible (s.31(2)(*c*), COPA).

**3.5.12**   Solid matter may lawfully enter a stream or water system if covered by any of the exemptions just mentioned. In general, however, it may not be put into a stream or watercourse without the permission of the appropriate river purification authority if it will impede the flow and possibly result in a substantial aggravation of pollution (s.31(1)(*b*)). Solid waste is similarly not to be allowed to enter controlled waters (s.31(1)(*c*)), although that from mines and similar workings can be dumped on land with the consent of the river purification authority, provided that no other method of disposal is reasonably practicable, and all practicable steps are taken to avoid it entering a water system. Under those circumstances, if notwithstanding compliance with these requirements, some matter enters inland waters, an offence has not been committed (s.31(3)). The Secretary of State has power to prohibit or restrict the carrying on of prescribed activities within a designated area without the consent of the local river purification authority in order that water pollution may be lessened (s.31(4)).

**3.5.13**   Unless with the consent of a river purification authority, it is an offence to disturb a deposit accumulated by a dam, weir or sluice with the result that the material is carried in suspension downstream. It is also an offence without such consent to allow any substantial amount of vegetation cut or uprooted in a stream, or falling into it, to remain in the stream. In both cases the consent of the river purification authority must not be unreasonably refused (s.49).

Under s.31(4) of the 1974 Act, the Secretary of State may by **3.5.14** regulation prohibit or restrict activities so as to prevent the entry of poisonous, noxious or polluting matter into any controlled waters. This power, however, cannot be used to regulate the entry of nitrates resulting from agriculture (s.31(9)). A separate local regime can exist to deal with that problem (see para. 3.8.3 below).

**Consent to Entry**

Other than the instances indicated above, a discharge or entry of **3.5.15** matter into controlled waters requires the consent of the appropriate river purification authority. In the absence of such consent, or where an entry of matter or a discharge does not comply with the terms of a consent, a person causing or knowingly permitting the event commits an offence (ss.31(1), (2), 32(1), COPA). As indicated above[20] causation is to be interpreted simply, without necessarily requiring proof of knowledge or intention.[21]

*Occasional Entry*

The consent of a river purification authority for single occurrences **3.5.16** presents no special problems. The authority has to be satisfied as to what is proposed, and may consent or consent subject to conditions. Special provisions are now made for the case of vessels in controlled waters (see below, Miscellaneous: Vessels).

*Continuing Discharges: Trade and Sewage Effluent*

Particular provision is made to control the entry of liquids into the **3.5.17** water system through trade and and sewage effluent. The sewerage system as such will be dealt with separately below.

By s.56 of the Control of Pollution Act 1974, "effluent" means any **3.5.18** liquid, including particles of matter and other substances in suspension in the liquid. By s.105 "trade effluent" includes any liquid (with or without particles of matter in suspension) discharged from premises used for any trade or industry, other than surface water and domestic sewage. Agricultural and horticultural premises, as well as premises used for scientific research or experiment are included. Whether or not the activities within premises are carried on for profit or otherwise, is not relevant for their classification. "Sewage effluent" includes effluent from a sewage disposal plant or sewage works of a local authority in its capacity as a sewerage authority (see below, Sewerage).

**3.5.19**  Except in enumerated instances, it is an offence to cause or knowingly to permit the discharge of trade or sewage effluent into controlled waters, or by a pipe from land in Scotland into the sea outside controlled waters or from any building or plant on to or into any land or into any waters which are not inland waters. Further, nothing other than trade or sewage effluent may be discharged from a sewer or a drain maintained by a roads authority (s.32(1), COPA).

**3.5.20**  Such a discharge is not unlawful if it is authorised by a consent from the relevant river purification board (to which we will come), or if the discharge takes place in an emergency to avoid danger to life or health, so long as the authority is notified as soon as possible. A licence granted under Part II of the Food and Environment Protection Act 1985 or an authorisation under Part I of the Environmental Protection Act 1990 for a prescribed process subject to central control will also make the discharge of trade or sewage effluent lawful.[22] In addition the Secretary can by statutory instrument exempt discharges of a type or within a specified area from control by the consent system.[23]

*Procedure*

**3.5.21**  An application for consent to a discharge is made to the appropriate river purification authority. The receipt of an application is publicly advertised in a local newspaper (s.36, COPA). The information that must accompany an application includes the site of the proposed discharge, the nature and composition of the discharge, the maximum to be discharged in any one day and the highest rate of discharge. (Falsification of data or recklessness as to its accuracy is an offence.) Where an unlawful discharge has taken place, the authority may require a consent application to be filed where it is likely there will be future occurrences. Consent given under these circumstances, however, does not eliminate the unlawful quality of the earlier occurrence.

**3.5.22**  It is the duty of the authority to deal with the matter within three months or such longer period as it may agree with an applicant. The

Secretary of State has power to call in particular applications (with or without representations having been made to him), or applications of a prescribed type (s.35, COPA), in which case the three-month limit does not apply. Applicants, the authority and interested parties are given opportunity to make representations whether the matter is dealt with by the Secretary or by an authority.

An application may be granted, refused, or granted subject to **3.5.23** conditions. Conditions listed in s.34(4) of the Control of Pollution Act as being reasonable for an authority to impose include: the place of discharge, the construction and maintenance of the outlet, the composition and temperature of the discharge, and its chemical composition, volume and rate of discharge. Other conditions can include the provision and operation of measuring apparatus, record-keeping and the forwarding of information to the authority. Most importantly, steps to be taken to minimise the effects of pollution by the discharge can be required. Finally, conditions can be varied as to time, and different conditions set for different periods.

A consent may not be unreasonably refused, and an appeal lies to **3.5.24** the Secretary of State on the grant, refusal or conditions of a consent (s.39, COPA). Each river purification authority maintains a register of applications and consents issued together with considerable detail as to their conditions. The register is open to public inspection.

*Failure to Comply with Consent*

Where a consent is in force, a failure to comply with its terms, **3.5.25** including any conditions, removes the protection the consent gives from prosecution for allowing trade or sewage effluent to enter the water system.

*Review of Consents*

Consents state the period for which they are valid, and are not **3.5.26** subject to review for a minimum of two years from the date on which they take effect without the agreement of the person making the discharge, unless the river purification authority considers it reasonable (s.38, COPA). This could apply where there is a significant change of circumstances. In addition the Secretary of State may intervene to require the terms of a consent to be altered, or even to be cancelled, in order to protect public health or the aquatic environment, following upon representations made to him, or to give effect to an international obligation (s.37(2), COPA).

**3.5.27**   The holder of a consent may himself ask for a review to be undertaken. In any event it is the duty of a river purification board from time to time to review consents it has issued, and their conditions. As a result of either such a review the authority may revoke a consent, alter its conditions or attach conditions to a previously unconditional consent (s.37, COPA).

*Information*

**3.5.28**   In order to carry out its functions as to consents a river purification authority has considerable powers to gain information, through access, inspection and requiring the giving of information. It is restricted as to the further disclosure of information that it obtains. Further, as indicated above, each river purification authority keeps a public record of applications for consents and a register open to public inspection of the consents that it has issued, and of their terms. In exceptional cases the Secretary of State may by certificate exempt the detail of an application and the terms of a consent from disclosure either in the public interest or on the ground that disclosure would unreasonably reveal trade secrets to an unreasonable extent (s.43, COPA).

## Sewerage

**3.6.1**   Apart from the various discharges of trade effluent into the water system, the major single pollutant of the waters of Scotland is the outpourings of the sewerage system. This system is subject to separate regulation down to the point at which sewage effluent is discharged into waters subject to the control of the river purification authorities. As such, sewerage largely falls outwith the scope of this chapter, but a brief sketch is necessary so that the whole picture of the control of water pollution may be understood.[24]

**3.6.2**   Sewerage is dealt with by the Sewerage (Scotland) Act 1968, as amended. Within its area sewerage is the responsibility of each regional or islands council acting as sewerage authority. Given the arrangements that have been established under the present system of local government, as well as those inherited by it, it is likely that if the regions are abolished a system not unlike the previous co-operative efforts of districts will be resurrected.

The duty of the sewerage authority is to provide and maintain the **3.6.3** public sewers necessary for domestic sewage, surface water and trade effluent and the necessary sewage treatments works, etc. It must lead a public sewer to a point where the owners of premises may at reasonable cost connect their drains or private sewers to the public system. The duty is, however, limited to provided what is necessary at reasonable cost. Owners connecting their buildings must give notice before connecting their systems, and receive permission to do so. There is no duty on the sewerage authority to provide or empty septic tanks. It may, however, resolve to empty domestic sewage septic tanks, and charge for the service. Trade effluent disposal would, under these circumstances, be for the trade or business to deal with, probably through the normal consent processes involving the river purification board dealt with above.

The use of the sewerage system mirrors to a degree the regulation **3.6.4** of the use of controlled waters. It is a general offence to put into the sewerage system anything which will damage it. Trade effluent is separately handled, requiring the consent of the sewerage authority. This consent may be subject to conditions. Only discharges which existed prior to 16 May 1973 (the date the 1968 Act was brought into force) and which have not been subsequently changed or altered are exempt from the requirement of consent. A sewerage authority may agree with the owner or occupier of trade premises as to the building of treatment works on the site of the premises.

The treatment and disposal of the contents of the sewer system is a **3.6.5** matter for the sewerage authority. At the final stage this may involve discharge into the water system, at which point the consent of the appropriate river purification authority is required, and conditions may have to be complied with, as noted above.

WATER SUPPLY

The providers of the public water supply are the other major actors **3.7.1** with powers and responsibilities affecting water pollution in Scotland. Water supply legislation is now largely codified by the Water (Scotland) Act 1980, as amended.[25] Water supply authorities are the regional and island councils for their areas, except where that pattern has been amended in the light of history or convenience. A Central Scotland Water Development Board also exists to cope with the peculiar requirements and conditions of that area.

**3.7.2**   It is the duty of a water authority to supply wholesome water to the public. This duty has been refined by ss.76A–76L of the 1980 Act.[26] These new sections and regulations made under them impose and provide mechanisms to secure implementation of the European Community Water Directives regarding fitness of water for human consumption. Water for food production has to meet similar standards under the Food Safety Act 1990, and regulations made under it.

**3.7.3**   To fulfil these duties and requirements water supply authorities have extensive powers to construct reservoirs and pipelines, as well as to seek and secure supplies of wholesome water. In the latter connection an authority has powers under ss.70–76 of the Water (Scotland) Act 1980 to prevent the contamination or pollution of water which may contribute to its water supply, and to require the owner or occupier of land to take steps for that purpose. In addition the water authority may itself enter into agreements as to land drainage, or in the last resort impose such an agreement in order that the purity of its water supplies shall not be prejudiced by the intermixture of foul water.

MISCELLANEOUS

**Agriculture and Horticulture** (see also below, Irrigation, Drought)

**3.8.1**   Agriculture and horticulture can produce problems for a water system. Various restrictions therefore apply which, in part at least, minimise and lessen the occasions on which agricultural operations and requirements cause water pollution. The major elements follow:

*Silage, Slurry and Oil*

**3.8.2**   A growing number of regulations deal with specific matters germane to the conduct of agriculture. In particular s.31A of the Control of Pollution Act permits the Secretary of State to make regulations about the custody, storage and use of potentially polluting material.[27] While much of this relates to other uses and abuses of these substances, an element of them is designed to secure that as little water pollution as possible is caused by their escapes into the water system.

*Nitrates*

Section 31B of the Control of Pollution Act allows the Secretary of **3.8.3** State to designate an area as a "nitrate sensitive area." He may then agree with owners of land in the area as to its management, or where necessary impose on them an order for its management including provisions as to prohibitions or restrictions as to how the land is to be worked. Compensation may be paid for such restrictions. By s.31C the agreement is registered in the Land Register of Scotland or the appropriate division of the Sasine Register, and is enforceable by the Secretary of State against successors of the person entering into the agreement, and anyone (e.g. a tenant) deriving title from him. Termination of the agreement may be agreed by the Secretary and the other party to an agreement or his successor. The making and modification of a Nitrate Sensitive Area order is governed by Schedule 1A to the Control of Pollution Act 1974.[28]

**Irrigation**

Modern agriculture and horticulture frequently require irrigation. **3.8.4** Water pollution can be increased if the flow of a river or stream is reduced below a critical point. The use of the stream for irrigation can have such an effect. On the request of the river purification authority the Secretary of State may by statutory instrument control the amount of water taken for any purpose, including irrigation, from controlled waters within a designated area. If an authority is not minded to make application in a suitable case, as he is under a duty to secure the conservation of water and the cleanliness of rivers, the Secretary of State may require it to apply for an order. When a control order is in place, it is an offence to abstract water for irrigation purposes except in terms of a licence issued by the authority. The licence may be limited or suspended when there is either drought or an abundance of water.[29]

**Drought**

Although, as just mentioned, water pollution may be significantly **3.8.5** increased by a lack of water in a watercourse, the maintenance of water supplies to the public can be given an overriding importance.

In the case of drought, powers exist to take water from various sources for supply purposes, as well as otherwise to control what is done with a water system, whether a river, stream or loch.

**3.8.6** In the case of drought, it used to be the responsibility of a water authority (i.e. an authority concerned with the supply of water to the public) to use its byelaw-making power to control the use of water. In acute circumstances orders prohibiting the use of water for hosepipes, or otherwise restricting the use of water, might be made.

**3.8.7** Such responsibilities will lie with the Secretary of State under Part III of the Natural Heritage (Scotland) Act 1991. By s.20 of the Act where by reason of an exceptional lack of rain there is a serious deficiency of supplies of water in any place, the Secretary of State may make an "ordinary drought order" or an "emergency drought order." These may be made only on the application of a water authority in the case of the emergency drought order, or on the application of either a water authority or a water development board in the case of the ordinary order. Ordinary orders authorise the authority or board to take water from any specified source to meet its needs, or to discharge to any specified place. They may allow the authority to prohibit or limit the use of water for specified purposes, although the Secretary can direct the authority as to the use it makes of that power. The order may also authorise the applicant to prohibit anyone from taking water from a source, and allow it to vary any arrangement it has entered into as to the taking, discharge or filtration and supply of water. Emergency orders can allow the applicant to prohibit or limit the use of water for such purposes as it thinks fit, and to supply by tankers, stand-pipes and so on. In the case of the emergency order, the Secretary of State can direct the applicant as to how it is to use the powers it has been given.

**3.8.8** An offence against a drought order is a criminal offence punishable by fine.

**Land Drainage**

**3.8.9** Many statutory provisions allow for the drainage of land in order to facilitate the enterprises that they authorise or encourage. The construction and maintenance of roads, railways or water transport systems such as canals, the safety of mines and the operation of mineral workings and hydro-electric schemes all are helped by the availability of statutory powers allowing for drainage. In addition water supply authorities have specific powers to construct or to require the construction of drainage works so as to ensure that foul waters are kept separate from the clean sources of supply which they require.

Apart from these measures, statutory schemes have existed since **3.8.10** the last century under which owners and occupiers of land can establish by official authority in the absence of agreement, drainage schemes to improve their land. Were this not the case, the artificial increase or alteration of the drainage of surface and other waters would constitute a nuisance to which neighbouring proprietors might object. A variety of statutes now govern such matters.[30] A river purification authority may be a party to a land drainage scheme, and might well have to be involved if there is any question of altering the flow of a stream, or adding polluting material to it.

**Fishing Offences**

Under various provisions it is an offence to put any noxious or **3.8.11** poisonous substances in or near water in order to take or destroy fish.[31]

**Vessels**

Pollution from vessels, particularly pleasure vehicles on rivers and **3.8.12** lochs, is an increasing problem.[32] To meet this, river purification authorities are to be given power to make byelaws applicable to any inland waters within their area (*i.e.* inland of the baselines of the territorial sea, and including lochs and rivers). Such byelaws can prohibit or otherwise regulate the keeping or using of vessels fitted with sanitary appliances (s.33, COPA). This last term includes appliances designed to permit polluting material to pass into the water, but not sinks, baths or showers. It is an offence punishable by a fine to contravene such a byelaw. As a corollary of these powers, the authorities have a duty to arrange for the collection and disposal of waste from vessels, to arrange facilities for the washing out of prescribed appliances, and to provide sanitary facilities onshore (s.47, COPA). These duties may be discharged for the river purification authority by a port local authority constituted under the Public Health (Scotland) Act 1897.

A further weapon in the armoury coping with the pollution of **3.8.13** controlled waters from vessels within its area is that a river purification authority may by byelaw require that vessels using waters in its area be registered by the authority or exempt from such registration (*i.e.* a particular type of boat could be so exempt). A reasonable registration charge may be imposed, but in that case no charge can be made on persons from registered vessels for the use of the onshore facilities mentioned at the end of the last paragraph (s.48, COPA; not yet in force).

## Waste[33]

**3.8.14**    It was indicated above that the entry of matter into a water system is not unlawful if it conforms to the terms of a waste management licence issued under Part II of the Environmental Protection Act 1990. But obviously other questions could arise, and some accommodation has to be reached between a waste regulation authority and a river purification authority as to the siting and operation of waste management sites. By s.36(6) of the 1990 Act, where a waste regulation authority proposes to issue a licence, it must refer the proposal to any river purification authority whose area includes any of the site(s) to be licensed, as well as to other agencies with interests that might be affected. The waste regulation authority must duly consider any representation made to it by the river authority. If the two authorities disagree as to the issue of a licence, or on conditions to be attached to it, either side can refer the matter to the Secretary of State, and a licence can be issued only in accordance with his decision on the matter.

## Entry and Enforcement

**3.8.15**    Finally it should be noted that in virtually every case mentioned or dealt with above, the appropriate authority or the Secretary of State has powers to enter on land or property, inspect, take samples and conduct other investigations to determine whether a licence, permission or other authority should be issued, whether such is being complied with, or whether an order or control or other enforcement procedure should be initiated. In some instances a duty is laid on the owners or occupiers of land and property to supply that information, where necessary establishing a monitoring system to provide the required information.

# Notes

*Further Reading*

E. Bain: "Water Supply," vol. 25, *Stair Memorial Encyclopaedia of the Laws of Scotland* (Edinburgh, 1988, Butterworths/Law Society of Scotland).

J. Ferguson: *The Law of Water and Water Rights in Scotland* (Edinburgh, 1907, W. Green).

W.M. Gordon: *Scottish Land Law* (Edinburgh, 1989, W. Green), Chapter 7, "Water and Water Rights," pp.150–189.

J. Keith: "Water Supply," vol. 15, *Encyclopaedia of the Laws of Scotland* (Edinburgh, 1933, W. Green).

F. Lyall: "Water," vol. 25, *Stair. Memorial Encyclopaedia of the Laws of Scotland* (Edinburgh, 1988, Butterworths/Law Society of Scotland).

C.D. Murray, J. Keith and J.F.G. Thomson: "Water and Water Rights" and J. Keith: "Water Supply," vol. 15, *Encyclopaedia of the Laws of Scotland* (Edinburgh, 1933, W. Green).

NOTES

[1] J. Ferguson, *The Law of Water and Water Rights in Scotland* (Edinburgh, 1907, W. Green and Sons); C.D. Murray, J. Keith and J.F.G. Thomson, "Water and Water Rights" and J. Keith, "Water Supply," vol. 15, *Encyclopaedia of the Laws of Scotland* (Edinburgh, 1933, W. Green); F. Lyall, "Water" and E. Bain, "Water Supply," vol. 25, *Stair Memorial Encyclopaedia*.

[2] See para. 1.1.6.

[3] See generally, Chap. 8.

[4] (1866) 5 M. 214 at 215–220.

[5] *McGavin* v. *McIntyre Bros.* (1890) 17 R. 818; *affd.* (1893) 20 R. (H.L.) 49.

[6] See below, Miscellaneous, Land Drainage (para. 3.8.9).

[7] See also "European Law," Chap. 11 below, especially para. 11.5.2 *et seq.*

[8] For detail see the updating annotations for the articles on "Water and Water Rights" and on "Water Supply" in the service volume for the *Stair Memorial Encyclopaedia of the Laws of Scotland.*

[9] s.135A of the 1973 Act, added by s.27 and Sched. 10, para. 6 of the Natural Heritage (Scotland) Act 1991.

[10] Added by Sched. 23 to the Water Act 1989.

[11] Lochs and ponds which do not drain are excluded, but may be added by order to the jurisdiction of a board.

¹² Controlled Waters (Lochs and Ponds) (Scotland) Order 1990, S.I. 1990 No. 120.

¹³ The breadth of the territorial sea is 12 nautical miles, one nautical mile being 1852 metres or 2025 yards (1.15 statute miles): Territorial Sea Act 1987 (c.49), the baselines for its measurement being established by that Act and by the Territorial Waters Orders in Council of 1964 and 1979 (printed at the end of the Statutory Instrument volumes for those years).

¹⁴ The quality of water supplied for public use is dealt with separately below; see paras. 3.7.1 *et seq.*

¹⁵ Added by Sched. 23 to the Water Act 1989.

¹⁶ The Surface Water (Classification) (Scotland) Regulations 1990, S.I. 1990 No. 121; the Surface Waters (Dangerous Substances) (Classification) (Scotland) Regulations 1990, S.I. 1990 No. 126. The latter has a schedule of dangerous substances and concentrations.

¹⁷ *Lockhart* v. *National Coal Board*, 1981 S.C.C.R. 9, 1981 S.L.T. 161; cf. *Alphacell Ltd.* v. *Woodward* [1972] A.C. 824, [1972] 2 All E.R. 475 (H.L.).

¹⁸ Effluent is defined by s.56 of the Control of Pollution Act as meaning "any liquid, including particles of matter and other substances in suspension in the liquid."

¹⁹ s.31(2)(*b*)(v) and (vi) COPA, added by Sched. 15, para. 16 of the Environmental Protection Act 1990. See also Chap. 5.

²⁰ para. 3.5.9.

²¹ See note 15.

²² Control of Pollution Act 1974, s.32(4), as amended by Sched. 15, para. 16 to the Environmental Protection Act 1990.

²³ See, *e.g.* the Control of Pollution (Exemption of Certain Discharges from Control) Order 1983, S.I. 1983 No. 1181, and the Control of Pollution (Exemption of Certain Discharges) (Variation) Order 1986, S.I. 1986 No. 1623.

²⁴ For detail see F. Lyall, "Water and Water Rights," vol. 25, *Stair Memorial Encyclopaedia of the Laws of Scotland*, sec. 14, paras. 429–500, "Sewerage," and the updating annotations for the section.

²⁵ See E. Bain, "Water Supply," vol. 25, *Stair Memorial Encyclopaedia of the Laws of Scotland*, and annotations in the Service Volume.

²⁶ Added by Sched. 22 to the Water Act 1989.

²⁷ See, *e.g.* the Control of Pollution (Silage, Slurry and Agricultural Fuel) (Scotland) Regulations 1991, S.I. 1991 No. 346.

²⁸ Added by Sched. 23, para. 8 to the Water Act 1989.

²⁹ The Spray Irrigation (Scotland) Act 1964 as amended will be replaced by Part II (ss.15–19) of the Natural Heritage (Scotland) Act 1991. The procedure for making of a control order will be governed by Sched. 5 to the 1991 Act.

## Notes

[30] See "Land Drainage," s.10 (paras. 363–374) of F. Lyall, "Water and Water Rights," vol. 15, *Stair Memorial Encyclopaedia*, and annotations volume.
[31] See also paras. 9.2.16–17.
[32] For marine pollution, see Chap. 10.
[33] See also Chap. 4, Waste.

# 4. Waste

**4.1.1** Part II of Environmental Protection Act 1990 (EPA) imposes new and more stringent controls on waste production, management, and disposal, extends the liability of those involved in the waste cycle by the introduction of a cradle-to-grave duty of care in respect of waste production, carriage, storage and disposal, and increases the powers of Waste Regulation Authorities (WRAs) to regulate waste management by the use of licensing powers. The duty of care for waste came into force in April 1992 and the waste licensing provisions are to be brought fully into force in April 1993.[1] The registration scheme for waste carriers was introduced in October 1991 and it was made an offence to carry waste without being registered from April 1992. Penalties for waste offences have been vastly increased: a maximum fine of £20,000 can be imposed on summary conviction and up to five years' imprisonment can be imposed on conviction on indictment if the offence relates to special waste.

## WASTE AND WASTE AUTHORITIES

### Waste

**4.2.1** Section 75 of the EPA defines waste as (1) any substance which constitutes a scrap material or an effluent or other unwanted surplus substance arising from the application of a process and (2) any substance or article which requires to be disposed of as being broken, worn out, contaminated or otherwise spoiled. Waste, however, does not include explosive substances under the Explosives Act 1875 and Part II does not generally apply to radioactive substances which are governed by the Radioactive Substances Act 1960.

This is a broad definition and the fact that material, effluent, a **4.2.2**
substance, or an article has some intrinsic value does not remove it
from the category of being waste. Whether a substance, material,
effluent or an article is waste is to be considered from the viewpoint
of the person discarding or disposing it and not from that of the
person acquiring it.[2]

## Controlled Waste

Controlled waste is defined by s.75(4) as "household, industrial **4.2.3**
and commercial waste or any such waste." That section also
differentiates between "household," "commercial" and "industrial"
waste and "special" waste.[3]

## Waste Authorities

The structure of waste regulation in Scotland is very different from **4.2.4**
that which is to operate in England and Wales. In Scotland the
functions of waste regulation authorities (WRAs); waste disposal
authorities (WDAs); and waste collection authorities (WCAs) generally
are combined in the islands and district councils (s.30). Each islands
or district council, however, must create administrative structures
(subject to the direction of the Secretary of State) which will keep
WRAs and WDAs at arm's length. Unlike England and Wales the
statutory obligation to create local authority waste disposal companies (LAWDCs) does not apply to Scotland (s.32(12)).

## WASTE MANAGEMENT LICENCES

Waste disposal licences under the Control of Pollution Act 1974 **4.3.1**
(COPA) are replaced by waste management licences (s.35). Sim-
ilarities exist between waste management licensing and liquor and
betting and gaming licensing, particularly in respect of the offences,
*e.g.* knowingly permitting, and in respect of licensing criteria, such
as a "fit and proper person."

It is necessary under s.35 to obtain a waste management licence **4.3.2**
from the WRA to authorise the following:
  A. the treatment, keeping or disposal of any specified descrip-
     tion of controlled waste in or on specified land ("a site
     licence");

B. the treatment or disposal of any specified description of controlled waste by means of specified mobile plant ("a mobile plant licence").

**Waste Management Licence Offences**

**4.3.3**  It is an offence for any person to deposit controlled waste, or knowingly to cause or knowingly to permit controlled waste to be deposited, in or on any land unless a waste management licence authorising the deposit is in force and the deposit is in accordance with the licence (s.33(1)).

**4.3.4**  It is an offence for any person to treat, keep, or dispose of controlled waste, or knowingly to cause or knowingly to permit controlled waste to be treated, kept or disposed of, in or on any land or by means of any mobile plant except under or in accordance with a waste management licence (s.33(2)).

**4.3.5**  It will be apparent that in relation to the first limbs of these offences the mere act of deposit, treatment, keeping or disposal is sufficient to attract criminal liability. However, in relation to the second limbs of these offences a test of knowledge must also be satisfied. In the case of the second limb of the first offence, where controlled waste is carried in and deposited from a motor vehicle, constructive knowledge is attributed to the person who controls the motor vehicle or is in a position to control the vehicle. In this case that person is treated as knowingly causing the waste to be deposited whether or not he gave instructions for that to be done. This in effect reverses the onus of proof but it should be noted that apart from this the knowledge of an employee has in some circumstances been imputed to the employer,[4] but in Scots law in general the knowledge of an employee who has sole charge of operations will not normally be imputed to the employer.[5]

**4.3.6**  Knowledge relates to knowledge of fact not law. If there is a *bona fide* (good faith) belief that there was an appropriate waste management licence in force it is likely that the courts would hold that an accused did not knowingly cause or knowingly permit the deposit, etc., of controlled waste to take place at an unlicensed site or an inappropriately licensed site. However, knowledge may be imputed from wilful ignorance.[6] The onus rests on the prosecution to establish "knowledge." In *Ashcroft* v. *Cambro Waste Products Ltd.*[7] (which concerned the offence of "knowingly permitting the deposit of controlled waste in contravention of a waste disposal licence" under s.3 of COPA) it was held that the prosecution only had to prove that the company knowingly permitted the deposit of the controlled waste. It was unnecessary for the prosecution also to prove that the company knowingly permitted the alleged breach of the licence conditions.

To "cause" means to give an express or positive order.[8] However, **4.3.7** if the accused does something which sets off a natural chain of events this will be sufficient.[9] To "permit" means to give a general or particular licence or authorisation but permission may be inferred from conduct.[10]

It was held in *Leigh Land Reclamation Ltd.* v. *Walsall MBC*[11] that a **4.3.8** deposit is made when waste has reached its final resting place with no realistic prospect of further examination and opportunity for rejection as unsuitable.

*Penalties*

The penalties for these offences are: **4.3.9**
   (i) Summary conviction: the maximum is six months' imprison-ment or a £20,000 fine or both;
   (ii) Conviction on indictment: maximum is two years' imprison-ment (five years' imprisonment in respect of special waste) or an unlimited fine or both.

These are serious penalties as directors, officers and senior employees obviously can be imprisoned, to which must be added the possibility of licences being revoked if the person in question is not regarded as a fit and proper person following conviction. There is also the effect of adverse publicity which may follow prosecution, far less conviction.

*Defences*

If it is established that there has been a *prima facie* breach of s.33 **4.3.10** it is open to the accused to avoid criminal liability if he can avail himself of one of the three defences open to him under s.33(7):
   (i) that all reasonable precautions were taken and all due diligence was exercised to avoid the commission of the offence; or
   (ii) that the acts were done under instruction from his employer and he did not know, and had no reason to suppose that the acts done by him constituted a s.33(1) offence; or

(iii) the acts were done in an emergency in order to avoid danger to the public and that as soon as reasonably practicable particulars of the acts were reported to the relevant WRA.

**4.3.11** The most contentious defence obviously will be the question whether the person charged with a s.33 offence took all reasonable precautions and exercised all due diligence to avoid the commission of the offence. It has been said that "all reasonable precautions" means setting up a system to ensure that things will not go wrong whereas "all due diligence" means seeing that the system works properly. This is a question of fact but it has been held that the larger the enterprise the higher the standard of care.[12]

**4.3.12** All reasonable precautions will obviously call for the accused to show that he made all relevant investigations to ascertain whether a waste management licence was in force, whether the deposit is in accordance with the licence, and to ascertain the exact nature of the waste to be deposited. It will also include ensuring that detailed written instructions were given to employees and contractors as to the deposit, treatment, storage and disposal of waste. This test cannot be satisfied by documentation alone.

**4.3.13** The exercise of due diligence to avoid a s.33(1) offence being committed, places a positive duty on the person to ensure that in practice an offence is not committed. This will involve the appropriate systems for monitoring, sampling and checking. It will also not be enough simply to rely on paper documentation to establish this defence.

**4.3.14** It has been held that a company took all reasonable precautions and exercised all due diligence when it had set up a careful and elaborate system of supervision[13] but spot checks have been held to be insufficient to amount to all reasonable precautions and due diligence.[14] It is not enough to satisfy these tests either to provide in a document that the other party will comply with statutory requirements[15] or to carry out sampling which is inadequate.[16] In *Byrne* v. *Tudhope*[17] it was held that a publican had failed to exercise due diligence when she failed to draw an employee's attention to his duties under the Licensing (Scotland) Act 1976.

**4.3.15** Other important offences created by s.33 relate to the breach of waste management licence conditions, which in itself is an offence, and to the treatment, keeping or deposit of waste in such a manner as to be a danger to the environment or to human life.

**Civil Liability For Waste**

Section 73(6) imposes civil liability on any person who deposits, **4.3.16**
treats or keeps waste in such a way as to commit an offence under
ss.33(1) or 63(2), which respectively relate to controlled and non-
controlled waste. It is a defence, however, if the damage was due
wholly to the fault of the person who suffered it or the damage was
suffered by a person who voluntarily accepted the risk of the damage
being caused. Liability under this provision does not prejudice any
liability arising otherwise.

**Clean-up Powers of WRA**

The WRA can require the clean-up of a site where controlled waste **4.3.17**
has been unlawfully deposited (s.59). The WRA must give a minimum
of 21 days' notice and must specify the steps to be taken to clean up
the site. There is a right of appeal to the sheriff by way of summary
application within the notification period. The sheriff may quash the
notice, if the appellant did not deposit or knowingly cause or
knowingly permit the waste to be deposited, or modify the requirement or dismiss the appeal. If an appeal is lodged the WRA action is
suspended. A person who fails to comply with an effective clean-up
order is liable on summary conviction to a fine not exceeding the
statutory maximum (currently £2000) plus a daily fine of £200 for
each day of continuing failure. The WRA may also clean up the site
itself and recover expenses from the person who was required to do
so. There is also provision for a WRA to take immediate action where
it is necessary to do so to avoid pollution or to protect human life.

**Application for Licences**

There are two types of waste management licences: site licences **4.3.18**
and mobile plant licences. A site licence is granted to the occupier
of the land whereas a mobile plant licence is granted to the operator
of the plant.

An application for a site licence is to be made to the WRA in whose **4.3.19**
area the land is situated (s.36(1)). The mobile plant licence is not site
specific but is issued to the applicant by the WRA in whose area the
operator has his principal place of business and allows the licensee
to operate the specified plant on any site. In general, the WRA has

four months in which to determine the application, after which the application is deemed to have been rejected and the applicant may appeal to the Secretary of State (ss.36(9), 43(1)).

## Grounds for Refusal of a Licence

**4.3.20**   A waste management licence is not to be issued for land for which planning permission is required unless there is an extant planning permission or an established use certificate for that use of the land (s.36(2)). In the case where only an established use certificate is available the WRA may refuse to grant a waste management licence if it is necessary to do so to prevent "serious detriment to the amenities of the locality" (s.36(3)(*c*)). Where there is an existing COPA waste disposal licence on the appointed day that licence becomes a site licence and is subject to the increased powers of the WRA under Part II of the EPA.

**4.3.21**   Apart from the question of the existence of a planning permission or an established use certificate, which is a question of fact, the grounds on which a WRA may refuse a waste management licence may be grouped into two categories: suitability of the applicant and environmental risk. These grounds call for an evaluation of suitability or environmental risk by the WRA and are likely to be the subject of dispute.

*Suitability of the Applicant*

**4.3.22**   Section 36(3) states that the WRA "shall not reject the application if it is satisfied that the applicant is a fit and proper person." Amongst the characteristics denoted by this eligibility test generally are: competence, good track record, and experience of the trade; knowledge, training and qualifications; ability; zeal; personal input and commitment; honesty; good conduct; financial creditworthiness and sound financial backing.

**4.3.23**   Section 74 of the EPA provides that a person is to be treated as not being a fit and proper person if it appears to the WRA that any of the following apply:

> (i) the applicant or another relevant person has been convicted of a relevant offence;
>
> (ii) the management of the activities which are or are to be authorised by the licence is not or will not be in the hands of a technically competent person, or

(iii) the applicant has not made or has no intention of making or is in no position to make adequate financial provision to discharge the obligations imposed by the licence.

The WRA has discretion to treat an applicant as being a fit and proper person notwithstanding conviction for a relevant offence and must have regard to guidance issued by the Secretary of State on "Relevant offences." "Technical competence criteria" may also be prescribed by the Secretary of State.

"Relevant persons" are defined by s.74(7) to be persons who at the **4.3.24** time of commission of the relevant offence fell into one of the following categories:

(i) employee, or

(ii) partner of the applicant or licence holder, or

(iii) body corporate of which the applicant or licensee was director, secretary or similar officer,

who either:

has been convicted of the relevant offence, or was the director, secretary, or similar officer of another body corporate when a relevant offence for which that body corporate was convicted was committed.

*Environmental Risk*

Where there is planning permission or an established use certifi- **4.3.25** cate in respect of the use of the land for waste management and the applicant satisfies the eligibility test of being a fit and proper person a presumption is raised in favour of the granting of a waste management licence. Section 36(3) states that in these circumstances the WRA shall not reject the application unless it is satisfied that the prevention of environmental damage makes it necessary so to do.

The environmental risk tests differ depending on whether or not **4.3.26** planning permission for the use has been granted or there is only an established use certificate. If the former, only the first two tests are applicable; if the latter, all three are applicable. There are three tests based on necessity to prevent pollution of the environment, harm to human health, and serious detriment to the amenities of the locality. The first two tests are based on the COPA tests but pollution to the environment is wider than pollution to water and harm to human health is more specific than danger to human health.

**4.3.27**    Where a WRA proposes to issue a licence (s.36(6)) it must refer the proposal to the River Purification Board (RPB), Health and Safety Executive (HSE) and if the WRA is not the district planning authority, the general planning authority. Where a Site of Special Scientific Interest (SSSI) may be affected Scottish Natural Heritage must also be consulted (s.36(7)). In the event of deadlock between the WRA and RPB in respect of the issue of the licence or its conditions there is provision for reference to the Secretary of State whose decision is final (s.36(6)).

**Licence Conditions**

**4.3.28**    A WRA is empowered to grant waste disposal licences "on such terms and conditions as appear to the WRA to be appropriate" (s.35(3)). It is specifically provided that such conditions may relate to the activities which the licence authorises, the precautions to be taken, and the works to be carried out in connection with or in consequence of those activities. In addition, it is provided that conditions may encompass pre-development and post-development activities; matters beyond the immediate control of the applicant and, in respect of special waste, the treatment, keeping or disposal of that waste (s.35(4)–(5)). It is a criminal offence to fail to comply with a waste management licence condition (s.33(6)).

**4.3.29**    The discretion of the WRA to impose conditions, is not unlimited. Section 35(6) empowers the Secretary of State to prescribe or proscribe waste disposal licence conditions by regulation. Conditions may also be struck down by the courts as being *ultra vires*. In *Attorney-General's Reference (No. 2 of 1988)*[18] a condition requiring that an industrial incinerator used for the purpose of disposal of hazardous waste "at all times be managed and operated so as to avoid creating a nuisance to the inhabitants of the neighbourhood" was struck down as being too wide in scope. Although the environmental risk tests have been widened by the EPA it is considered that this remains a correct statement of the law.

**Variation of Licence Conditions**

**4.3.30**    The WRA may on its own initiative or on application modify waste management licence conditions (s.37(1)). However, if the WRA takes the initiative its discretion is limited by the need to satisfy itself that the modification is desirable and is unlikely to require unreasonable expense on the part of the licence holder.

A WRA may only consider a variation of management licence **4.3.31** conditions to the extent which it considers is required for the purpose of ensuring that the activities authorised by the licence do not cause pollution of the environment or harm to human health or become seriously detrimental to the amenities of the locality (s.37(2)); and to the extent required by regulations (s.35(6)).

The WRA has extensive power to relax or tighten up on licence **4.3.32** conditions. A waste management licence-holder faced with an undesirable modification of a licence condition or the rejection of an application for a variation of the conditions of a waste management licence may appeal to the Secretary of State (s.43(1)(c)). The consultation requirements (s.36) also apply to waste management licence conditions variation (s.37(5)).

**Supervision of Licensed Activities**

The WRA is under a duty to supervise the activities authorised by **4.3.33** the licence (s.42(1)). Its duty includes an obligation to take such steps as are necessary to ensure compliance with licence conditions and that the activities authorised by the licence do not cause pollution of the environment, do not cause harm to human health, and do not become seriously detrimental to the amenities of the locality. Where there is a likelihood of water pollution the WRA must consult the RPB (s.42(2)).

The WRA is empowered to authorise in writing an officer of the **4.3.34** WRA in the case of emergency to carry out necessary work (s.42(3)). The cost of such work is recoverable from the licence holder or from the former holder of a surrendered licence unless the licence holder or former licence holder can establish there was no emergency requiring such work or the expenditure was unnecessary (s.42(4)).

**Revocation and Suspension of a Licence**

A WRA may partially or fully revoke a licence if it appears to the **4.3.35** WRA that the holder of the licence has ceased to be a fit and proper person by reason of his having been convicted of a relevant offence, or that the continuation of the activities authorised by the licence would cause pollution of the environment of harm to human health or would be seriously detrimental to the amenities of the locality affected, and the pollution, harm or detriment cannot be avoided by modifying the conditions of the licence (s.38(1)).

**4.3.36** Where the WRA considers that the holder of the licence has ceased to be a fit and proper person by reason of the management of the activities having ceased to be in the hands of a technically competent person, the WRA may revoke the licence insofar as it authorises the carrying out of the activities specified in the licence or such of them as the authority specifies in revoking the licence.

**4.3.37** The WRA may suspend a waste disposal licence if it appears that either the licence holder has ceased to be a fit and proper person by reason of the management of the activities authorised by the licence having ceased to be in the hands of a technically competent person, or that serious pollution of the environment or serious harm to human health has resulted, or is about to be caused, by the activities to which the licence relates or the happening or threatened happening of an event affecting those activities, and that the continuing to carry on those activities (or any of those activities) in the circumstances will continue or, as the case may be, cause serious pollution of the environment or serious harm to human health (s.38(6)).

**4.3.38** There is clearly an overlap between the grounds for revocation and suspension of a licence. However, it is clear from the greater stringency of the environmental detriment tests that the object of suspension differs from the object of revocation of a waste management licence. The option of suspension is considered to be only appropriate in cases of the utmost gravity, emergencies, and circumstances of a more than temporary nature.

**4.3.39** The effect of partial or full revocation of a waste management licence releases the licence holder from further obligations and rights to the extent of the revocation (s.38(5)). On partial revocation therefore the licence holder must comply with those conditions specified by the WRA to remain in force.

**4.3.40** Where a waste disposal licence is suspended the licence for the specified activities ceases to have effect. During suspension, however, the licence holder is bound to comply with the conditions of the licence and the WRA may require the licence holder to take such measures to deal with the pollution or the harm as the WRA considers necessary (s.38(8)–(9)). It is an offence to fail without reasonable excuse to take such measures (s.38(6)).

**Transfer of Licences**

The WRA is obliged to transfer a waste management licence if it is **4.3.41** satisfied that the transferee is a fit and proper person (s.40(4)). The procedure for transfer of a licence requires a joint application for transfer to be made in the prescribed form to the WRA by the licence holder and the proposed transferee, accompanied by the licence itself, and the specified fee (ss.40, 41).

**Surrender of Licence**

EPA 1990 imposes stricter controls than COPA in respect of the **4.3.42** surrender of waste management licences. Whereas under COPA it is possible to surrender a waste disposal licence at any time to the authority under the EPA a site licence may be surrendered to the WRA only if the WRA accepts the surrender (s.39(1)). The WRA is only to accept the surrender of a site licence if it is satisfied that the condition of the land arising from the treatment, keeping or disposal of waste is unlikely to cause pollution or harm to human health (s.39(6)). WRAs will be unlikely to accept willingly the surrender of site licences because by doing so they will be unable to recover costs of remedial action in respect of closed landfills.

*The Procedure for Licence Surrender*

Application for the surrender of a licence must be made by the **4.3.43** licence holder, providing the prescribed information and evidence. On receiving an application for surrender of a site licence the WRA must inspect the land (s.39(4)). The WRA has discretion to require the licence holder to provide further information or evidence (s.39(4)). The WRA must determine whether the condition of the land is likely or unlikely, in consequence of waste treatment, keeping or disposal, to cause pollution of the environment or harm to human health. An application is deemed to be rejected if not determined within three months. The WRA must consult the RPB (and the general planning authority if the WRA is not a district planning authority). If the RPB opposes surrender of the licence either the RPB or the WRA may refer the matter to the Secretary of State whose decision is final (s.39(8)).

*Certificate of Completion*

**4.3.44**　If the surrender is accepted by the WRA, it is obliged to issue a certificate of completion stating that it is satisfied that the condition of the land is unlikely to cause pollution of the environment or harm to human health (s.39(9)). On the issue of the certificate of completion the site licence ceases to have effect (s.39(9)).

**4.3.45**　It should be kept in mind that the issue of a certificate of completion will not release waste disposal companies or purchasers of reinstated land from civil liability under the common law for nuisance or negligence or liability for criminal offences or clean-up costs under the Public Health (Scotland) Act 1897 or other environmental legislation.

**Licence Fees**

**4.3.46**　The 3Ps (the polluter pays principle) are most clearly evident in the scheme for licence fees and charges in connection with waste licence applications. The Secretary of State is to draw up a licence scheme by regulation (s.41(2)) and that scheme is to provide for charges which will be sufficient to enable the WRAs to recover the full costs of regulation.

**Appeals**

**4.3.47**　Given the powers of WRAs to regulate the granting of waste management licences and the suspension of licensed operations, and their power to revoke or suspend licences, it is important that there are rights of appeal against their decisions to an independent body. Section 43 of the EPA provides for appeal to the Secretary of State by licence holders, applicants for licences and proposed transferees. Appeal may be made against the rejection or deemed rejection of an application for a licence or for a modification of the conditions of a licence, against the imposition of licence conditions, against the modification of licence conditions, against the suspension or revocation of a licence, and against the rejection or deemed rejection of an application for the transfer of a licence.

**4.3.48**　The Secretary of State may appoint a person to hear any matter on the appeal but retain the power of final decision or may delegate the decision to a person appointed by him. The appeal may be made by written representation, or may, and must if a party so requests, take the form of a hearing which may be held, wholly or partly in private (s.43(2)). The WRA is bound by the decisions of the Secretary of State or the person empowered by the Secretary of State to determine the appeal (s.43(3)). The Secretary of State may make regulations in respect of appeals. In particular, these regulations may deal with the time-limits for making an appeal, the manner of making an appeal, and the manner in which appeals are to be considered.

The effect of appealing to the Secretary of State against the **4.3.49** decision of the WRA varies depending on the circumstance of appeal. In general where the appeal is against the modification of licence conditions or the revocation of a licence the decision of the WRA is ineffective until the appeal is either dismissed or withdrawn. However, lodging an appeal has no effect on the decision of the WRA where the notice effecting the modification or revocation states that in the WRA's opinion it is necessary for the purpose of preventing or minimising pollution of the environment or harm to human health that the appeal should not suspend the effect of the appeal pending determination. Where the appeal is against the suspension of a licence, making an appeal has no effect on the decision of the WRA.

There is provision for compensation where the WRA has acted **4.3.50** unreasonably in suspending the licence or in excluding the operation of the general principle in the case of licence condition modification or revocation that its decision is to have no effect until dismissal or withdrawal of the appeal, and there is provision for arbitration in the event of dispute or as to entitlement to compensation or to the amount of compensation (s.43(7)).

## Licence Application Offences

It is an offence in connection with applying for a licence; applying **4.3.51** for modification of licence conditions; applying for the surrender of a licence; or applying for the transfer of a licence for a person to do any of the following: to make a statement which is false in any material particular; recklessly to make any statement which is false in any material particular.

PUBLIC REGISTERS RELATING TO WASTE

It is the duty of a WRA under s.64 to maintain a public register **4.4.1** containing prescribed information containing prescribed particulars of or relating to licences granted, applications for licences, applications for licence modifications, notifications of licence modifications, notices of revocation or suspension of licences, notices imposing requirements on licence holders, appeals relating to WRA decisions, certificates of completion, conviction of licence holders, discharge of the WRA functions in respect of supervision of licensed operators and closed landfills, directions given to the WRA by the Secretary of State, resolutions made by a WRA in respect of land occupied by a WDA, and such other matters relating to the treatment, keeping or disposal of waste or pollution of the environment as may be prescribed and a statement of exclusion of confidential information under s.66.

**4.4.2**  There are two categories of excluded information: information affecting national security (s.65) and commercially confidential information (s.66). The exclusion of commercially confidential information is limited by the ability of the Secretary of State to override commercial confidentiality in the public interest (s.66(7)). There is a right of appeal to the Secretary of State against the refusal of the WRA to treat information as being commercially confidential (s.66(1)).

**4.4.3**  If on an application for information to be treated as being commercially confidential and hence excluded from the register the WRA does not make a determination within 14 days the information is deemed to be commercially confidential (s.66(3)). It should be noted that the protection against the entry of information in the public register lasts for only four years unless the person who provided the information applies for the exclusion to continue to operate and the WRA determines that the information remains commercially confidential (s.66(8)). Information is only commercially confidential if in relation to any individual or person that information, if contained in the register, would prejudice to an unreasonable degree the commercial interests of that individual or person (s.66(11)).

THE DUTY OF CARE FOR WASTE

**4.5.1**  The most important innovation of Part II of the Environmental Protection Act 1990, is the duty of care for waste contained in s.34 of the Act. The duty of care, however, does not stand in isolation as it cannot be brought into force until each WRA has established a register of carriers under the Control of Pollution (Amendment) Act

# The Duty of Care for Waste

1989. The government issued the Controlled Waste (Registration of Carriers and Seizure of Vehicles) Regulations[19] in October 1991 and initiated a rolling programme for establishment of a waste carriers registration scheme. The duty of care for waste also came into force in April 1992.

## Who is Liable?

The duty of care applies to each stage of the waste chain from **4.5.2** production to final disposal or cradle to grave. The categories of persons liable under the duty therefore are any person involved in the import, production, carriage, keeping, treatment, disposal or brokerage, providing the broker has control of the waste. Households are exempt from the duty of care in respect of their own household waste (s.34(2)).

## What is the Duty?

The duty of care relates to controlled waste and the obligation on **4.5.3** those liable under this duty is to take all such measures in their particular capacities as are reasonable in the circumstances to prevent the unlawful management of waste (s.33), to prevent the escape of waste from his control or that of any other person and to ensure that on transfer (a) waste is transferred to an authorised person; and (b) the waste is accompanied by a written description of the waste sufficient to enable other persons to avoid contravention of s.33 and to comply with the duty of care in respect of the escape of waste.

Breach of the duty of care is a criminal offence (s.34(6)). **4.5.4**

Section 34(5) empowers the Secretary of State to make regulations **4.5.5** imposing detailed requirements in respect of the duty of care and those liable under it in relation to documentation, the retention of documents and the furnishing of documents or copies of documents.

## Code of Practice

The Secretary of State is obliged after consultation with representa- **4.5.6** tive bodies to prepare and issue a Code of Practice. A final version was issued in November 1991. The Environmental Protection (Duty of Care) Regulations 1991[20] require all those subject to the duty of care for waste to make records of waste received and assigned, and to keep records and to make them available to the WRA. The purpose of the Code of Practice is to provide practical guidance on how to discharge the duty of care and it is provided that the Code of Practice is to be admissible in evidence.

**4.5.7** Breach of the Code *per se* is not a criminal offence but the court must take account of the Code of Practice in determining any question arising in proceedings where it appears to the court that the Code is relevant to that question.

**4.5.8** The Code of Practice gives step-by-step advice on the identification and description of waste, management of waste, transfer of waste to an authorised person, receiving and holding waste and monitoring compliance. The revised Code of Practice also provides a useful checklist, guidance on how to obtain expert help and advice, and a model waste-transfer note.

**4.5.9** It is important to emphasise that compliance with the guidance provided by the Code may not be sufficient to discharge the duty to take all reasonable measures in the circumstances as particular circumstances may dictate that more onerous or less onerous steps should be taken to comply with the duty. Therefore it may be possible for the prosecution to establish that although the accused complied with the Code in all respects he did not comply with the duty of care.

**4.5.10** The duty of care applies to waste producers, etc., in their own capacity. The object of the duty of care is to ensure that adequate steps are taken at each stage in the waste production/disposal chain to ensure that waste is properly described, consigned and handled.

CARRIAGE OF WASTE

**4.6.1** Subject to specified exceptions, any person who transports controlled waste to or from any place in Great Britain in the course of any business of his or otherwise with a view to a profit must be registered to do so.

**4.6.2** The Control of Pollution (Amendment) Act 1989 makes it an offence to transport controlled waste without being registered. It is not an offence, however, to transport controlled waste between different places within the same premises or to transport controlled waste by air or sea if that waste is being exported from Great Britain (s.1(1)).

**4.6.3** Under the Controlled Waste (Regulation of Carriers and Seizure of Vehicles) Regulations 1991[21] each Waste Regulation Authority is required to establish and maintain a register of waste carriers and to set out the basis on which the registration system operates and provide guidance on the seizure of vehicles used for fly-tipping and the enforcement of registration of waste carriers and the seizure of vehicles.

The Duty of Care requires that if controlled waste is transferred it is **4.6.4** only transferred to an authorised person. "Authorised person" includes any person registered with a Waste Regulation Authority as a carrier of controlled waste and any person who is exempt by virtue of Regulations made under s.1(3) of the 1989 Act. Regulation 2 of the Regulation of Carriers Regulations 1991 sets out persons exempt for the purposes of s.1(3). These include charities and voluntary organisations, waste collection authorities, British Rail when carrying waste by rail and ship operators where waste is to be disposed of under licence at sea.

## CLOSED LANDFILLS

Section 61 of EPA imposes a duty on WRAs periodically to inspect **4.7.1** their areas to detect whether any land is in such a condition, by reason of relevant matters affecting the land, that it may cause pollution of the environment or harm to human health. This duty does not apply where there is a site licence in force in respect to the land. "Relevant matters" are defined as follows: the concentration or accumulation in, and emission or discharge from, the land of noxious gases or noxious liquids caused by deposits of controlled waste in the land. The principal purpose of this provision is to oblige WRAs to take steps to avert the danger arising from the gathering of methane gas in landfills.

The WRA is given rights of entry and inspection for this purpose. In **4.7.2** addition, the WRA is obliged to take remedial action where the condition of the land is likely to cause pollution of the environment or harm to human health due to the relevant matters affecting the land. The reasonable costs of remedial actions are recoverable from the owner of the land for the time being (not the owner when the deposit of controlled waste occurred) unless the WRA pursuant to s.39 accepted the surrender of the waste management licence which authorised the activities in the course of which the waste was deposited.

**4.7.3**　As the surrender of a waste management licence under s.39 will deprive the WRA of the opportunity of recovering the costs of remedial action in respect of closed landfills it is unlikely that WRAs will willingly accept their surrender. There is, however, a right of appeal against refusal or deemed refusal of the surrender of a waste management licence.

### PUBLIC REGISTERS OF LAND WHICH MAY BE CONTAMINATED

**4.8.1**　Section 143 of the Environmental Protection Act 1990 imposes a duty on planning authorities to compile and maintain registers of land in their area which is or has been put to a contaminative use. Contamination is not synonymous with pollution and land may be registered without actually being contaminated—the register is a register of land which is or has been put to a contaminative use and not a register of contaminated land. It is doubtful if investors or purchasers will take on board the distinction between contaminated land and land which is or has been put to a contaminative use or between contamination and pollution.

**4.8.2**　According to the Consultation Paper issued by the Scottish Office in July 1991, planning authorities were scheduled to begin compiling the registers from April 1, 1992 and the registers were to be open to public inspection from April 1, 1993. Regulations on the form of the registers, contaminative uses of land, and the information to be included in the registers were due in April 1992. However, there has been some slippage and definite dates for the introduction of these proposals are uncertain at present.

**4.8.3**　The key definitions are contained in s.143(6) of EPA: "contaminative use" means any use of land which may cause it to be contaminated with noxious substances; "land subject to contamination" means land which is being or has been put to a contaminative use; "substance" means any natural or artificial substance, whether in solid or liquid form or in the form of a gas or a vapour. According to the Consultation Paper, "land" is to include any ground, soil or earth, houses or other buildings, the air space about it, but excludes all mines or minerals beneath it; land used for partial and ancillary purposes which form part of the primary use is also included.

**4.8.4**　From the viewpoint of the landowner or the financial institution the consequences of the registration of land in the registers will be seriously to affect the value of the land. There is no compensation for the blighting effects of registration, no appeal against registration, and no procedure for removing land from the register after it has been registered even if the land is cleaned up.

A list of contaminative uses will be set out in the regulations. **4.8.5** However, a list of proposed contaminative uses appears in Annex C of the Consultation Paper and includes agriculture (burial of deceased livestock), coal, petroleum and minerals, gasworks, power stations, metal production, chemical production, engineering, explosives and electrical components, food processing (pet foods and animal feedstuffs), animal by-product processing (rendering, etc., but excluding slaughterhouses and butchering), paper, pulp and printing, timber and timber products, textiles, rubber, transport, waste disposal and dry cleaning. In addition to uses which are widely recognised as being sources of possible contamination, *e.g.* chemical production, the list includes other less obviously contaminative uses, such as dry cleaning, transport and printing.

In compiling the registers planning authorities will rely on disparate **4.8.6** sources of information such as Ordnance Survey and other maps, the Scottish vacant land survey, waste disposal licence records, records of premises under the Radioactive Substances Act 1960, planning registers, records of burial sites of dead animals, river purification records, local archives and societies, industrial sources and local knowledge.[22]

As can be seen, the sources range from the objective to the **4.8.7** subjective. Bearing in mind that there is no right of appeal against registration and that a property cannot be removed from the registers, even if decontaminated, some concern must be expressed about the use of the less objective sources of information for registration purposes.

Obviously land which has not been put to a contaminative use will **4.8.8** not be in these registers. However, the fact that land is not in the register does not necessarily mean that it is not contaminated or polluted. For example, the following will not be in the register: land which is contaminated with naturally-occurring contaminative substances such as radon gas and arsenic, land which has been contaminated by unauthorised dumping of waste (fly-tipping), land contaminated by accidental spillage of harmful materials, land contaminated by activities on adjacent or nearby sites.

The registers must meet the requirements of the EC Directive on **4.8.9** Freedom of Access to Information on the Environment.[23] The Directive recognises the need to protect commercially confidential information but clearly the onus lies on the landowner to establish why such information should not be fully available to the public. Recent experience of Integrated Pollution Control (which deals with the much more sensitive area of industrial processes) does not augur well for landowners who hope to exclude information about their land from the Register, as almost without exception pleas for the exclusion of information from the IPC Registers on the ground of commercial confidentiality have been rejected.

*Further Reading*

S. Ball and S. Bell: *Environmental Law*, Chapter 12 (London, 1991, Blackstone).
S. Garbutt: *Waste Management Law—A Practical Handbook* (London, 1992, Chancery).
S. Tromans: *Environmental Protection Act 1990* (London, 1991, Sweet & Maxwell).

NOTES

[1] The Consultation Paper on the creation of a Scottish Environment Protection Agency (see para. 1.1.6) suggests that this timetable may have to be reviewed in the light of the proposed administrative changes.
[2] *Kent C.C.* v. *Queensborough Rolling Mill Co.* (1990) 2 L.M.E.R. 28: material from a demolition site of former pottery was waste notwithstanding its subsequent use as infill material; *R.* v. *Rotherham M.B.C., ex p. Rankin* [1990] J.P.L. 503: contaminated solvents considered waste notwithstanding that after the removal of contaminants the solvents could be re-used.
[3] "Special Waste" is defined fully by the Control of Pollution (Special Waste) Regulations 1980 (S.I. 1980 No. 1709, as amended by S.I. 1988 No. 1790).
[4] *Hawker* v. *Robinson* [1973] Q.B.178
[5] *Noble* v. *Heatley*, 1967. S.L.T. 26.
[6] *Smith of Maddiston Ltd.* v. *McNab*, 1975 S.L.T. 86; *MacPhail* v. *Allan and Dey Ltd.*, 1980 S.L.T. (Sh.Ct.) 136; *Knox* v. *Boyd*, 1941 J.C. 82.
[7] [1981] 1 W.L.R. 1349; [1981] 3 All E.R. 699.
[8] *Price* v. *Cromack* [1975] 1 W.L.R. 988; [1975] 2 All E.R. 113.
[9] *Lockhart* v. *N.C.B.*, 1981 S.L.T. 161; *Alphacell Ltd.* v. *Woodward* [1972] A.C. 824.

## Notes

[10] *Smith of Maddiston* v. *MacNab, supra.*
[11] [1991] Crim. L.R. 298.
[12] *Garrett* v. *Boots Chemists Ltd.*, July 16, 1980.
[13] *Tesco Supermarkets Ltd.* v. *Nattrass* [1972] A.C. 153.
[14] *Simmons* v. *Potter* [1975] R.T.R. 347.
[15] *Riley* v. *Webb* [1987] Crim. L.R. 477; *Garrett* v. *Boots Chemists Ltd.* (*supra*); *Taylor* v. *Lawrence Fraser (Bristol) Ltd.* (1977) 121 Sol. J. 157.
[16] *Rotherham Metropolitan B.C.* v. *Raysun (U.K.)*, *The Times*, April 27, 1988.
[17] 1983 S.C.C.R. 337.
[18] [1990] 1 Q.B. 77.
[19] S.I. 1991 No. 1624.
[20] S.I. 1991 No. 2839.
[21] S.I. 1991 No. 1624. See also Scottish Environment Department, Circular 18/1991.
[22] Appendix 2 of the Consultation Paper contains fuller details on these sources.
[23] Directive 90/313/EEC.

# 5. Integrated Pollution Control

**5.1.1** Increasing concern for the environment and consideration of how to protect it most effectively are themes which have come to greater and greater prominence in recent years. The Environmental Protection Act 1990 (EPA) contains in its provisions on Integrated Pollution Control (IPC) the most significant British legislative effort so far to achieve a comprehensive and all-embracing system of control over all (or at least most) aspects of certain potentially polluting processes. It is substantially prompted by EC law, such as the Air Framework Directive,[1] and allows future EC rules and international agreements to be carried into effect in the United Kingdom (s.156), for example by prescribing emission standards which must then be complied with by operators and adopted by enforcing authorities (s.3).

**5.1.2** IPC is introduced by Part I of EPA and, in general terms, deals with processes in which the discharges affecting all environmental media are regulated. Both fixed and mobile plant can fall under IPC. This Part also brings in new provisions for Local Authority Air Pollution Control, which is dealt with more fully in Chapter Two. Many of the rules apply to both, and in this chapter, while the provisions of the Act described also relate to Local Authority Air Pollution Control in many cases, Air Pollution Control is not considered as such.

**5.1.3** IPC deals with some of the situations formerly regulated under the Control of Pollution Act 1974 (COPA). To avoid overlap of the regulatory systems, the Disposal of Controlled Waste (Exceptions) Regulations 1991[2] exempt from regulation under COPA the deposit of controlled waste on land, or the use of plant, etc., for disposing of controlled waste to the extent that such activities are or form part of any process subject to IPC. This does not, however, exempt the final disposal of controlled waste by deposit on land. Such disposal is covered by EPA, Part II.

THE ENFORCING AUTHORITY

In Scotland, at present, there is no single authority dealing with **5.2.1**
pollution matters, although there are proposals to create a Scottish
Environment Protection Agency with responsibility for all forms of
pollution control.[3] Air pollution is the responsibility of local authorities
(see Chapter 2). For IPC proper, responsibility is split between:
1. *Her Majesty's Industrial Pollution Inspectorate* (HMIPI), a
   central body of some 16 inspectors based in Edinburgh with
   a total staff of under 30. HMIPI are the successors of the
   Alkali Inspectorate and still have some duties under the Alkali
   Acts, although these are to be superseded, in time, by EPA.[4]
2. *The River Purification Authorities (RPAs).* Mainland Scotland
   is divided into seven areas, each the responsibility of a River
   Purification Board established under s.135 of the Local
   Government (Scotland) Act 1973,[5] while in the islands areas,
   the islands councils act as the River Purification Authorities.
The division of responsibility between HMIPI and the RPAs is laid **5.2.2**
down in regulations under EPA, s.5[6]
In summary, the responsibilities are as shown in this table.

| Environmental Media Affected | Enforcing Authority |
|---|---|
| Air only | HMIPI |
| Air and land | HMIPI |
| Air and Water | HMIPI |
| Water only | RPAs |
| Water and land | RPAs |
| Land only | HMIPI |

The non-enforcing authority is the "Consulted Authority."
The costs of the enforcing and consulted authorities are met from **5.2.3**
fees charged to those regulated. Separate fees are charged for initial
applications and applications for variations, together with a "subsis-
tence charge" paid annually to cover the costs of monitoring, etc.
Separate fees are charged for each component of a process.

THE BASICS OF IPC

The basic principle is contained in s.6(1) which states that no person **5.3.1**
shall, after certain prescribed dates, carry on a *prescribed process*
except in accordance with the *conditions* of an *authorisation* granted

by an enforcing authority. To do otherwise is an offence under s.23(1).

**What Processes Come under IPC?**

**5.3.2**  For the purpose of Part I of the Act, processes are prescribed by the Environmental Protection (Prescribed Processes and Substances) Regulations 1991 ("the PP & S Regs.").[7] Schedule 1 to the Regulations divides processes into six broad industrial areas, each with subdivisions. Each process is categorised as either Part A or Part B. Part A processes are subject to IPC, but Part B processes only to Local Authority Air Pollution Control. Schedules 4, 5 and 6 to the PP & S Regs. specify the prescribed substances whose release into the environmental media of air or water and on to land respectively must comply with the conditions of an authorisation. Schedule 2 to the PP & S Regs. deals with their interpretation. In particular, if Part A and B processes are carried on together, the whole operation falls under IPC. There are very limited exemptions for vehicles, domestic activity and for cases where the amounts of substances released are trivial (PP & S Regs., reg. 4).

**When Does IPC Apply to my Process?**

**5.3.3**  The dates at which the new IPC system comes into force for various processes are laid down in Part III of Sched. 3 to the PP & S Regs.

**5.3.4**  All new processes are covered by IPC from April 1, 1992.

**5.3.5**  For existing processes, applications for authorisation have to be made in accordance with the timetable in para. 18 of Sched. 3 to the PP & S Regs. The dates vary from April 1, 1992 for furnaces or boilers over 50 megawatts to May 1, 1995 for the recovery of oil or solvents. The date by which one must comply, however, is the date at which application for authorisation is refused or granted, so existing plant can continue to operate under any earlier provisions or licences after the dates on the timetable, provided that application for their authorisation under IPC has been made at the time laid down (PP & S Regs., reg. 19).

**5.3.6**  An existing process is one which was carried on at some time in the 12 months up to April 1, 1992, *or* was to be carried on at works under construction or contracted for before April 1, 1992, *and* which has not ceased to be carried on for a period of 12 months between April 1, 1991 and the authorisation date (PP & S Regs., regs. 20, 21).

**How to go about Obtaining an Authorisation**

The rules covering applications for authorisation are contained in **5.4.1** Part I of Sched. 1 to EPA and in the Environmental Protection (Applications, Appeals and Registers) Regulations 1991[8] ("the AA & R Regs."). Paragraph 2 of the AA & R Regs. specifies the very full information which the applicant must supply. The enforcing authority can require further information to be furnished. (EPA Sched. 1, para. 1). Failure to furnish information means that the authority may refuse to proceed with the application. The appropriate fee must be paid with the application (s.6(2)).

HMIPI or an RPA, if not the enforcing authority, will be the **5.4.2** consulted authority. Copies of applications must be passed to a consulted authority by the enforcing authority within 14 days, to allow observations to be made, generally within two months.[9]

Publicity is an important part of the scheme of the EPA. All **5.4.3** applications for authorisation must be advertised in the press,[10] and full details of any application with any further information supplied by the applicant are kept in a register which is open for inspection by the public (s.20). There is a general exemption from publicity for information affecting national security (s.21), but commercially confidential information only has limited protection (s.22). When applying, a claim must be made for confidentiality which is determined by the authority or on appeal by the Secretary of State. If the authority does not make a determination on commercial confidentiality within 14 days of the application, it is treated as having determined that the information is confidential, and it will be excluded from the register. If the authority itself thinks that information obtained otherwise than from the applicant or from the holder of an authorisation might be confidential, it must notify the person to whom it relates, and give him an opportunity to object to its inclusion in the register (s.22(4)). There are only 21 days in which to appeal to the Secretary of State against a determination that information is not to be treated as confidential. The Secretary of State can direct that certain information, even if commercially confidential, shall be included in the registers (s.22(7)). Time limits affect confidential information excluded from the register. After four years, commercially confidential information will cease to be treated as such, unless the person who gave it applies to the authority for it to remain confidential (s.22(8)).

**5.4.4** While there is no requirement in the Act for holders of authorisations to have particular qualifications, authorities are not to grant authorisations unless they consider that the applicant will be able to comply with the conditions which would be imposed (s.6(4)). Previous difficulties or even convictions may not be relevant in deciding this, and the applicant for an authorisation is not required to be a "fit and proper" person.[11]

**5.4.5** As well as publicity by advertisement, there is a considerable list of persons and bodies who must be consulted about any application.[12] Note that this list includes regional and islands councils, but not district councils.

*Determination by the Secretary of State*

**5.4.6** The Secretary of State can issue directions to an authority (s.6(5)) requiring it to grant or refuse an authorisation. He can also call in an application for his decision (Sched. 1, para. 3) in which case the applicant can require the Secretary of State either to hold a local inquiry or to let him appear before a person appointed by the Secretary of State to state his case.[13]

*Time Limits for Decision*

**5.4.7** The Authority normally has four months from receiving the application within which to determine it. The applicant can agree to a longer period (Sched. 1, para. 5), unless the Secretary of State intervenes. If the authority does not do so, the applicant can notify the authority in writing that he is taking this as a deemed refusal and appeal to the Secretary of State. If commercial confidentiality or national security matters have to be decided, the four month period starts from the date on which those matters are finally disposed of.[14]

**Conditions in Authorisations**

**5.4.8** All authorisations are granted subject to conditions. These are critical for the practical implementation of the system of IPC. Conditions once imposed, however, do not last indefinitely. The authority

# OUTLINE IPC AUTHORISATION PROCEDURE

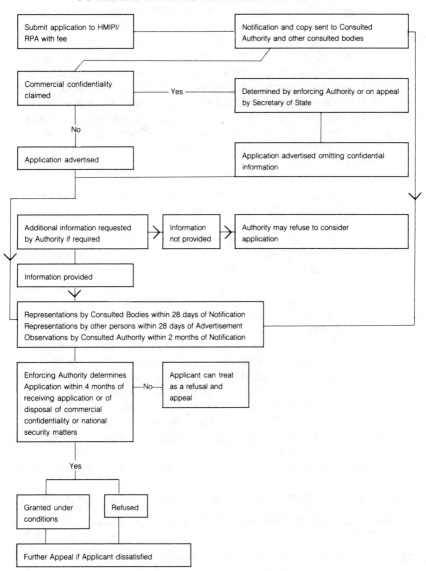

| Submit application to HMIPI/RPA with fee | Notification and copy sent to Consulted Authority and other consulted bodies |

| Commercial confidentiality claimed | — Yes — | Determined by enforcing Authority or on appeal by Secretary of State |

No

| Application advertised | Application advertised omitting confidential information |

| Additional information requested by Authority if required | Information not provided | Authority may refuse to consider application |

| Information provided |

Representations by Consulted Bodies within 28 days of Notification
Representations by other persons within 28 days of Advertisement
Observations by Consulted Authority within 2 months of Notification

| Enforcing Authority determines Application within 4 months of receiving application or of disposal of commercial confidentiality or national security matters | —No— | Applicant can treat as a refusal and appeal |

Yes

| Granted under conditions | Refused |

| Further Appeal if Applicant dissatisfied |

must review them not less often than every four years (s.6(6)). The Secretary of State may alter this four-year period by regulation (s.6(7)).

**5.4.9**  Conditions are imposed by the enforcing authority but if HMIPI is the consulted authority, it may require an RPA to impose conditions relating to releases of prescribed substances into land, and if an RPA is the consulted authority, it can require HMIPI to impose conditions on the release of prescribed substances to water, but not air.[15]

**5.4.10**  If a condition requires information to be supplied to the enforcing authority, application can be made for the information to be treated as commercially confidential, and thus to be omitted from the public registers (s.22(2)).

**5.4.11**  Conditions can be considered in four categories.

1.  The general condition requiring the process to be carried on using the Best Available Techniques Not Entailing Excessive Cost (BATNEEC):
    (a)  To prevent the release of prescribed substances, or to keep this to a minimum and render the released substances harmless.
    (b)  To render harmless any other substance which might cause harm if released (s.7(4)).
    This condition does not apply to matters where specific conditions regulate the operation of the process (s.7(6)).
2.  Such specific conditions as the authority considers appropriate in order to achieve the objectives in s.7(2), that is:
    (a)  That BATNEEC will be used in carrying on the process.
    (b)  To comply with EC or international law.
    (c)  To comply with limits, standards, etc., set by the Secretary of State under other relevant enactments (s.7(12)).
    (d)  To comply with plans made by the Secretary of State under EPA, s.3(5).
3.  Such conditions as the Secretary of State directs under s.7(3).
4.  Such other conditions as the authority think appropriate.

*BATNEEC (Best Available Techniques, Not Entailing Excessive Cost)*[16]

**5.4.12**  An understanding of this idea is essential to understanding the role of conditions for IPC. Some explanation of both parts of the expression is required, which takes us back to the EC directives. These, such as the Dangerous Substances Directive,[17] refer to the "Best Available Technology." Use of the United Kingdom phrase "Best Available Techniques" is intended to indicate that more than technology is required.

"Techniques" refers to the plant or apparatus used in carrying on **5.4.13** the process and also to other matters such as the way in which this is used, the staff employed, their level of training and supervision, and their methods of work. Items such as these can therefore be specified in a condition in an authorisation.

"Best Available" indicates firstly that the technique is to be the **5.4.14** most effective in preventing, rendering harmless or minimising the emission of prescribed and other harmful substances; and secondly, that the techniques, or more probably technology, are generally accessible. If the technology is available only from a monopoly supplier overseas, it is still "available" but the contrary would be the case if it could not be obtained by customers in general—for example, because it was a defence secret. It may be that two or more techniques are equally effective. If so, each of them qualifies as the "Best."

The phrase "Not Entailing Excessive Cost" provides scope for **5.4.15** argument. "Excessive" is always a matter of opinion. It appears that there is a presumption that the best available techniques are to be used.

Whether or not he can be allowed to use a cheaper technique **5.4.16** which is less effective is something on which the applicant must negotiate with the authority, and this will be a matter of degree. In some cases a technique at half the cost which is, say, 75 per cent as effective as the best available, might be acceptable if the danger is not very great. In others, the substances involved might be considered so dangerous that the extra cost of the "best available" technique may be inescapable.

The authority must also consider factors such as the length of time **5.4.17** that a technique will be in use. An existing plant may not be capable of adaptation now to use the best available techniques except at great expense, but the operator may intend to replace it anyway in a few years, when upgrading can readily take place. In such cases, the applicant would no doubt try to persuade the inspector that the existing arrangements should be allowed to continue. The economic position of an industry can apparently be taken into account.

*Guidance*

**5.4.18**    By s.7(11) authorities are obliged to have regard to Guidance Notes issued by the Secretary of State. These are of the greatest practical importance in any negotiation with the enforcing authority. There are two kinds, general guidance for certain industrial sectors, and more specific guidance for particular processes. At present all the Guidance Notes having been produced by the H.M. Inspectorate of Pollution (for England and Wales) (HMIP).

**5.4.19**    The General Guidance Notes so far issued correspond to the first five chapters within Sched. 1 to the PP & S Regs. They list the international obligations and EC directives applicable to that chapter, summarise the types of processes falling under the subdivisions of the chapter, and the reason for prescribing them. They also contain emission limits and advice on the requirement for sampling and monitoring. The Specific Guidance Notes deal with various individual processes within the chapters of the PP & S Regs., for example, there are separate notes on the incineration of clinical, municipal and chemical waste. The notes contain details of the level of releases that may be permitted, and the practical requirements to achieve BAT-NEEC. Details of typical types of plant used and their relative advantages and disadvantages are given, together with notes on the kind of techniques that may be used to avoid pollution, and for compliance monitoring. The notes also contain advice on the detail that must be provided when applying for an authorisation.

*Best Practicable Environmental Option (BPEO)*[18]

**5.4.20**    It is the purpose of IPC to look at potentially polluting processes "in the round." IPC covers cases where more than one environmental medium may be affected. In these cases, an additional requirement is imposed by s.7(7). BATNEEC has still to be applied to the process, but with the aim of minimising pollution to the environment as a whole by adopting the Best Practicable Environment Option (BPEO). BPEO is not defined in EPA but was discussed in the 12th Report of the Royal Commission on Environmental Pollution,[19] where it was defined as the option which provides "the most benefit or least damage to the environment as a whole . . . in the long as well as the short term." Once again, identification of the BPEO can only be made by careful consideration of all the factors affecting any process.

*Content of Conditions*

As well as the general purposes for which conditions are **5.4.21**
imposed—compliance with objectives, etc.—EPA contains a number
of provisions which specify the matters which may be put in
conditions.

1. A condition may impose limits on the amount or composition
   of a substance used in, or produced by, a process over a
   period of time.
2. A condition may require prior notification of any change in
   the way a process is carried on (s.7(8)).
3. A condition may not be imposed purely for securing the
   health of persons at work (s.7(1)). In practice, however, this
   might be very hard to differentiate from more general aims to
   be achieved by imposing a condition.
4. A condition may not regulate the final disposal of controlled
   waste by deposit in or on land (s.28(1)). Waste on land is
   generally dealt with in EPA, Part II.[20] This might seem to be an
   area where IPC is less "integrated" than it could be.
   However, in these cases the authority is obliged to inform the
   local Waste Regulation Authority, *i.e.* the district or island
   council, that the authorisation will result in waste needing to
   be disposed of on land. It may be the case that regulations
   under Part II of EPA (s.33(3)) will exempt certain plants from
   regulation under Part II, but if this is done for plants regulated
   under IPC, the conditions will still not regulate final disposal
   to land.

## VARIATION OF AUTHORISATIONS

There are numerous provisions in the Environmental Protection Act **5.5.1**
1990 dealing with variation of authorisations. This has to be seen
against the background of the BATNEEC principle. If scientific
knowledge or technology moves on, the original approval for the
carrying on of a process may not meet new standards, and thus
changes will be needed. It is definitely not the case that having been
given authorisation, one acquires an indefinite right to operate a
process, notwithstanding that it has later been discovered, for
example, to be more polluting than originally believed. It will also be

the case that operators of processes will find new ways of carrying these on and this may also need a change in the authorisation. Variations then are in two broad categories:

1. Those imposed by the authority (s.10); and
2. Those requested by the holder of an authorisation (s.11).

## Variations Imposed by the Authority

**5.5.2**     Variations imposed by the authority are promulgated by the service of a variation notice on the holder of the authorisation. This must specify the changes in the authorisation and the date or dates on which they are to take effect. This will happen unless the notice is withdrawn (s.10(3)). A variation notice also requires the holder to notify the authority within a set period as to what he has to do to comply, and will also require him to pay a fee. Some variations may be minor, others may involve a "substantial change" in the way in which the process is carried on. A "substantial change" is defined as a substantial change in the type, amount or any other characteristic of the substances released from the process (s.10(7)). Note, however, that a small reduction in the permitted limit for emission of a prescribed substance, for example, may involve tearing down existing plant if it cannot be made to reach the standard laid down, and its replacement with new equipment. The upheaval might be substantial, but the change might not be substantial enough to require notification by the authority. If the authority considers that a change in the authorisation will involve such a "substantial change" it must notify the holder (s.10(5)). It must also notify the consulted bodies, who are the same as for initial applications, of the actions which the holder is to take in order to comply with the variation. The time limit for notification is 14 days (A.A. & R. Regs., reg. 4) and for responses by the consulted bodies, 28 days (Sched. 1, reg. 6(7)). In "substantial change" cases, the holder must also advertise the action which he is to take and a further 28 days are allowed after the advertisement for any representations to be made to the authority. The Secretary of State has powers (s.10(6)), to direct authorities as to the exercise of the variation powers.

**5.5.3**     If the holder appeals against a variation notice, this does not suspend operation of the notice pending the appeal (s.15(9)). There is a potential difficulty here, because the period within which action must be taken according to the notice may expire before the appeal is determined. While no offence is specified in EPA, s.23 for failure to obey a variation notice, as it will have effect on a certain date, if the holder has not altered the way in which his process is carried on accordingly, he will be operating in breach of a condition, and thus in breach of s.6(1).

## Variation Applied for by the Holder

There are a number of possible routes for dealing with such a **5.5.4** variation. Different rules cover cases where the process is in actual operation, or where not. A holder can apply for a determination as to whether or not a change will require a variation, or may apply directly for the variation.

Variation will probably be required where is there "relevant **5.5.5** change" in the manner of operating. A "relevant change" is one *which is capable* of altering the substances released or affecting the amount or any other characteristic of those substances (s.11(11)). There is nothing to say that a mere reduction in releases is not a "relevant change." Thus almost any significant alteration to the process will mean that the need for a variation must be considered.

If the process is not being carried on, the holder must apply **5.5.6** directly for a variation (s.11(5)), supplying such information as is prescribed and paying the fee (A.A. & R. Regs., reg. 3(3)(*b*) and 3(4)). This application includes an indication of the changes which the holder wishes the authority to make to the authorisation. After consultation, and advertisement in the case of "substantial changes," the authority may grant or refuse the variations.

If the process *is* being carried on, the holder can either apply **5.5.7** directly for a variation, if he is to make a "relevant change" which he considers will require variation (s.11(6)) or notify the authority of the changes he proposes to make, and request it to determine whether or not the change will breach a condition, (s.11(1)) (an "application for a determination") and whether or not the authority would vary the conditions. The authority may require further information to be furnished by the applicant (s.11(7)). The authority must notify the holder:

1. Whether the change will breach a condition.
2. If not, whether the authority is likely to vary the conditions.
3. If it would involve a breach, whether the authority would consider varying the conditions.
4. Whether or not the proposed change is "substantial" (s.11(2)).

No time limit is set down within which the authority must respond to the applicant.

**5.5.8** In any case where the conditions have to be varied to allow the change to proceed, the authority notifies the holder of the variations which it is "likely to consider making" and the holder applies for the variation in the ordinary way. His application will be referred to consulted bodies and advertised if it is a "substantial change" (s.11(3), (4)–(8)).

If a holder applies directly for a variation, the authority can treat that application as an application for determination. This variation procedure applies to all other provisions of an authorisation, as well as actual conditions in an authorisation (s.11(10)).

**5.5.9** The procedures for variations applied for by the holder are most easily understood by a diagram.

ENFORCEMENT PROCEDURES

**5.6.1** As IPC deals with the processes most likely to cause environmental harm, EPA provides a variety of increasingly strong powers which regulatory authorities may use to enforce compliance. In increasing order of severity, these are; enforcement notices; prohibition notices; and revocation of the authorisation. The enforcing authority must notify the consulted authority in writing on or before taking any enforcement action.[21]

## Enforcement Notices

**5.6.2** Enforcement notices may be served if an authority considers that:
1. A condition of an authorisation is likely to be breached by the person carrying on the process, or
2. The condition is actually being contravened (s.13(1)).

The notice must state the authority's opinion, namely, that there is a likelihood of a breach, or an actual breach, and specify the matter constituting the contravention or making it likely that a contravention will arise. The notice must also specify the steps to be taken to remedy the situation and the period within which this must be done. The Secretary of State may direct an authority as to the exercise of its powers under the enforcement notice procedure (s.13(2)). Note that an appeal against an enforcement notice does not suspend its operation (s.15(9)).

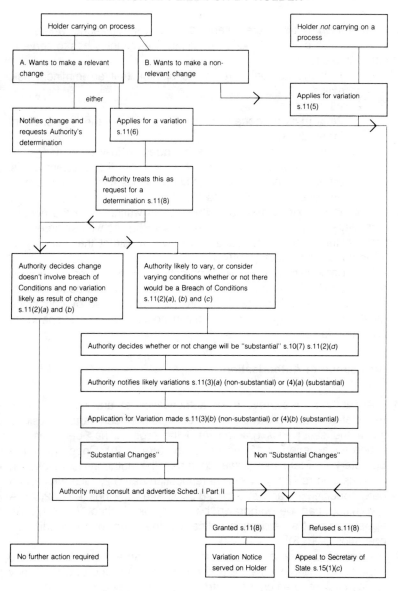

*Enforcement Procedures*

## VARIATION APPLIED FOR BY HOLDER

| Holder carrying on process | Holder *not* carrying on a process |

A. Wants to make a relevant change

B. Wants to make a non-relevant change

Applies for variation s.11(5)

either

Notifies change and requests Authority's determination

Applies for a variation s.11(6)

Authority treats this as request for a determination s.11(8)

Authority decides change doesn't involve breach of Conditions and no variation likely as result of change s.11(2)(*a*) and (*b*)

Authority likely to vary, or consider varying conditions whether or not there would be a Breach of Conditions s.11(2)(*a*), (*b*) and (*c*)

Authority decides whether or not change will be "substantial" s.10(7) s.11(2)(*d*)

Authority notifies likely variations s.11(3)(*a*) (non-substantial) or (4)(*a*) (substantial)

Application for Variation made s.11(3)(*b*) (non-substantial) or (4)(*b*) (substantial)

"Substantial Changes"

Non "Substantial Changes"

Authority must consult and advertise Sched. I Part II

Granted s.11(8)

Refused s.11(8)

No further action required

Variation Notice served on Holder

Appeal to Secretary of State s.15(1)(*c*)

## Prohibition Notices

**5.6.3**    Prohibition notices are intended to cover situations where an imminent risk of serious pollution exists. The authority has to serve a notice specifying:
1. That the authority are of the opinion that an imminent risk exists.
2. What the risk is.
3. What must be done to remove the risk and the time allowed for so doing.
4. That the authorisation is suspended, wholly or in part, until the prohibition notice is withdrawn. If the suspension is partial, the notice can specify conditions that apply to a part authorised to continue (s.14(3)).

**5.6.4**    Prohibition notices must be withdrawn in writing once the necessary steps to comply have been taken (s.14(5)). As with enforcement notices, the Secretary of State has power to direct the authority in performing their duties (s.14(4)).

**5.6.5**    Note particularly that a prohibition notice can be served whether or not the holder is complying with the conditions of his authorisation, and may relate to aspects of the process not covered by conditions (s.14(2)). Appeal against a prohibition notice does not suspend its operation (s.15(9)).

## Revocation of Authorisation

**5.6.6**    An authority may revoke an authorisation at any time (s.12(1)). Revocation is also allowed if a process has not been carried on since the authorisation was granted, or if the process has been discontinued for a period of 12 months or more (s.12(2)). Once again, the Secretary of State has power to direct the authority to revoke an authorisation (s.12(5)). Notice of revocation can only take effect on a date specified in, and at least 28 days after, the notice (s.12(3)). A revocation can be withdrawn before it takes effect (s.12(4)). An appeal against a revocation notice has the effect of suspending its operation (s.15(8)).

**5.6.7**    Whether or not a process is being "carried on" is therefore important. A single instance of the carrying-on of the operation may be insufficient to amount to "carrying-on" the process.

An appeal to the Secretary of State is competent in four cases **5.7.1**
(unless the decision made was by his direction), and is also always
competent in four more (s.15). Appeals are available against:
1. Refusal to grant an authorisation;
2. Conditions in an authorisation;
3. Refusal of a variation of an authorisation sought by the
   holder;
4. Revocation of an authorisation (the appeal suspends the
   revocation);

and an appeal will always lie:

5. Against a variation notice ⎫ The appeal does not
6. Against and enforcement notice ⎬ suspend operation of
7. Against a prohibition notice ⎭ the notice

8. Against refusal of commercial confidentiality for information
   (s.22(5)). The information is not put on the Register pending
   determination of the appeal.

Appeals are heard either by the Secretary of State or by someone **5.7.2**
appointed to act in his place. Any matter involved in an appeal can
be referred to an appointed person, presumably along the same lines
as an inspector in a planning appeal (s.15(3)).

**Time Limits**

This table summarises the time limits within which notice of appeal **5.7.3**
must be given (A.A. & R. Regs., reg. 10).

| *Cases referred to above* | *Time* |
| --- | --- |
| Cases 1, 2 and 3 | Within six months of decision or deemed refusal |
| Case 4 | Before the revocation takes effect |
| Cases 5, 6 and 7 | Within two months of the date of the notice |
| Case 8 | Within 21 days of the determination |

The Secretary of State can allow more time for notice of appeal to be
submitted in cases 1, 2 and 3 and 5, 6 and 7.

## Method of Determining Appeals

**5.7.4** An appeal or appeals can be determined by written representations to the inspector appointed by the Secretary of State or by a hearing. The hearing may be held in public or private, or a mixture of both, as the inspector may decide (A.A. & R. Regs., reg. 13). The Secretary of State when deciding an appeal can cancel, modify or impose conditions and can modify enforcement, etc., notices.

**5.7.5** The A.A. & R. Regulations (regs. 9–12) contain further provisions about the conduct of appeals, content of notices of appeals, publicity where the appeal is to be by way of public hearing, notification of appeals to consulted bodies and those who made representations to the authority, and on numerous other matters.

POWERS OF INSPECTORS

**5.8.1** Inspectors have extensive powers including power to require information to be furnished, to enter premises, to seize and destroy dangerous items, to make investigations and to take measurements and samples. Obstruction of an inspector and failure to comply with his requirements are offences (ss.17–19).

OFFENCES AND THE ONUS OF PROOF—OTHER REMEDIES

**5.9.1** Offences are set out in s.23 of EPA and cover a wide variety from carrying on a process without authorisation, which appears to be an offence of strict liability, to impersonating a pollution inspector. Also, by s.157 of EPA, any director, manager, secretary or other officer of a corporate body will also be criminally liable if his consent, connivance or neglect contributed to the commission of the offence.

**5.9.2** Two other points should be particularly noted.
   (1) An authority, if they think the criminal sanctions inadequate to ensure compliance with the Act, may take proceedings, for example for interdict, in the sheriff court or Court of Session (s.24).
   (2) In a charge for failure to comply with the general condition in all authorisations under s.7(4), it is for the accused to show that there was no better BATNEEC than that actually used.

## Notes

However, it should be noted that the general condition does not apply to matters which are regulated by specific conditions.

As well as the criminal sanctions, the courts have power (s.25) to **5.9.3** order anyone convicted of an offence to remedy the matter for which they were convicted. This could include changing working practices to avoid a repetition, or actually putting to rights the damage caused.

### TRANSFER OF AUTHORISATIONS

As authorisation is of the manner of carrying on a process, rather **5.10.1** than of an individual or company, authorisations can therefore be transferred to successors as owners or occupiers of a plant, and the transferee must notify the authority in writing within 21 days of the fact of the transfer (s.9). As authorities are directed by s.6(4) not to grant authorisations to persons who may be unable to implement the conditions of an authorisation, any intending transferee should investigate in advance with the authority whether or not he is considered to be able to carry on the process in accordance with the authorisation. If the authority does not think he is, it would be bound to revoke the authorisation.

*Further Reading*

S. Ball and S. Bell:  *Environmental Law*, Chapter 10 (London, 1991, Blackstone).

S. Tromans:  *Environmental Protection Act 1990* (London, 1991, Sweet & Maxwell).

NOTES

[1] Directive 84/360/EEC.
[2] S.I. 1991 No. 508.
[3] See para. 1.1.6.
[4] See paras. 2.2.1 *et seq.*
[5] See para. 3.5.4.
[6] The Environmental Protection (Determination of Enforcing Authority, Etc.) (Scotland) Regulations 1992 (S.I. 1992 No. 530).
[7] S.I. 1991 No. 472 as amended by S.I. 1991 No. 836 and S.I. 1992 No. 614.

⁸ S.I. 1991 No. 507.
⁹ Environmental Protection (Determination of Enforcing Authority etc.) (Scotland) Regulations 1992 (S.I. 1992 No. 530), reg. 4.
¹⁰ AA & R Regs., reg. 5.
¹¹ Contrast paras. 3.4.22 *et seq.*
¹² AA & R Regs., reg. 4, implementing Sched. 1.
¹³ AA & R Regs., reg. 8.
¹⁴ Environmental Protection (Authorisation of Processes) (Determination Periods) Order 1991 (S.I. 1991 No. 513), para. 2.
¹⁵ Environmental Protection (Determination of Enforcing Authority, etc.) (Scotland) Regulations 1992 (S.I. 1992 No. 530), Reg. 5.
¹⁶ See paras. 2.5.1 *et seq.*
¹⁷ Directive 76/464/EEC.
¹⁸ See paras. 2.5.1 *et seq.*, especially para. 2.5.5.
¹⁹ Cm. 310 (1987).
²⁰ See Chap. 4.
²¹ Environmental Protection (Determination of Enforcing Authority etc.) (Scotland) Regulations 1992 (S.I. 1992 No. 530), reg. 6.

# 6. Planning Law

Planning legislation has been with us now for 80 years. However, no **6.1.1**
statement of its objectives is to be found in the principal Act, the
Town and Country Planning (Scotland) Act 1972. An adequate
statement is to be found in a consultation paper, *Review of the
Management of Planning*, issued by the Scottish Development
Department in 1977. Planning, says the paper, "was initially, and still
is mainly, a means of controlling and guiding the use of land and the
processes of change in the environment."

Underlying this statement is an acknowledgment that the market, if **6.1.2**
left to itself, will not allocate land in a way which adequately safeguards
the environment. The abuses of the industrial revolution provided ample
evidence of that. Intervention is required. This has been achieved by
appropriating to the State the right to develop land: since 1948[1] a
landowner has had no more than the right to continue the existing use
of the land. Development can only be carried out if a licence, a grant of
planning permission, is first obtained from the planning authority. In
deciding whether to grant planning permission, the authority will have
regard to the likely effect of the proposal on the environment and to
other considerations. If the likely effects are regarded as unacceptable,
the development will not be allowed to proceed. The landowner is not
entitled to compensation in that event.

To secure a measure of consistency and continuity in the licensing **6.1.3**
process, decisions are made within a framework of policy guidance.
However, the process is flexible. The policy is not binding and each
proposal is looked at on its merits.

The planning process is not intended to be wholly reactive. The **6.1.4**
emphasis is very much on planning authorities guiding the processes
of change in the environment. Planning policy has an important role
to play in this. Planning authorities also have powers to enter the
market and acquire land to implement policy. However, resource

constraints have severely limited this aspect of the process in recent years and this description of planning law focuses mainly on the control of development proposals.

**6.1.5**    There is a tendency to regard the development control process as a largely negative function. This is too simplistic. Planning authorities have an important role to play in ensuring that development happens in an environmentally acceptable way. Negotiations between a developer and the authority to put a proposal into an acceptable form are a key part of the process; and conditional consents and planning agreements are intended to ensure that development remains that way.

**6.1.6**    The process outlined above is what is sometimes referred to as "mainstream planning control." This is the subject of this chapter. However, the 1972 Act also incorporates a number of special regimes of control. The felling of trees, for example, is not subject to mainstream control; but because of their contribution to the landscape, trees are subject to a separate system of control.[2] Proposals to alter or extend buildings of architectural or historic interest or groups of such buildings may be subject to mainstream control; but because of the importance attached to safeguarding the nation's supply of interesting buildings, they are subject also to a concurrent system of control.[3] Mineral working differs from other forms of development in that it is essentially destructive of the land. Because of this, it is subject not only to mainstream control but to additional controls.[4] Advertisements may have an impact on the landscape or townscape out of proportion to their size and are subject to a separate regime of control.[5] For reasons of safety, provisions exist for subjecting the introduction of hazardous substances on to land to an additional system of control.[6] These provisions have yet to be brought into force. Finally, where the condition of land adversely affects amenity, planning authorities have power to secure the abatement of these adverse effects.[7] Such action is beyond mainstream control.

**6.1.7**    Although some of these controls may at times offer important environmental safeguards, limitations on space preclude a description of them in this chapter. What follows is a description of mainstream planning control.

ADMINISTRATION

**6.2.1** Overall responsibility for the administration of the town and country planning legislation in Scotland rests with the Secretary of State for

Scotland. He acts in planning matters through the Scottish Office Environment Department. The day-to-day operation of the legislation rests for the most part with district, regional and general planning authorities.

The Secretary of State's role in planning may be said to fall into two **6.2.2** parts. First of all, he secures a measure of consistency and continuity between the different levels at which planning is administered. Secondly, he ensures that planning is administered at the different levels in line with national policy.

The Secretary of State has a number of instruments at his disposal **6.2.3** to fulfil his role. He has extensive power under the 1972 Act to make subordinate legislation and has used this power to adjust the scope of planning (see paras. 6.4.4 and 6.4.14) and to prescribe procedures. His issues circulars and other forms of guidance (see para. 6.3.2) on matters of policy and procedure. He determines appeals against planning authority decisions and in this way is the final arbiter on matters of planning merit. Structure plans, the top tier of the development plan, are subject to his approval. Finally, he has the power under the 1972 Act to issue directions to planning authorities with regard to a wide range of planning matters; directions may be specific or general in their application.

Below the Secretary of State are the district, regional and general **6.2.4** planning authorities. The Local Government (Scotland) Act 1973 introduced a two-tier planning system in the regions of Central, Fife, Grampian, Lothian, Tayside and Strathclyde. The regional councils as "regional planning authorities" are responsible for the preparation of the structure plan (see para. 6.3.7) and have certain reserve powers with regard to local plans (see para. 6.3.10) and development control. The district councils as "district planning authorities" have primary responsibility for local plans and for development control.

In Borders, Dumfries and Galloway and Highland Regions and in **6.2.5** the three Islands areas the regional or islands councils are all-purpose planning authorities, referred to as "general planning authorities."

District, regional and general planning authorities may delegate **6.2.6** planning functions to a committee or sub-committee of the council, to a suitably qualified officer or to another local authority (1973 Act, s.56).

**6.3.1** The essential characteristic of Scottish planning is that it is a system of discretionary development control operating within a framework of indicative policy guidance. Those engaged in the development control process will wish to know where to find such guidance. Such guidance is issued at national, regional and local levels.

**National Policy Guidance**

**6.3.2** The Secretary of State is under no obligation to issue statements of national policy on planning matters but in order to fulfil his role in the planning system (see para. 6.2.2) he quite often does so. The principal sources at the present time are national planning guidelines, circulars and planning advice notes, although the first two are going through a process of change.[8]

**6.3.3** National planning guidelines define land resources having national significance which should be safeguarded by planning authorities from or for development. An example are the guidelines for skiing which identify a number of primary areas in Scotland where there is to be a presumption in favour of development and a number of reserved areas where there is to be a presumption against development. Other guidelines safeguard areas of landscape and nature conservation interest. The national planning guidelines are in process of being replaced by national planning policy guidelines containing locational or policy guidance to planning authorities.[8]

**6.3.4** Circulars have been widely used in the past to convey national policy guidance on land-use matters, to explain new legislation and to deal with procedural matters. Occasionally they have been used to offer an interpretation of the law on such matters as the use of planning conditions and agreements. In future, circulars will no longer be used to convey policy guidance on land-use matters; that will be the function of the new national planning policy guidelines.[9]

**6.3.5** Planning advice notes set out advice on good planning practice on specific issues: for example, the siting and design of new housing in the countryside.

**6.3.6** Copies of relevant national policy guidance may be obtained on request from the Scottish Office Environment Department, New St Andrew's House, Edinburgh, EH1 3SZ. The Department is to prepare and maintain an index to all national planning publications.

**Regional Policy Guidance**

Regional and general planning authorities are required by s.5 of **6.3.7**
the 1972 Act to prepare a structure plan covering the whole or a part
of their area. The structure plan is the top tier of the development
plan for an area and is prepared by the regional or general planning
authority. It is intended to be problem-orientated. It should single out
for consideration in the plan those land use issues which are
significant at the national or regional level and in respect of which
action is required. It is not map-based; it comprises a written
statement supplemented by diagrams.[10]

The stages in the preparation of a structure plan are: **6.3.8**
(1) survey of the plan area and preparation of report;
(2) consultation with specified bodies;
(3) opportunity for the public to participate in the formulation
process;
(4) making of the plan and submission to the Secretary of State
for approval;
(5) opportunity for objection;
(6) an examination in public at the minister's discretion: a
probing discussion of selected key issues by invited parties
led by a person appointed by the minister;
(7) rejection or approval of the plan by the minister in whole or in
part. Approval may be with or without modifications or
reservations.

The intention is that the structure plan should be kept up to date. **6.3.9**
With this in mind, authorities are required to monitor and review the
plan and may submit proposals for alteration from time to time.

**Local Policy Guidance**

The second tier of the development plan for an area comprises one **6.3.10**
or more local plans. A local plan, or plans, must be prepared by
district or general planning authorities for all parts of their area (1973
Act, s.176(1)). This process is still under way. A local plan should
provide a firm framework within which decisions on planning applications can be made. It consists of a map and a written statement.[11] A
local plan must conform generally to the relevant structure plan (1972
Act, s.9(9)).

**6.3.11**   The stages in the preparation and adoption of a local plan are:
  (1) survey of the plan area, in so far as this has not already been done;
  (2) consultation with specified bodies;
  (3) opportunity for the public to participate in the formulation exercise;
  (4) preparation of plan and opportunity for objection;
  (5) consideration of objections by planning authority—an objector may require to be heard at a public inquiry;
  (6) the planning authority may adopt the plan as originally prepared or as modified to take account of objections.

**6.3.12**   The intention is that the local plans should be kept up to date. With this in mind, planning authorities are required to monitor and review their local plan or plans and may make proposals for alteration from time to time.

### Other Policy Guidance

**6.3.13**   Structure and local plans together will progressively replace the old style development plans prepared under earlier legislation. Until they do, these old-style plans will have some residual influence.

**6.3.14**   Regional and general planning authorities may at any time prepare and send to the Secretary of State a regional report consisting of planning policy proposals (1973 Act, s.173). After an initial round of such reports in 1976, they are now little used in practice. Their function is unclear.

**6.3.15**   Planning authorities sometimes prepare non-statutory policy statements dealing with specific land use issues. There are no prescribed procedures. Such statements can have an important influence on development control decisions and those engaged in the planning process should check for their existence.

OBTAINING PLANNING PERMISSION

### Development

**6.4.1**   Planning permission must be obtained for the development of land (1972 Act, s.20(1)). "Development" is, therefore, a key word in the development control process. If an activity is not development it is beyond the control of the planning authority.

"Development" is defined in s.19(1) of the 1972 Act as:  **6.4.2**

"the carrying out of building, engineering, mining or other operations in, on, over or under land, or the making of any material change in the use of any buildings or other land."

Certain activities are specifically excluded from the definition **6.4.3** (s.19(2)). These include:

(1) works which affect only the interior of a building or which do not materially affect the external appearance of a building;

(2) the use of any buildings or other land within the curtilage of a dwelling-house for any purpose incidental to the enjoyment of a dwelling;

(3) the use of land for the purposes of agriculture or forestry;

(4) the demolition of any description of building specified in a direction given by the Secretary of State—the demolition of a building is treated as a building operation but it has been proposed that the minister should direct that the demolition of a building that does not contain a dwelling should not constitute development[12];

(5) a change from one use to another within the same class specified in an order made by the Secretary of State.

The Secretary of State has made such an Order, the Town and **6.4.4** Country Planning (Use Classes) (Scotland) Order 1989.[13] Art. 3 provides that where a building or other land is used for a purpose in one of the 16 classes specified in the Schedule to the Order, the use of that building or land for any other purpose in the same class is not to be taken to involve development. The classes group together broadly similar uses of the land, for example, shops (class 1), general industrial (class 5).

It is generally fairly easy to determine when an activity will fall within **6.4.5** the scope of the first part of the definition of development—an operation of one sort or another. Determining when a material change of use has taken place can be more difficult. The change must be "material," in other words, it must be significant and not merely trivial in planning terms.

Where multiple uses are being carried on on land, it is necessary **6.4.6** to distinguish between the primary use (or primary uses) and uses which are merely ancillary. Ancillary uses may come and go and do not constitute development. In considering whether a proposed change would be material, it is the primary use against which this should be judged.

**6.4.7**    Where multiple uses occur it will be helpful in determining whether a proposed change in one of the uses is material to begin by identifying the planning unit. The planning unit is the area of land to be looked at in considering the materiality of the proposed change. The answer to the question "is the change material?" may depend on the area selected for consideration. The planning unit is generally taken to be the unit of occupation—the area occupied as a single holding by an occupier or occupiers. However, where within that unit two or more physically separate areas are occupied for different primary activities, the planning unit is the unit of activity: *Burdle* v. *Secretary of State for the Environment*.[14]

**6.4.8**    The mere discontinuance of a use is not development. Even if the intention is to abandon the use, it seems that the planning permission for that use may be reactivated at a later stage—*Pioneer Aggregates (UK) Ltd.* v. *Secretary of State for the Environment*[15]—provided it has not been extinguished in the meantime by the commencement of some other use.

### Development not Requiring Planning Permission

**6.4.9**    Certain activities, although constituting development within the meaning of s.19 of the 1972 Act, do not require planning permission. These include:

    (1) where an enforcement notice (see para. 6.6.4 below) is served in respect of unauthorised development, the resumption of the immediately preceding lawful use (1972 Act, s.20(9));

    (2) development by the Crown on Crown land (as defined in s.253(7) of the 1972 Act). An informal consultation procedure set out in SDD Circular 21/1984 is followed instead.

### Deemed Planning Permission

**6.4.10**    In certain cases, planning permission may be deemed to granted for an activity. These cases include:

    (1) development by a local authority of land in respect of which they are the planning authority. The authority must follow a separate procedure prescribed in the Town and Country Planning (Development by Planning Authorities) (Scotland) Regulations 1981,[16] completion of which confers a deemed planning permission;

(2) certain cases, for example, the construction of a power station or the laying of a cross-country pipeline, where a public body or utility is required to obtain an authorisation for development under some other statutory procedure.

## Enterprise Zones

An Enterprise Zone Scheme, made by the Secretary of State under **6.4.11** the Local Government, Planning and Land Act 1980 for a period of 10 years to encourage economic development in certain areas of physical and economic decline, will grant a general planning permission for specified activities within the enterprise zone. Other activities in the zone will require a grant of planning permission in the normal way. Three such zones exist in Scotland at the present time and a fourth is to be designated shortly. A fifth has already reached its term date.

## Simplified Planning Zones

In similar fashion, a simplified planning zone made by a planning **6.4.12** authority under powers conferred by the Housing and Planning Act 1986 will grant a general planning permission for specified activities within the zone. Few such zones have yet been made. The more relaxed planning regime of the zone is intended to encourage investment in an area identified as suitable for development.

## Development Orders

Planning permission may be granted by development Order, a **6.4.13** piece of subordinate legislation made by the Secretary of State under s.21 of the 1972 Act. An Order may be special in the sense that it applies to a defined area. Examples are the special development orders made for five of the six new town development corporations in Scotland granting planning permission for development within the new town area in accordance with the new town master plans.

Alternatively, an Order may have general application throughout **6.4.14** Scotland. The Town and Country Planning (General Permitted Development) (Scotland) Order 1992[17] by Art. 3 grants planning permission for the activities listed in the 23 Parts of Schedule 1 to the Order. These include development within the curtilage of a dwelling-house, certain agricultural and forestry buildings and operations, industrial and warehouse development and mineral exploration. The permission granted by the Order may be conditional and may be subject to tolerances. The purpose of the Order is to remove from planning control certain categories of relatively minor development or development carried on by bodies having a public character such as statutory undertakers.

## Making a Planning Application

**6.4.15**     An application for planning permission is made to the appropriate district or general planning authority. It must be accompanied by: the appropriate fee[18]; a certificate stating that the applicant is the owner or that the owner, and any agricultural tenant, has been notified; and a certificate that neighbours[19] have been notified.

**6.4.16**     An application may be made in outline or for full planning permission. An outline planning permission settles the principle of the proposed use but reserves for later approval certain matters of detail.

## Environmental Impact Assessment

**6.4.17**     European Community Directive 85/337 on the assessment of the effects of certain public and private projects on the environment has been implemented for the purposes of development control by the Environmental Assessment (Scotland) Regulations 1988.[20] The Regulations, which are explained in SDD Circular 13/1988, require that an environmental assessment should accompany a planning application for one of the nine categories of development listed in Schedule 1. These are large, complex developments such as crude oil refineries, thermal power stations, integrated chemical installations and waste disposal installations. The planning authority must not grant planning permission for such development unless they have first taken account of the assessment.

**6.4.18**     Schedule 2 to the Regulations lists 11 categories of development where the planning authority have a discretion to ask for an environmental assessment before determining a planning application. An applicant may appeal against a request by an authority for such a statement to the Secretary of State. The categories in Schedule 2 include certain agricultural developments, some of the activities undertaken by the extractive and energy industries, the processing of metals, some infrastructure projects, and certain activities associated with the chemical and food industries.

SDD Circular 13/1988 states that the purpose of environmental **6.4.19** assessment is to draw together expert quantitative analysis and qualitative assessment of the likely environmental effects of the proposed development in a systematic way so that these effects may be properly evaluated by the planning authority. Information about the content of an environmental statement is provided in Schedule 3 to the Regulations.

The 1988 Regulations also apply to certain electricity, road and **6.4.20** land drainage projects. SOEnvD Circular 26/1991 and General Order No. 27A will also apply the spirit of the Regulations to Provisional Orders made under the Private Legislation Procedure (Scotland) Act 1936 which authorise the carrying out of works. Other regulations require environmental assessment to be undertaken prior to the carrying out of prescribed activities which are beyond planning control. These are the Environmental Assessment (Afforestation) Regulations 1988,[21] the Environmental Assessment (Salmon Farming in Marine Waters) Regulations 1988,[22] and the Electricity and Pipeline Works (Assessment of Environmental Effects) Regulations 1990.[23]

## Consultations

The Town and Country Planning (General Development Procedure) **6.4.21** (Scotland) Order 1992[24] requires a planning authority to consult with specified bodies where appropriate and to have regard to their response when determining a planning application. Statutory consultees among bodies charged with safeguarding the environment include the river purification boards and Scottish Natural Heritage.

## Publicity

Apart from the requirement on the applicant to notify owners of the **6.4.22** subject land and neighbours, the planning authority must give public notice of applications:

(1) which fall within one of the 15 classes of "bad neighbour development." These classes are set out in Schedule 2 to the Town and Country Planning (General Permitted Development) (Scotland) Order 1992 and may involve development which would be likely to have an adverse environmental impact;

(2) which constitute a departure from the development plan;
(3) which affect the character of a conservation area or the setting of a listed building;

and must have regard to any response. All planning applications must also be deposited in the planning register maintained by the planning authority which is open for public inspection.

**Call-in**

**6.4.23**   The Secretary of State has required planning authorities to notify him of certain planning applications[25] so that he can decide whether to call them in from the planning authority in order to make the decision himself. These are applications raising issues of national importance. A notable example of an application called in because of environmental considerations was the proposal in 1982 to extend skiing on Cairngorm into Lurcher's Gully.

**6.4.24**   In those areas of Scotland where a two-tier planning system is in operation (see para. 6.2.4 above), the regional planning authority must be notified of applications and may call in for decision those applications where the proposed development does not conform to the structure plan or where it raises a major planning issue of general significance.[26]

**Determination of an Application**

**6.4.25**   When determining an application, the planning authority must have regard to the development plan, so far as material, and to any other material consideration (1972 Act, s.26). Once s.58 of the Planning and Compensation Act 1991 is brought into force, the determination will have to be made in accordance with the plan unless material considerations indicate otherwise (1972 Act, s.18A).

**6.4.26**   The term "material consideration" is not defined in the Act and the scope of the term has given rise to considerable uncertainty. In *Stringer* v. *Minister of Housing and Local Government*[27] Cooke J. defined these other considerations as "any consideration which relates to the use and development of land." He went on to say that "whether a particular consideration falling within that broad class is material in any given case will depend on the circumstances." These two tests provide no more than very general guidance. The initial decision as to the materiality of a consideration and the weight to be given to it rests with the planning authority and with the Secretary of State on appeal.

The list of material considerations is open-ended and much will **6.4.27** depend on the particular circumstances of a case. Environmental factors are, of course, often important in the determination of planning applications. By way of illustration of more specific factors, the following considerations have, in particular circumstances, been held to be material:

(1) compatability with other uses,
(2) the effect on private interests,
(3) the desirability of retaining the existing use,
(4) the risk of creating an undesirable precedent,
(5) circulars and other policy statements,
(6) the need for the development in economic terms,
(7) the financial consequences of the development,
(8) personal circumstances.

Given the nature of planning, there will be occasions when **6.4.28** "planning" considerations are also taken into account in other systems of regulation, including other systems of environmental regulation. An example would be the control of neighbourhood noise. It has sometimes been suggested that planning powers should not be used to control matters which are specifically dealt with in other legislation but this is not a suggestion which has found much favour in the courts: *Esdell Caravan Parks Ltd.* v. *Hemel Hempstead RDC.*[28]

The planning authority may grant planning permission uncondi- **6.4.29** tionally, grant it subject to conditions or they may refuse permission (1972 Act, s.26).

### Conditions

The planning authority have power to impose "such conditions as **6.4.30** they think fit" (1972 Act, s.26). Such conditions may regulate the development or use of land under the control of the applicant, whether or not it is part of the application site, and may require the carrying out of works (1972 Act, s.27).

Although the power is expressed in very broad terms, the courts **6.4.31** require that conditions should serve a planning purpose, be fairly and reasonably related to the subject-matter of the application and should not be unreasonable in the administrative law sense: *Newbury District Council* v. *Secretary of State for the Environment.*[29] They must also be sufficiently certain.

**6.4.32** In addition to the qualifications laid down by the courts, the Secretary of State has also given guidance on the scope of the power to impose conditions. SDD Circular 18/1986 states that, in deciding whether to impose a condition, the planning authority should consider whether they would refuse the application without it. If they would not, the condition requires some special justification. The Circular lays down the following tests which a condition should satisfy: necessity, relevance to planning, relevance to the development in question, enforceability, precision, reasonableness in all other respects. The Circular goes on to give guidance on the use of conditions to deal with particular circumstances such as restrictions on occupancy and the future management of the development.

**6.4.33** In practice conditions are extensively used by planning authorities to control a wide range of matters relating to the environment. Conditions may be used, for example, to secure landscaping and tree planting, to monitor and control various aspects of pollution, and to safeguard environmentally important parts of a site.

**6.4.34** A condition will be unreasonable if it requires the fulfilment of some obligation which is beyond the control of the applicant, for example, the provision of landscaping on land outwith the application site which is not controlled by the applicant. However, in *Grampian Regional Council* v. *Secretary of State for Scotland*[30] it was held that a condition could properly be imposed which made the commencement or occupation of the development contingent on the happening of a specified event, provided there was a reasonable prospect of the contingency occurring. Such a negatively worded condition could enable permission to be granted, for example, where it would otherwise have to be refused because of the lack of off-site landscaping.

**Planning Agreements**

**6.4.35** Section 50 of the 1972 Act enables a planning authority to enter into an agreement with any person interested in land with a view to restricting or regulating the development or use of the land. If recorded in the Register of Sasines or in the Land Register for Scotland, such an agreement will be enforceable at the instance of the planning authority against singular successors.

**6.4.36** Such agreements are almost invariably triggered by a planning application. They are used by planning authorities in practice to enhance their development control powers, including the control of matters of environmental concern. They overcome limitations on the control that can be secured by condition and they open up the prospect of alternative and possibly more effective enforcement mechanisms. SDD Circular 22/1984 gives advice on the scope of agreements. In summary, it suggests that obligations in an agreement should be reasonably related to and in proportion to the requirements of the proposed development.

Although the words "restricting or regulating" in s.50 have a **6.4.37** negative flavour, it is generally accepted that provided the overall purpose of an agreement can be said to be regulatory of a development, individual obligations in an agreement may be positive and not just restrictive.

Such agreements must serve a planning purpose and must not be **6.4.38** unreasonable in the administrative law sense—*R.* v. *London Borough of Gillingham, ex p. F. Parham Ltd.*[31]—although just how much of a limitation is imposed by this second test is uncertain. It is not clear whether, like conditions, they must also be fairly and reasonably related to the subject-matter of the planning application to which they are linked.

In determining the related planning application, the planning authority **6.4.39** are likely to be influenced by the outcome of the negotiations over the agreement. The matters to which an authority may have regard in determining an application have been described in para. 6.4.25 above. If the agreement is to influence the decision, it would seem that the matters dealt with in it may have to be heralded in the development plan or fall within the meaning of "other material considerations."

## The Planning Authority's Decision

The period within which the planning authority are to give notice of **6.4.40** their decision is two months. The period is extended to three months where the application is called in by the regional council. The period may be extended by agreement with the applicant.

A planning permission enures for the benefit of the land. However, **6.4.41** it must be acted upon within five years of the grant or such other period specified in the grant, otherwise it lapses. The time limit is slightly different where planning permission is granted in outline (see para. 6.4.16) (1972 Act, s.39). Mineral permissions have a defined life. Unless otherwise stated, this will be 60 years.

## Revocation and Discontinuance

**6.4.42**   A planning authority may by order revoke or modify a planning permission at any time before it has been implemented (1972 Act, s.42). Where a permission has been implemented, the authority may by order require the discontinuance of the use or the alteration or removal of buildings or works (s.49). Except for an unopposed revocation order, both sorts of order require confirmation by the Secretary of State, although it should be noted that the power to revoke a planning permission is exercised when the order is made. In both cases, there is provision for objection, for a hearing before a person appointed by the Secretary of State, and for compensation for loss arising from an order.

## Compensation and purchase notices

**6.4.43**   No compensation is payable for a refusal of planning permission or for the imposition of onerous conditions.

**6.4.44**   However, the legislation recognises that the effects of regulation can sometimes be every bit as severe as expropriation and provision is made in such cases for the service of a purchase notice (1972 Act, s.169). In order to serve a purchase notice following an adverse planning decision, it is necessary to show that the land is incapable of reasonably beneficial use in its existing state and that the land cannot be put to reasonably beneficial use by implementing any permission that has been granted or which is promised. It is not enough that land is of less use or value as a result of an adverse planning decision; that will often be the case. The test is whether it is incapable of reasonably beneficial use: *R. v. Minister of Housing and Local Government, ex p. Chichester RDC.*[32]

**6.4.45**   The purchase notice procedure operates like an inverse compulsory purchase order. The notice must be served within 12 months of the adverse decision. If the notice is resisted by the planning authority, it is referred to the Secretary of State for a decision. If the notice is accepted or confirmed, the authority must buy the subject land at its market value.

## Appeal

**6.5.1**   An applicant may appeal to the Secretary of State against a refusal of planning permission or against the imposition of onerous conditions. The appeal must be made within six months of the decision. There is no right of appeal against a grant of planning permission.

The appeal is an administrative rather than a judicial procedure. **6.5.2**
Although certain procedures must be followed to ensure fairness, the
decision-maker is free to consider the evidence led against the
background of national or local policy.

An appeal may be pursued through written submissions, basically **6.5.3**
an exchange of correspondence, or, at the request of the appellant
or the planning authority, by way of a public inquiry. In an effort to
speed up the proceedings, most appeals are now dealt with by
written submissions. The appeal process is conducted by a reporter
from the Scottish Office Inquiry Reporters' Unit and in the great
majority of appeals the decision has been delegated to the reporter
as an "appointed person," again with a view to speeding up the
process. With a few important appeals raising issues of national
importance the process will culminate in a report to the Secretary of
State who will make the decision.

The conduct of appeals is governed by procedural rules. For those **6.5.4**
inquiries where the decision is to be made by the Secretary of State
the relevant rules are the Town and Country Planning (Inquiries
Procedure) (Scotland) Rules 1980.[33] Where the decision following an
inquiry is delegated to an appointed person, the rules are the Town
and Country Planning Appeals (Determination by Appointed Persons)
(Inquiries Procedure) (Scotland) Rules 1980.[34] Written submission
appeals are governed by the Town and Country Planning (Appeals)
(Written Submissions Procedure) (Scotland) Regulations 1990.[35]

Planning appeals often deal with matters of interest not just to the **6.5.5**
appellant and the planning authority but to the wider public. This is
particularly so where a proposed development raises issues of
environmental concern. Persons falling within certain prescribed
categories (generally referred to as "Section 26 parties") who have
made representations on the appeal or application have a right to be
heard. The person conducting the appeal has a discretion to hear
other interested third parties and in practice they will be heard if they
have something relevant to say.

## ENFORCEMENT

Part V of the 1972 Act, as amended, makes provisions for the **6.6.1**
enforcement of planning control. These provisions are to be substantially enhanced by the Planning and Compensation Act 1991. This

description of the provisions in Part V anticipates the bringing into effect of the changes in the 1991 Act.

**6.6.2** A breach of planning control occurs when development is carried out without planning permission or when there is a failure to comply with a condition subject to which planning permission has been granted (1972 Act, s.83A). A breach of planning control is not automatically an offence. Formal enforcement action begins with a notice procedure designed to secure compliance. Criminal sanctions may be invoked only if the notice procedure fails to remedy the position.

**6.6.3** There are two separate notice procedures. First of all, where there is a breach of a condition, the authority may serve a "breach of condition" notice requiring compliance with the condition. There is no appeal against such a notice and failure to comply within the time allowed will render the responsible person guilty of an offence punishable on conviction by a fine.

**6.6.4** Secondly, in respect of any breach of control, the planning authority may serve an "enforcement notice." This, too will require compliance within a specified period of time. There is a right of appeal to the Secretary of State on prescribed grounds against such a notice (1972 Act, s.85, as amended) and the consequence of an appeal is to suspend the effect of the notice pending final determination of the matter. Failure to comply with an enforcement notice is an offence and the penalties have been considerably enhanced by the 1991 Act. The planning authority may also be in a position to take direct action to secure compliance.

**6.6.5** Somtimes the consequence of a breach of control in terms of pollution, hazard or effect on landscape or nature conservation may be so serious that the planning authority will want to bring it to a halt straight away rather than waiting for the outcome of an appeal against an enforcement notice. In such a case, they may serve a stop notice after the enforcement notice requiring specified activity to stop until such time as the outcome of the enforcement notice is determined (1972 Act, s.87). There is no appeal against a stop notice and failure to comply is an offence. The penalties following conviction have been substantially enhanced by the 1991 Act.

**6.6.6** However, if the stop notice is withdrawn or if an appeal against the related enforcement notice succeeds on one of the legal grounds in s.85 of the 1972 Act, the planning authority may have to compensate for any loss resulting from the service of the stop notice. The prospect of a compensation claim inhibits the use of stop notices.

*Blight*

## THE ROLE OF THE COURT OF SESSION IN PLANNING CONTROL

Any person aggrieved by a decision of the Secretary of State on an **6.7.1** application for planning permission which he has called in for decision or on an appeal against a refusal of planning permission, the imposition of onerous conditions, the service of an enforcement notice or by certain other decisions and orders under the 1972 Act, may apply to the Court of Session under s.233 of the 1972 Act for the order or decision to be quashed. The validity of structure and local plans may also be challenged by way of application under s.232.

Just who is encompassed by the term "aggrieved person" is not **6.7.2** clear but it is probable that in the context of appeal decisions it would include, not only owners and tenants of the subject land, the appellant and the planning authority who are directly affected by the decision, but also anyone who took part in the appeal process.

The application must be made within six weeks of the date of the **6.7.3** decision in question. There are two possible grounds on which the application may be made. The first is that the decision was outwith the powers of the Act. The second is that there has been a failure to comply with a procedural requirement which has caused substantial prejudice to the applicant.

A successful application under ss.232 or 233 may result in the **6.7.4** order, plan or decision in question being quashed. The court will not substitute its own decision; it will be for the decision-maker to make a fresh decision.

Those planning actions and decisions, which are not subject to the **6.7.5** statutory application procedure in ss.232 and 233, are subject to the general supervisory jurisdiction of the Court of Session. Thus, a person wishing to question the validity of a decision by a planning authority, for example to grant or refuse planning permission, may apply to the Court of Session for judicial review. However, such person must qualify title and interest and, although the applicant would clearly qualify, it is not clear whether the increased standing of the public in the development control process in recent years through bad neighbour and neighbour notification would be sufficient.

## BLIGHT

Blight is generally taken to refer to the depressing effect on the value **6.8.1** of property resulting from proposals which imply either the public acquisition of the property or disturbance of the existing use. For example, a proposal to build a new major road, extend an airport or construct a high-speed rail link will have a depressing effect not only on the value of property to be acquired for the work but on property nearby which will suffer serious disturbance, including environmental disturbance such as noise, fumes, dust and so on, from the construction and subsequent use of the work.

**6.8.2** The 1972 Act in Part IX makes some provision to alleviate hardship on the part of those whose property is earmarked for eventual acquisition. A person who can show that the proposed works are sufficiently advanced in their planning to cast a blight on the value of his or her property may serve a "blight notice" on the responsible body. They must, however, have an interest which qualifies for protection.[36] The provisions do not protect everyone suffering from blight; only the most serious cases.

**6.8.3** If the blight notice is accepted or confirmed on a reference to the Lands Tribunal for Scotland, the responsible body must acquire the property at its market value—ignoring the effects of blight.

**6.8.4** For those whose property is not required for the works but who will suffer disturbance from its construction and use, there are three possible remedies. First of all, the responsible body may be empowered to buy up the interests of those who are most seriously disturbed.[37] Secondly, the responsible body may be in a position to take steps to mitigate the effects of disturbance by, for example, noise insulation.[38] Thirdly, those disturbed may qualify for compensation equal to the depreciation in the value of their property.[39]

*Further Reading*

R. Henderson: *Planning in Scotland: a Basic Guide* (Dundee, 1985, Park Place Publishing).

J. Rowan-Robinson and E. Young: *Planning by Agreement in Scotland*, (Edinburgh, 1989, W. Green and the Planning Exchange).

E. Young: *Scottish Planning Appeals* (Edinburgh, 1991, W. Green).

E. Young and J. Rowan-Robinson: *Scottish Planning Law and Procedure* (Edinburgh, 1985, Hodge).

*Scottish Planning Sourcebook* (and updates ed. R. Henderson), (Dundee, 1989, Hillside Publishing).

*Stair Memorial Encyclopaedia of the Laws of Scotland*, vol. 23: "Town and Country Planning" (1991).

*Notes*

1 The year when comprehensive planning control was first introduced in Scotland.
2 1972 Act, ss.57–60, 98 and 99, as amended; the Town and Country Planning (Tree Preservation Order and Trees in Conservation Areas) (Scotland) Regulations 1975 (S.I. 1975 No. 1204) as amended.
3 1972 Act, ss.52–56, 92–97, 262–262B, as amended; the Town and Country Planning (Listed Buildings and Buildings in Conservation Areas) (Scotland) Regulations 1987 (S.I. 1987 No. 1529); SDD Circular 17/1987, "New Provisions and Revised Guidance Relating to Listed Buildings and Conservation Areas"; Memorandum of Guidance on Listed Buildings and Conservation Areas, SDD Historic Buildings and Monuments Directorate, 1987.
4 1972 Act, as amended by the Town and Country Planning (Minerals) Act 1981; Town and Country Planning (Compensation for Restrictions on Mineral Workings) (Scotland) Regulations 1987 (S.I. 1987 No. 433); SDD Circular 22/1987 "Town and Country Planning (Minerals) Act 1981."
5 Town and Country Planning (Control of Advertisements) (Scotland) Regulations 1984 (S.I. 1984 No. 467) as amended.
6 1972 Act as amended by the Housing and Planning Act 1986, Pt. VI and the Environmental Protection Act 1990; see para. 1.5.4.
7 1972 Act, ss.63 and 63A as substituted by the Local Government and Planning (Scotland) Act 1982, s.48 and Sched. 2 and further substituted by the Housing and Planning Act 1986, s.53 and Sched. 11.
8 Scottish Office Environment Department consultation paper, "Review of Planning Guidance," 1991.
9 *Ibid.*
10 For further information about structure plans, see the 1972 Act, ss.5–8; the Town and Country Planning (Structure and Local Plans) (Scotland) Regulations 1983 (S.I. 1983 No. 1590); Planning Advice Note 37; and SDD Circular 32/1983.
11 For further information about local plans, see the 1972 Act, ss.9–13; the Town and Country Planning (Structure and Local Plans) (Scotland) Regulations 1983; Planning Advice Note 30; and SDD Circular 32/1983.
12 s.44 of the Planning and Compensation Act 1991, which will bring demolition within the definition of "development," is not in force at the time of writing. And see SOEnvD consultation paper, "New Planning Controls over the Demolition of Houses," September 1991.
13 S.I. 1989 No. 147; and see SDD Circular 1989/6.
14 [1972] 1 W.L.R. 1207.
15 [1985] A.C. 132.
16 S.I. 1981 No. 829, as amended by the Town and Country Planning (Development by Planning Authorities) (Scotland) Amendment Regulations 1984 (S.I. 1984 No. 238).

[17] S.I. 1992 No. 223.
[18] These are set out in the Town and Country Planning (Fees for Applications and Deemed Applications) (Scotland) Regulations 1990 (S.I. 1990 No. 2474), as amended by S.I. 1991 No. 2765.
[19] Defined in Art. 10 of the Town and Country Planning (General Development Procedure) (Scotland) Order 1992 (S.I. 1992 No. 224).
[20] S.I. 1988 No. 1221.
[21] S.I. 1988 No. 1207.
[22] S.I. 1988 No. 1218.
[23] S.I. 1990 No. 1442.
[24] S.I. 1992 No. 224.
[25] Town and Country Planning (Notification of Applications) (Scotland) Direction 1988, attached as Annex A to SDD Circular 29/1988.
[26] Local Government (Scotland) Act 1973, s.179(1) and (2)(*a*) and (*b*) as substituted by the Local Government and Planning (Scotland) Act 1982, s.66 and Sched. 3. See also SDD Circular 29/1988.
[27] [1970] 1 W.L.R. 1281.
[28] [1966] 1 Q.B. 895.
[29] [1981] A.C. 578.
[30] 1984 S.C. (H.L.) 58; 1984 S.L.T. 197.
[31] [1988] J.P.L. 336.
[32] [1960] 1 W.L.R. 587.
[33] S.I. 1980 No. 1676.
[34] S.I. 1980 No. 1677.
[35] S.I. 1990 No. 507.
[36] 1972 Act, s.181.
[37] Land Compensation (Scotland) Act 1973, s.24, as amended by the Planning and Compensation Act 1991, s.76.
[38] Land Compensation (Scotland) Act 1973, s.18; and see the Noise Insulation (Scotland) Regulations 1975 (S.I. 1975 No. 460).
[39] Railways Clauses Consolidation (Scotland) Act 1845, s.6, as applied by the Acquisition of Land (Authorisation Procedure) (Scotland) Act 1947; also the Land Compensation (Scotland) Act 1973, Pt. 1.

# 7. Noise

## INTRODUCTION

Noise pollution of the environment can be controlled by the common **7.1.1**
law. The main common law control of noise takes the form of remedy
by way of the law of nuisance. A number of unconnected statutes
also have a bearing on noise. The various controls are discussed
below.

## NUISANCE

Noise nuisances which have been the subject of litigation in the **7.2.1**
United Kingdom include a wide variety of noises from various
sources. The list includes noise from printworks,[1] building works,[2] a
sawing mill,[3] singing,[4] domestic birds,[5] cattle,[6] horses,[7] a power
station,[8] petrochemical works,[9] an unruly family,[10] powerboats,[11] a
children's playground,[12] a military tattoo,[13] and the firing of guns.[14]

### Elements of Nuisance

Essentially the courts will protect the enjoyment of the land one **7.2.2**
occupies from any form of unreasonable interference by others. In
order to ascertain if a nuisance exists in law the courts take a variety
of factors into account. None of these factors is *per se* conclusive.
The list of factors discussed below may not be exhaustive. Furthermore the courts do not give one factor prominence over another in
determining whether any given state of affairs constitutes a
nuisance.[15]

### *Social Utility of the Defender's Conduct*

The court may take some account of the value of the defender's **7.2.3**
conduct to society in general. The more socially useful the
defender's conduct is, the less likely the court would consider his

conduct unreasonable.[16] The courts have, however, carefully avoided constructing a hierarchy in terms of social worth, of the various activities which have been the subject of nuisance actions. While the courts obviously recognise the social value of, for example, manufactories, it is impossible to predict whether the courts would regard an opera house as more valuable to society than (say) a cinema or swimming pool and so be less willing to regard noise from the opera house a nuisance than noise from a cinema or swimming pool.[17]

*Motive of the Defender*

**7.2.4**     The courts take into account the extent to which, if any, the state of affairs complained of is motivated by spite. If spite is present the courts readily incline to the view that a nuisance exists. The leading cases on the significance of spite in the law of nuisance all relate to noise. In *Christie* v. *Davie*[18] the plaintiff's family annoyed the defendant by frequently playing musical instruments. The defendant decided to retaliate by banging tin trays on the party wall. It was held that the defendant had created a nuisance. In *Hollywood Silver Fox Farm Ltd.* v. *Emmett*[19] the plaintiff's company bred foxes on his land. The defendant objected to this practice and therefore decided to create a cacophony by shooting along the boundary which separated his property from that of the plaintiff.[20] The plaintiff succeeded in a nuisance action.

*Locality*

**7.2.5**     The nature of the relevant locality where the nuisance exists is taken into account. The leading Scottish case is *Inglis* v. *Shotts* where the Lord Justice-Clerk stated pithily:
"Things which are forbidden in a crowded community may be permitted in the country. What is prohibited in enclosed land may be tolerated in the open."[21]

**7.2.6**     The rationale of such a judicial approach can be explained on the grounds that courts expect people who live in localities where a certain state of affairs is commonplace to have become habituated to it and therefore less disposed to becoming adversely affected by it. For example the noise from the unloading of ships in a port is less likely to constitute a nuisance than a similar level of noise from a newly established discotheque situated in the same locality. The nature of the locality is only relevant when the adverse state of affairs complained of solely affects the plaintiff's comfort.[22] The locality principle becomes redundant therefore when physical damage accrues as a result of the alleged nuisance complained of.[23] For example if noise and vibration from factory operations damaged the foundations of a nearby building it would be quite irrelevant that the defender's factory was situated in an industrial area. There is no authority as to how the courts would apply the locality principle if the defender's factory were situated in an industrial area but the pursuer's premises were situated in a residential area. In the absence of authority it is suggested that if indeed in such a case the locality test were applicable, the relevant locality would be that of the pursuer.

*Duration and Intensity*

The length of time the relevant state of affairs lasts and its intensity **7.2.7** are taken into account.[24] The authoritative dissenting judgment of Pollock C.B. in *Bramford* v. *Turnley* phrased in quaint language is worthy of repetition here:

"A clock striking the hour or a bell ringing for some domestic purpose may be a nuisance, if unreasonably loud and discordant of which the jury alone must judge; but although not unreasonably loud if the owner for some whim or caprice, made the clock strike the hour every ten minutes or the bell ring continually, I think a jury would be satisfied in considering it to be a very great nuisance."[25]

*Time of Day*

The time of day the state of affairs complained of exists is taken **7.2.8** into account. Noise therefore which is created during the night is more likely to constitute a nuisance than one which occurs during the day.[26] It is unlikely that the time of day is relevant in relation to alleged nuisances other than noise.

*Sensitivity of the Pursuer*

The courts are not indulgent to the oversensitive. This general **7.2.9** principle is well illustrated in nuisance law in *Heath* v. *Brighton Corporation*[27] where the plaintiff, who possessed hypersensitive hearing, failed in his nuisance action since it was proved that a person of normal hearing would not have been affected in the circumstances.

*A State of Affairs*

**7.2.10**    The pursuer needs to show that the enjoyment of his property is prejudiced by a state of affairs. In other words the alleged nuisance must have some flavour of permanence. It cannot simply be transitory in nature. In practice, however, as far as noise nuisance is concerned, the relevant adverse state of affairs normally takes place over a period of time, in which case the requirement of the existence of a state of affairs would be automatically satisfied.

*Fault Required*

**7.2.11**    Case law is now weighted heavily in favour of the proposition that *culpa* or fault is required on the part of the defender before a successful action in nuisance at common law can lie.[28] The requisite *culpa* is not however identical to fault in the law of negligence. *Culpa* in the Scots law of nuisance seems to be of wider scope. The distinction, however, has not been comprehensively discussed by the courts.[29]

**Who is Liable?**

*The Author*

**7.2.12**    Generally the person who creates the nuisance is liable at common law for any nuisance created. He need have no proprietary interest in the land on which the nuisance exists.[30] Therefore musicians who use unoccupied premises for band practice could be successfully sued if they caused undue annoyance to adjoining proprietors.

*The Occupier*

**7.2.13**    The occupier of the premises concerned will normally be the relevant defender in a noise nuisance action.[31] In practice the author of the nuisance and the occupier will usually be the same individual.

*The Landlord*

**7.2.14**    Sometimes premises which have the capacity to cause a nuisance are let. Generally speaking the courts are unwilling to allow landlords to absolve themselves of legal liability in respect of such nuisances even in the face of a lease which purports to absolve the landlord of liability.[32]

## The Licensor of the Nuisance

The person who authorises a nuisance will normally be liable **7.2.15** especially if he makes no effort to abate the nuisance concerned. The leading case is now *Webster* v. *Lord Advocate*.[33] The Lord Ordinary, Lord Stott, in the Outer House of the Court of Session held the Secretary of State for Scotland liable for authorising the holding of the Edinburgh Military Tattoo, the noise from which *inter alia* was alleged to cause a nuisance. It was held irrelevant that the contract between the Secretary of State and the Tattoo Policy Committee included a condition that no nuisance was to be created, since no effort had been made by the former to monitor the activities of the licensees or to enforce the condition of the licence. It is possible that the court might adopt a different attitude if satisfied that the licensor was capable of making and in fact did make a genuine effort to ensure that his licensee did not create a nuisance. This point can only be clarified by future decision.

## Defences, etc.

## Statutory Authority

It is possible for Parliament to sanction the creation and conti- **7.2.16** nuance of a nuisance. The leading case is *Allen* v. *Gulf Oil Refining Ltd.*[34] There, occupiers of property which was situated in the vicinity of a huge oil refinery were affected *inter alia* by oil smut and noise emanating from the plant. A private Act of Parliament had authorised the establishment and operation of the plant. The House of Lords[35] held that the oil company had a complete defence since the Act had sanctioned the existence and operation of the refinery, the necessary consequence of which was the creation of the nuisance. Whether any statute authorises a nuisance therefore depends on its construction. The court in such circumstances would have to satisfy itself that the defender conducted his activities without negligence and furthermore took reasonable measures to mitigate the relevant nuisance.[36]

*Prescription*

**7.2.17**   As far as nuisance is concerned the law will not allow the pursuer to succeed if he has acquiesced in the face of a nuisance for 20 years or more.[37] Furthermore the nuisance must remain substantially constant in nature over the period and constitute an actionable nuisance.[38] In practice the defence is mainly applicable to noise nuisance actions. The leading case is now *Webster* v. *Lord Advocate*[39] where Lord Stott stated *obiter* in relation to the noise from the performance of the Edinburgh Military Tattoo that while the programme of events varied in detail, the sound content of the Tattoo was broadly similar each year and therefore the defence of prescription would possibly have been appropriate.

*Coming to a Nuisance*

**7.2.18**   It is no defence that the pursuer has come to a nuisance and thereby implicitly accepted its presence at the outset. The leading case is again *Webster* v. *Lord Advocate*[40] where the pursuer moved into a flat adjoining the Edinburgh Castle esplanade in the knowledge that by so doing she would be within earshot of the noise of the performance of the Tattoo. The Lord Ordinary accepted the view of both counsel in the case that it was immaterial for the purpose of the defence of prescription that the pursuer had come to the nuisance.[41]

**Common Law Remedies**

*Damages*

**7.2.19**   The court has power to award damages to compensate the pursuer for the infringement of the enjoyment of his property. The court can take into account the extent to which the pursuer has been discomfited as well as the physical injury caused to the property of the pursuer.

*Interdict*

**7.2.20**   The court can grant an interdict to prevent recurrence of the noise nuisance in question. The interdict is a flexible tool. It can be used to abate the nuisance in question but at the same time allow the operations whence the nuisance emanates to continue. Such flexibility can be illustrated by the following nuisance cases which all concern the English equivalent to the interdict, namely the injunction to which similar principles apply. In *Dunton* v. *Dover District Council*[42] the relevant noise emanated from a children's playground. The injunction restricted the opening of the playground to between 1000 and 1830 hours and then only to children under the age of 12. In *Kennaway* v. *Thompson*[43] the noise nuisance was generated by powerboats operating on the lake which adjoined the plaintiff's premises. The Court of Appeal granted an injunction which prevented the defendant boat club from holding more than one international event, two national events and three club events per racing season. In addition no boat capable of creating more than 75dB(A) was to be used on the club's water. The injunction also restricted the use of motorboats employed to pull waterskiers to the extent that not more than six could be used at any one time. As a general rule the terms of the interdict require to be precise and must leave the defender in no doubt as to what requires to be done in order to comply with its terms.[44]

## Declarator

In some cases a pursuer who alleges he has been or is being **7.2.21** affected by a nuisance may apply to the court for a declarator that his legal rights are being infringed. For example the court could make a declaration to the effect that the defender, a factory occupier, had created a sufficient level of noise to constitute a nuisance in law.

## STATUTORY CONTROLS: CONTROL OF POLLUTION ACT 1974

The most important legislation dealing expressly with the problem of **7.3.1** noise is Part 3 of the Control of Pollution Act 1974. Section 58, repealed in England and Wales but still in force in Scotland, sets out the relevant procedure the local authority is required to follow to abate a noise nuisance. Most noise nuisances will be dealt with by a local authority acting under the powers conferred by this section. Subsection (1) provides:

"Where a local authority is satisfied that noise amounting to a nuisance exists, or is likely to occur or recur, in the area of the local authority, the local authority shall serve a notice imposing all or any of the following requirements—

> (*a*) requiring the abatement of the nuisance or prohibiting or restricting its occurrence or recurrence;
>
> (*b*) requiring the execution of such works, and the taking of such other steps, as may be necessary for the purpose of the notice or as may be specified in the notice;

and the notice shall specify the time or times within which the requirements of the notice are to be complied with."

Under subsection (2) the relevant notice requires to be served on the person responsible for the nuisance or, if that person cannot be found, or the nuisance has not yet occurred, on the owner or occupier of the premises from which the noise is emitted or could be emitted.

**7.3.2** The term "nuisance" used in the section bears its ordinary meaning at common law.[45] Therefore when the courts are considering whether a given noise constitutes a nuisance under the section similar rules to those mentioned above would be employed.[46] However the general utility of the section is to some extent circumscribed by the fact that the relevant noise is required to emanate from premises. In *Tower Hamlets London Borough Council* v. *Manzoni and Walder*[47] some traders in an open market incurred the obloquy of certain members of the public by offering live animals for sale. Demonstrations were organised. The demonstrators created a great deal of noise. The local authority served notice on the demonstrators under s.58(1) of the Act. It was held on appeal that s.58 had to be read as a whole. Therefore the noise referred to had to be emitted from premises before the provisions of the Act could be invoked. The terms of the abatement notice require to be precise and practicable in their terms.[48] Whereas subsection (1) requires the notice to specify the time or times within which the notice is to be complied with, it has been held that it is not necessary for the relevant notice to specify a time limit for the prohibition of the recurrence of the nuisance.[49] It has also been held in proceedings under the section that it is not necessary for the prosecution to prove that a particular occupier of property has been adversely affected by the relevant noise.[50] It is sufficient furthermore to the prosecution to rely solely on other evidence including expert evidence.[51] The notice can be worded to have immediate effect.[52] Under subsection (4) if a person on whom a notice is served fails to comply with its provisions without reasonable excuse[53] he commits an offence.

The person served with a notice in Scotland may appeal to the **7.3.3**
sheriff against the notice within 21 days from the service of the notice
(s.58(3)). It has been held that failure to appeal against such a notice
deprives the accused of the right to challenge the terms of the notice
at any subsequent trial.[54] A concession is made in respect of noise
from industrial sources. Section 58(3) provides:

"In proceedings for an offence [under subsection 4] in respect of
noise caused in the course of a trade or business it shall be a
defence to prove that the best practicable means have been used for
preventing, or for counteracting the effect of the noise."

Section 72(2) of the Act defines the expression "best practicable **7.3.4**
means" as "reasonably practicable having regard among other
things to local conditions and circumstances, to the current state of
technical knowledge and to the financial implications." Under subsection (3) of section 72:

"The means to be employed include the design, installation,
maintenance and manner and periods of operation of plant and
machinery, and the design, construction and maintenance of buildings and acoustic structures." Therefore the expression "best practicable means" applies not only to equipment which may be a source
of a noise complaint but also to the relevant building in which the
equipment is contained. If, for example a factory owner failed to
provide suitable insulation to the external walls of his premises as a
result of which noise from plant in the factory caused a nuisance he
would be unable to avail himself of the defence provided it was held
to be reasonably practicable to provide the insulation.

Normally noise nuisances will be abated by a local authority **7.3.5**
invoking the provisions of s.58 of the Act. However it may sometimes
happen that the relevant local authority for a variety of reasons, is
unwilling to take appropriate measures to abate a noise nuisance. In
such a case the provisions of s.59 could be invoked. That section
confers on the occupier of premises who is aggrieved by such a
nuisance the right to take summary proceedings (as far as Scotland
is concerned) before the sheriff court. There is no authority as to the
meaning of "aggrieved" in the section. However, it is suggested that
the word simply means adversely or prejudicially affected by the
relevant noise. Section 59(2) empowers the court, if satisfied that a
nuisance exists or that it could recur to make an order for either or
both of the following:

"(*a*) requiring the defendant to abate the nuisance, within a time specified in the order, and to execute any works necessary for that purpose;

(*b*) prohibiting a recurrence of the nuisance, and requiring the defendant, within a time specified in the order, to execute any works necessary to prevent the recurrence."

Under subsection (4) a person who without reasonable excuse[55] contravenes any requirements of an order under subsection (2) commits an offence under the Act. The defence of best practicable means is also available under subsection (5).

**7.3.6** The section does not allow the court to award damages to the successful litigant. Therefore appropriate action at common law may be more appropriate for individuals who seek compensation for the discomfort they have been subjected to. It seems that s.59 has been little used in the United Kingdom. This may be due to some extent to local authorities being willing to remedy noise nuisance under s.58 or simply legal practitioners being unaware of the existence of the section.

**Construction Sites**

**7.3.7** Building operations present a particular problem as far as noise is concerned. Machinery which is commonly employed for excavating, lifting, cutting, demolishing, etc., has the capacity to generate loud and often disagreeable noise. The capacity of building sites to create a nuisance in the environment is increased by the fact that people tend to be more adversely affected by noise to which they are unaccustomed. Since building site operations are generally of only temporary duration the residents in the vicinity do not have time to become habituated to the relevant noise and so are more pre-disposed to being discomfited. The 1974 Act therefore gives special prominence to construction sites. Section 60 confers both wide and detailed powers on local authorities in relation to noise from con-struction sites. The section applies to:

"(*a*) the erection, construction, alteration, repair or maintenance of buildings, structures or roads;

(*b*) breaking up, opening or boring under any road or adjacent land in connection with the construction, inspection, mainte-nance or removal of works;

(*c*) demolition or dredging work; and

(*d*) (whether or not also comprised in paragraph (*a*), (*b*) or (*c*) above) any work of engineering construction."
Under subsection (2) a local authority is empowered to serve a notice imposing requirements as to the way in which the works are to be carried out. The terms which the local authority can stipulate in the notice require to be both practical and precise.[56] An important point is that the section does not lay down any requirement that a nuisance should exist before notice is served.

Subsection (3) provides that the local authority may by appropriate **7.3.8** notice specify the plant or machinery which is or is not to be used and the hours during which the works may be carried out. The notice may also specify the level of noise which may be emitted from the premises. Under subsection (4) the local authority must have regard to the provisions of any code of practice issued under Part 3 of the Act and the best practicable means to minimise the noise. The relevant notice requires to be served on the person who appears to the local authority to be carrying out or going to carry out the works and on other persons appearing to the local authority to be responsible for or to have control over the works. Therefore notice could be served on the relevant building contractor as well as the person commissioning the works (if they are different persons) such as the owner or occupier of the land concerned. The notice may specify the time within which its terms are to be complied with and may require the person on whom notice is served to execute works as opposed simply to refrain from creating noise (s.60(6)). The person served with a notice under s.60 may appeal against the notice as far as Scotland is concerned to the sheriff court within 21 days from the service of the notice (s.60(7)). It is a defence in relation to proceedings under s.58 (which deals with noise nuisances) to prove that the alleged offence is covered by a notice served under s.60 (s.58(6)(*a*)).

It can be seen therefore that the possibility of the appropriate local **7.3.9** authority serving notice under s.60 could constitute a constant threat to a building contractor who requires to know at the outset how long the building works will be in progress and the type of machinery he will employ on site. Section 61 therefore allows a person who intends to carry out building works to apply to the local authority for consent. If, as in most cases in Scotland, the relevant building works require a warrant in terms of s.6 of the Building (Scotland) Act 1959 the request for approval must be made at the same time as application for building warrant. The application must contain particulars of the works and the method by which they are to be carried out and, perhaps more importantly, the steps proposed to be taken to minimise the noise resulting from the works. Under subsection (4) if the local authority considers it would not serve notice under s.60 it must give its consent to the application. A local authority when considering whether to grant consent must address its mind to the provisions of subsection (4) of s.60. If consent is in fact granted, the local authority can reduce the nuisance potential of the site by attaching relevant conditions to a consent and limiting or qualifying the consent to allow for any change of circumstances and limiting the duration of the consent.

**7.3.10** The applicant can appeal to the sheriff court against the refusal of a local authority to grant consent or against any condition or qualification attached to the consent. It is in the interests of a person who intends to carry out building works, to obtain consent under s.61 since in any proceedings for an offence under s.60(8) of the Act it is a defence to prove that the alleged contravention amounted to the carrying out of works in accordance with a consent given under s.61. A further consequence of a consent given under s.61 is that it precludes a local authority from serving notice under s.58 (which deals with general noise nuisance) provided the noise emanates from a state of affairs sanctioned by a consent notice (s.58(6)(*a*)). Consent under s.61 does not however preclude an occupier aggrieved by an alleged noise nuisance taking action under s.59.

**Noise in Streets**

**7.3.11** Street noise received express legislative attention for the first time in 1960 when it came within the ambit of the Noise Abatement Act of that year. Section 62 of the Control of Pollution Act 1974 (which in effect repeals and re-enacts the appropriate provision of the 1960 Act) proscribes the use of a loudspeaker in a street between nine in the evening and eight in the following morning for any purpose. The section also makes it an offence to use a loudspeaker in a street at any other time for the purpose of advertising any trade or business. The section exempts the operation of loudspeakers by certain classes of persons including police, fire brigade and ambulance purposes. The section also exempts the use of a loudspeaker (for example a loudspeaker integrated in a car radio system) to entertain or communicate with the occupant of a vehicle provided the loud-speaker is not operated so as to give reasonable cause for annoyance to persons in the vicinity (s.62(2)). An important exemption in practical terms is that made in respect of the operation of a loudspeaker between noon and seven in the evening of the same day provided that the loudspeaker is fixed to a vehicle used for the purposes of sale of a perishable commodity (for example ice cream) for human consumption and is operated so as not to give reasonable cause for annoyance to persons in the vicinity (s.62(3)).

## Noise Abatement Zones

The Act introduces a new concept in noise control by way of noise **7.3.12** abatement zones. Under s.63 a local authority is empowered to designate all or any part of its area a noise abatement zone. The relevant order must specify the classes of premises to which it applies. Local authorities therefore have considerable discretion to control noise in their areas.

The procedure for setting up a noise abatement zone is set out in **7.3.13** Schedule 1 to the Act. Prior to initiating such a scheme the local authority need not make a prior inspection of the area concerned[57] although such an inspection would in practice be administratively prudent. Provision is made in the Schedule to the Act for the proposals to be adequately publicised to allow individuals who have a proprietary interest in the relevant premises to make objections to the district council concerned. In turn the local authority must consider objections prior to making the appropriate order under s.63.

After the noise abatement zone has been established the local **7.3.14** authority is required to measure the level of noise emanating from the premises concerned and record the same in a register known as the noise level register which must be kept by the authority.[58] After recording the noise level the local authority must serve a copy of that record on the owner and occupier concerned (s.64(3)). Any person on whom a notice is served can appeal to the Secretary of State against the record. The latter has complete powers of review and he can give such directions to the local authority as he thinks fit. In turn the local authority must comply with the directions (s.64(4)). Under s.65(1) the level of noise recorded in the noise level register in relation to any premises must not be exceeded except with the written consent of the local authority concerned. The local authority's consent may be given conditionally (s.65(2)). An applicant for consent may appeal to the Secretary of State against the local authority's decision within three months of the date of the decision (s.65(4)). Again, the Secretary of State can review the local authority's decision. It is an offence to emit noise from any premises in contravention either of subsection (1) or of a condition attached to a consent (s.65(5)). The sheriff court when convicting a person of such an offence, if satisfied that the offence is likely to recur, may make an order requiring the execution of any works necessary to prevent it continuing or recurring. It is an offence to contravene such an order without reasonable excuse (s.65(6)). Default powers are given to the local authority if the order is contravened by the relevant individual failing to carry out the necessary works (s.69).

**7.3.15**  Section 66(1) gives a local authority power to reduce the level of noise emanating from any premises situated in a noise abatement zone if the noise is of such a level that it is not acceptable having regard to the purposes for which the order was made and that a reduction in that level would afford a public benefit. The noise reduction notice may specify particular times, or particular days, during which the noise level is to be reduced and may require the noise level to be reduced to different levels for different times or days. In Scotland a person served with a noise reduction notice can appeal to the sheriff against the notice. It is an offence to contravene a noise reduction notice without reasonable excuse.[59] Section 69(2) gives a local authority power to carry out works in default of the person on whom a noise reduction notice is served. Under s.67(1) if it appears to the local authority that a new building is going to be constructed in a noise abatement zone or that the use of an existing building will be changed by reason of which in either case the terms of the noise abatement order will apply, the local authority may either on its own initiative or on the application of the owner or occupier of the premises or a person who satisfies the local authority that he is negotiating to acquire an interest, determine the level of noise which will be acceptable from those premises. Appeal against this pre-determined level can be made to the Secretary of State within three months of the date the applicant owner or occupier is notified of the decision of the local authority concerned (s.67(3)).

**Miscellaneous Provisions**

**7.3.16**  Section 68 of the Act allows the Secretary of State to make regulations for reducing noise from plant or machinery and limiting the level of noise which may be caused by any plant or machinery used in connection with building works. Under s.71 he can make codes of practice for minimising noise.[60]

## Town and Country Planning (Scotland) 1972

Planning control and its effect on the environment is dealt with **7.4.1** elsewhere in this work.[61] Therefore only brief mention can be made here of its significance in the context of noise. Effective prophylactic measures against the source of environmental noise can often be taken at the development stage of the relevant building by the appropriate planning authority imposing conditions on the granting of planning permission under s.26(1)(*a*) of the 1972 Act, since considerations of noise would rank as a material consideration in terms of this section. The planning authority's powers are wide in this context. The authority could for example impose conditions governing the distance between the relevant premises and (say) existing dwellinghouses. It could also and perhaps most importantly, impose conditions governing levels of noise which could lawfully be emitted from the premises.

## Civic Government (Scotland) Act 1982

An interesting inclusion in the 1982 Act is s.54(1) which provides: **7.4.2** "Any person who—
(*a*) sounds or plays any musical instrument;
(*b*) sings or performs; or
(*c*) operates any radio or television receiver, record player, tape recorder or other sound-producing device,
so as to give any other person reasonable cause for annoyance and fails to desist on being required to do so by a constable in uniform, shall be guilty of an offence and liable, on summary conviction, to a fine not exceeding £50."

Subsection (3) makes certain exceptions in relation to certain types of vehicles and loudspeakers, for example loudspeakers used by the police or fire brigade.

**Byelaws**

**7.4.3**    Since Victorian times local authorities have used their various byelaw-making powers to deal with the problem of noise nuisance. Indeed the famous case of *Kruse* v. *Johnston*[62] centred on the legality of a byelaw which purported to make certain types of street music illegal. As far as Scotland is concerned local authorities have power under s.201(1) of the Local Government (Scotland) Act 1973 to make byelaws *inter alia* for the prevention and suppression of nuisances. Obviously such a power could be used to make byelaws to suppress noise nuisances.

**Health and Safety Legislation, etc.**

**7.4.4**    Under s.3 of the Health and Safety at Work, etc., Act 1974 a duty is placed on every employer to conduct his undertaking in such a way as to ensure so far as is reasonably practicable, that persons not in his employment are not exposed to risks to their health or safety. Clearly therefore such a duty would cover, for example, risks posed to occupiers of land by noise and vibration from industrial and commercial premises.

**Public Health (Scotland) Act 1897**

**7.4.5**    Section 16(1) of the Act provides that any premises or part thereof of such a construction or in such a state as to be a nuisance or injurious or dangerous to health is deemed to be a statutory nuisance. It is possible therefore that if the external walls of a house were so constructed that they permitted noise to easily permeate them, or if the premises were situated so close to a noise source that the occupiers were unduly discomfited, such premises would fall within the scope of the Act. There is no Scottish authority. However in *Southwark London Borough Council* v. *Ince*[63] it was held that it was quite legitimate to take external factors into account when considering if premises constituted a nuisance under s.92(1)(*a*) of the Public Health Act 1936[63a] which corresponds to s.16 of the 1897 Act. In the *Southwark* case the occupiers of dwelling-houses successfully brought an action against the owners of the houses on the grounds that noise and vibration from passing trains and traffic was prejudicial to the health of the occupiers concerned.

Under s.16(6) of the 1897 Act, any work, manufactory, trade or business, injurious to the health of the neighbourhood or so conducted as to be injurious or dangerous to health, ranks as a statutory nuisance and is therefore liable to be dealt with by the relevant local authority. From the available evidence it seems that local authorities have rarely, if ever, invoked this subsection in relation to noise, probably on account of the potential difficulty of proving a causal nexus between a given noise source and the alleged injury to health.

## Licensing (Scotland) Act 1976

Section 38(1)(*f*) of the Act allows a licensing board to make **7.4.6** byelaws for the setting out of conditions which may be attached to licences for the improvement of standards of, and conduct in licensed premises. The appropriate board could therefore make conditions relating to noise from licensed premises. Under subsection (3) the board, when granting a licence, may attach to the licence any condition set out in a byelaw. Such power would be particularly relevant in relation to premises incorporating, for example, discotheques and juke boxes.

## Aircraft Noise

The relevant controls over aircraft noise can be roughly divided **7.4.7** into those which relate to the control of noise from the flight or navigation of aircraft and those which specifically relate to the control of noise from aerodromes.

### Flight Noise

Under s.76(1) of the Civil Aviation Act 1982 no action may lie *inter* **7.4.8** *alia* in respect of nuisance by reason only of the flight of the aircraft over any property so long as the provisions of any Air Navigation Order and any Order made under s.62 (which relates to Orders made during times of war and emergency) have been complied with and furthermore there is no breach of s.81 (which proscribes dangerous flying). Section 60(2) of the Act allows Orders in Council to be made to regulate air navigation. Under Article 3(1) of the Aircraft Navigation Order 1989[64] an aircraft may not fly over the United Kingdom unless it is registered in the manner prescribed by the Order. However, under para. (6) of Sched. 2 to the Order an unregistered aircraft may fly over the United Kingdom if its flight is in accordance with procedures which have been approved by the Civil Aviation Authority (CAA) in relation to flight over any congested area of a city or town. Under Article 95(1) the CAA may direct the operator or commander of any aircraft not to make the particular flight, etc., if the aircraft would be flown in such a way that Article 3 would be contravened.

**7.4.9** Under Article 5(1) of the Air Navigation (Noise Certification) Order 1990[65] no aircraft to which the Order applies may take off or land in the United Kingdom unless a noise certificate has been granted in relation to the aircraft. Paragraph (2) of the article makes certain exceptions to this requirement. Article 6 requires the CAA to issue a noise certificate if it is satisfied the aircraft complies with the appropriate standards specified in the article in relation to noise made by the aircraft. The CAA is empowered to direct the appropriate operator or commander not to make a particular flight if the provisions of Article 5 would be infringed.

**7.4.10** The noise from low flying aircraft presents an obvious problem. Regulation 5(1) of the Rules of the Air Regulations 1991[66] prohibits low flying by aircraft, an expression which is defined by the Regulations. No aircraft other than a helicopter is allowed to fly over any congested area of a city, town or settlement. Regulation 5(*c*) prohibits low flying by a helicopter except with the permission in writing of the CAA.

*Aerodrome Noise*

**7.4.11** Section 77(1) of the Civil Aviation Act 1982 allows provision to be made by way of an appropriate Air Navigation Order, for regulating the conditions under which noise and vibration may be caused by aircraft on aerodromes. Under subsection (2) of the Act no action may lie in respect of nuisance by reason only of the noise and vibration caused by aircraft on an aerodrome so long as the provisions of the Order are complied with. The appropriate current Order is the Air Navigation Order 1989.[67] Under s.78(1) of the Act, the Secretary of State may designate certain aerodromes in relation to which certain requirements concerning the minimising of noise and vibration, apply.[68] Under s.78(3) the Secretary of State can prohibit aircraft taking off or landing at a designated aerodrome during certain periods. Under subsection (6) the Secretary of State may give to the person managing a designated aerodrome appropriate directions for the purpose of avoiding, limiting or mitigating the effect of noise and vibration connected with the taking-off or landing at the aerodrome. The duties imposed by the aforementioned subsections are enforceable by order of the Court of Session.

Under s.79 of the Act, the Secretary of State may, by statutory **7.4.12** instrument, make a scheme requiring a person managing a designated aerodrome to make a grant towards the cost of insulating such buildings or part of such buildings against noise.

## Traffic Noise

Section 41(1) of the Road Traffic Act 1988 allows the Secretary of **7.4.13** State to make regulations governing *inter alia*, the use of motor vehicles on roads and the conditions under which they can be used. Power is also given to make regulations relating to the construction and equipment of vehicles. Under subsection (2)(*c*) such regulations can make provision *inter alia* for noise. Section 42 makes it an offence for a person to fail to comply with any regulations made under s.41. The main regulations presently governing the construction and use, etc., of vehicles are the Road Vehicles (Construction and Use) Regulations 1986.[69] Under reg. 54 every vehicle propelled by an internal combustion engine requires to be fitted with an exhaust system including a silencer both of which require to be maintained in good and efficient working order. Regulations 56–58 inclusive make provision in respect of noise limits which vehicles must not exceed. Under regulation 97 no motor vehicle may be used in such a manner as to cause any excessive noise which could have been avoided by the exercise of reasonable care on the part of the driver. Under s.54 of the 1988 Act the Secretary of State is empowered to make regulations requiring the type approval of vehicles with regard to their design, construction and equipment. If he approves a vehicle as a type he must issue a certificate stating that the vehicle complies with the relevant type approval. A plethora of type approval regulations have been made. The contents of the vast majority of this legislation have no bearing on noise. However the Motor Vehicles (Type Approval) (GB) Regulations 1984[70] make provision relating to noise and silencers in respect of vehicles.

Brief mention should be made here of s.56(1) of the Countryside **7.4.14** (Scotland) Act 1967[71] which allows a local authority to make byelaws *inter alia* requiring the use of effectual silencers on pleasure boats. Byelaws can also be made to control the use on land or waterways of vehicles including hovercraft and boats as well as the landing and taking-off of aircraft.

### Land Compensation (Scotland) Act 1973

**7.4.15**    Section 18(1) of the 1973 Act allows the Secretary of State to make regulations imposing a duty or conferring a power on responsible authorities to insulate buildings or make grants in respect of such insulation against noise caused or expected to be caused by the construction or use of public works. Under reg. 3(1) of the Noise Insulation (Scotland) Regulations 1975[72] where the use of a highway first open to the public after October 16, 1972 (or in respect of which an additional carriageway has been or is to be constructed since that date) causes or is expected to cause noise at a level not less than the level specified in the regulations, the appropriate highway authority is required to either carry out or make the appropriate grant in respect of relevant insulation work. Subject to certain exceptions grant may only be made in respect of dwellings and other buildings used for residential purposes (reg. 7).

### Noise from Household Appliances, etc.

**7.4.16**    Regulation 3 of the Household Appliances (Noise Emission) Regulations 1990[73] prohibits the manufacturer or importer of an appliance manufactured or imported by him on or after February 28, 1990 from marketing any appliance unless the provisions of reg. 4 are complied with. Regulation 4 provides that where a manufacturer or an importer of an appliance takes any steps to inform any person to whom the appliance is to be or may be marketed, of the level of airborne noise emitted by the appliance, the level requires to be determined in accordance with Article 6(1) of the EC Directive set out in the Schedule to the Regulations.[74]

### Building Standards (Scotland) Regulations 1990[75]

**7.4.17**    The above Regulations apply to the construction of new buildings. Part H is intended to protect occupants of dwellings from excessive noise transmitted from other parts of the building by imposing requirements as to the structural design of such buildings. Part H does not deal with external noise sources such as that generated by road traffic, nor does it apply to a wholly detached dwelling.

*Further Reading*

*Stair Memorial Encyclopaedia of the Laws of Scotland*, vol. 9, "Environment" (Section 7) (Edinburgh, 1987, Butterworths)

D. Hughes: *Environmental Law* (2nd ed., London, 1992, Butterworths)

C. Kerse: *Noise* (London, 1975, Oyez)

F. Lyall: *Air, Noise, Waste and Water* (Glasgow, 1982, Planning Exchange), Chap. 3

F. McManus: *Environmental Health Law in Scotland* (Aldershot, 1989, Avebury)

C.N. Penn: *Noise Control* (London, 1979, Shaw and Sons)

A.J. Waite: "Statutory Controls on Construction Site Noise" (1990) 6 Const.L.J. 97

Cmnd. 2056, "Noise", Final Report of Committee on the Problem of Noise (1983, H.M.S.O.)

H.L. Paper 1981–82 "Noise in the Environment" (Select committee on the European Communities)

Report of the Noise Review Working Party (The Batho Report) (1990, HMSO) Cm. 1200 "This Common Inheritance" (Part 4) (1990, HMSO)

NOTES

[1] *Rushmer* v. *Polsue and Alfieri* [1906] 1 Ch. 234.
[2] *Andreae* v. *Selfridge & Co. Ltd.* [1938] Ch. 1.
[3] *Gilling* v. *Gray* [1910] T.L.R. 39.
[4] *Motion* v. *Mills* [1897] 13 T.L.R. 427.
[5] *Leeman* v. *Montague* [1936] 2 All E.R. 167.
[6] *London Brighton and South Coast Railway* v. *Truman* (1886) 11 App.Cas. 45.
[7] *Ball* v. *Ray* (1873) 8 Ch.App. 467.
[8] *Halsey* v. *Esso Petroleum Co.* [1961] 1 W.L.R. 683.
[9] *Allen* v. *Gulf Oil Refining Ltd.* [1981] A.C. 1001.
[10] *Smith* v. *Scott* [1973] Ch. 314.
[11] *Kennaway* v. *Thompson* [1981] Q.B. 88.

¹² *Dunton* v. *Dover District Council* (1978) 76 L.G.R. 87.

¹³ *Webster* v. *Lord Advocate*, 1984 S.L.T. 13.

¹⁴ *Hollywood Silver Fox Farm Ltd.* v. *Emmett* [1936] 2 K.B. 468.

¹⁵ See generally paras. 8.2.1 *et seq.*

¹⁶ *Harrison* v. *Southwark and Vauxhall Water Co.* [1891] 2 Ch. 409.

¹⁷ See N. Whitty: *Stair Memorial Encyclopaedia of the Laws of Scotland*, vol. 14, para. 2072; *cf.* para. 8.2.28 *infra.*

¹⁸ [1893] 1 Ch. 316.

¹⁹ [1936] 2 K.B. 468.

²⁰ The effect of loud noises on vixen is to deter mating, impede whelping and provoke infanticide! See also *Western Silver Fox Ranch Ltd.* v. *Ross and Cromarty County Council*, 1940 S.L.T. 144.

²¹ (1881) 8 R. 1006 at 1021. See also *Bramford* v. *Turnley* (1862) 31 L.J.Q.B. 286.

²² *St. Helen's Smelting Co.* v. *Tipping* (1865) 11 H.L.Cas. 642.

²³ *Lord Advocate* v. *Reo Stakis Organisation*, 1982 S.L.T. 140. See also *Swinton* v. *Pedie* (1837) 15 S. 775.

²⁴ *Harrison* v. *Southwark and Vauxhall Water Co.* [1891] 2 Ch. 409.

²⁵ (1862) 31 L.J.Q.B. 286 at 346. See also *Lord Advocate* v. *Reo Stakis Organisation*, 1980 S.L.T. 237 at 238 where Lord Jauncey, in the Outer House, stated that the critical question (as to whether a nuisance exists) is whether what the defender was exposed to was *plus quam tolerabile* when due weight was given to the surrounding circumstances of the offensive conduct and its effects.

²⁶ *Bramford* v. *Turnley* (1862) 31 L.J.Q.B. 286.

²⁷ (1909) 98 L.T. 718.

²⁸ See *Sedleigh-Denfield* v. *O'Callaghan* [1940] A.C. 880; *Goldman* v. *Hargrave* [1967] 1 A.C. 645; *Leakey* v. *National Trust for Places of Historic Interest and Natural Beauty* [1980] Q.B. 485, and *RHM Bakeries (Scotland) Ltd.* v. *Strathclyde Regional Council*, 1985 S.L.T. 214.

²⁹ See *Stair Memorial Encyclopaedia*, vol. 14, "Nuisance," paras. 2087–2108 incl.

³⁰ *Slater* v. *McLellan*, 1924 S.C. 854.

³¹ See, *Sedleigh-Denfield* v. *O'Callaghan* (see note 25).

³² See, *Mint* v. *Good* [1951] 1 K.B. 517; *Brew Bros.* v. *Snax (Ross) Ltd.* [1970] 1 Q.B. 612; *Heap* v. *Ind Coope and Allsop* [1940] 2 K.B. 476. See also *Tetley* v. *Chitty* [1986] 1 All E.R. 663.

³³ 1984 S.L.T. 13.

³⁴ [1981] A.C. 1001. See also *Gillingham B.C.* v. *Medway (Chatham) Dock Company Ltd.* [1992] J.P.L. 458, where it was held that the grant of planning permission could provide a defence to a nuisance action provided the state of affairs complained of fell within the scope of the planning permission granted.

³⁵ Lord Keith dissented.

## Notes

[36] See also *Department of Transport* v. *North West Water Authority* [1984] A.C. 336.
[37] s.8 of the Prescription and Limitation (Scotland) Act 1973.
[38] *Sturges* v. *Bridgman* (1879) 11 Ch.D. 852.
[39] 1984 S.L.T. 13; 1985 S.L.T. 36.
[40] *Ibid.*
[41] 1984 S.L.T. 13 at 14.
[42] (1978) 76 L.G.R. 87.
[43] [1981] Q.B. 88.
[44] *Webster* v. *Lord Advocate*, 1985 S.L.T. 61.
[45] *A. Lambert Flat Management Ltd.* v. *Lomas* [1981] 1 W.L.R. 898.
[46] See paras. 7.2.2–7.2.11.
[47] [1984] J.P.L. 437.
[48] *Strathclyde Regional Council* v. *Tudhope* 1983 S.L.T. 22, 1982 S.C.C.R. 286. See also *R.* v. *Fenny Stratford Justices ex p. Watney Mann (Midlands) Ltd.* [1976] 1 W.L.R. 1101.
[49] *R.* v. *Birmingham Justices Clerk, ex p. Guppy* (1988) 86 L.G.R. 264.
[50] *A. Lambert Flat Management Ltd.* v. *Lomas* [1981] 1 W.L.R. 898.
[51] *Cooke* v. *Adatia* (1989) 153 J.P. 129.
[52] *Strathclyde Regional Council* v. *Tudhope, supra.*
[53] In *Wellingborough District Council* v. *Gordon, The Times*, November 9, 1990 it was decided that the holding of a birthday celebration was not a reasonable excuse for creating a noise nuisance.
[54] *Stagecoach Ltd.* v. *McPhail*, 1988 S.C.C.R. 289.
[55] See note 53 above for the meaning of "reasonable excuse."
[56] *Strathclyde Regional Council* v. *Tudhope, supra.*
[57] *Morganite Special Carbons Ltd.* v. *Secretary of State for the Environment* (1980) 256 E.G. 1105.
[58] See The Noise Level (Measurements and Registers) (Scotland) Regulations 1982 (S.I. 1982 No. 660).
[59] See note 53 above for the meaning of "reasonable excuse."
[60] See the Control of Noise (Code of Practice for Construction Sites) (Scotland) Order 1982 (S.I. 1982 No. 601) and the Control of Noise (Codes of Practice for Construction and Open Sites) (Scotland) Orders 1985 (S.I. 1985 No. 145) and 1987 (S.I. 1987 No. 1730).
[61] See Chap. 6.
[62] [1898] 2 Q.B. 91.
[63] *The Times*, May 16, 1989; (1989) 21 H.L.R. 504.
[63a] See now s.79(1)(*a*) of the Environmental Protection Act 1990.
[64] S.I. 1989 No. 2004 (as amended by S.I. 1990 No. 2154 and S.I. 1991 No. 1726).
[65] S.I. 1990 No. 1514, made under s.60 of the Civil Aviation Act 1982.
[66] S.I. 1991 No. 2437.
[67] S.I. 1989 No. 2004. See Art. 83.

*Noise*

[68] The Civil Aviation (Designation of Aerodromes Order 1981 (S.I. 1981 No. 651) made under s.29B of the Civil Aviation Act 1971 (now s.80 of the 1981 Act) does not designate any Scottish airport.

[69] S.I. 1986 No. 1078 (amended by S.I. 1986 No. 1597; S.I. 1987 No. 676; S.I. 1987 No. 1133; S.I. 1988 No. 271; S.I. 1988 No. 1102; S.I. 1988 No. 1177; S.I. 1988 No. 1524; S.I. 1988 No. 1871; S.I. 1989 No. 1478; S.I. 1989 No. 1695; S.I. 1989 No. 1865; S.I. 1989 No. 1695; S.I. 1990 No. 317; S.I. 1990 No. 1131; S.I. 1990 No. 1981; S.I. 1990 No. 2125; S.I. 1990 No. 2212; See also the Motor Cycle Noise Act 1987 (as amended by the Consumer Protection Act 1987 which requires suppliers of exhaust systems, etc., and silencers for motor cycles to comply with such requirements as may be prescribed by regulations made by the Secretary of State. The Act is not yet in force.

[70] S.I. 1984 No. 981 (amended by S.I. 1985 No. 1072; S.I. 1987 No. 524; S.I. 1988 No. 1103; S.I. 1988 No. 1669; S.I. 1989 No. 1580; S.I. 1989 No. 2262; S.I. 1990 No. 94; S.I. 1990 No. 1839; S.I. 1991 No. 1022; S.I. 1991 No. 820).

[71] Amended by s.11 of the Countryside (Scotland) Act 1981 (c. 44).

[72] S.I. 1975 No. 460.

[73] S.I. 1990 No. 161.

[74] Directive 86/594/EEC; see para. 11.5.19.

[75] S.I. 1990 No. 2179.

# 8. Civil Liability for Environmental Harm

Civil liability for environmental harm may arise either at common law **8.1.1** or under a specific statutory provision. At common law liability may arise from a variety of principles. Under the law of delict, for example, an individual who has suffered harm from exposure to toxic substances at work may seek to recover damages. Under the law of nuisance a person may be found liable for damaging his neighbour's property or disturbing his enjoyment of it. For many years land law and the law of nuisance have together regulated the rights of riparian proprietors to draw water from or make deposits into rivers. Land law, in the form of servitudes, also applies to the drainage of water from one person's land to another's. Trespass or encroachment may found a claim for damages in respect of a physical intrusion on to land by another. Questions of liability are not only relevant to those who have suffered or caused harm, but also to those who may become liable for the activities of others, for example, as employers, landlords, or purchasers of or lenders over property.

The expression "toxic torts" has been coined to cover the main **8.1.2** areas of liability for environmental harm. In general, where such harm is inflicted on the three media of soil, air or water the law of nuisance is more likely to be invoked in response than any other civil remedy. Nuisance, therefore, is worthy of particular study. It is worth remembering, however, that in addition to the common law of nuisance there are also statutory nuisances and specific areas of civil liability imposed by statute. These matters will be touched upon after an examination of the common law.

## Nature of Nuisance

In Scots law nuisance is a comparatively modern cause of action[1] **8.2.1** and one where the basis of liability occasioned no small degree of confusion, at least up until the decision of the House of Lords in *RHM Bakeries (Scotland) Ltd.* v. *Strathclyde Regional Council*.[2] Nuisance arises where one person so uses his property as to occasion serious disturbance or substantial inconvenience to his neighbour or material damage to his neighbour's property.[3] Such a baldly stated principle requires amplification. What sort of disturbance or damage is regarded as actionable? Does liability arise only where there is fault? What interests in property may sue or be sued? What degree of geographical proximity is implied in the concept of a neighbour? Where does the onus of proof lie? What defences are available?

**8.2.2**    Disturbance or damage will be actionable where the injury sustained by a neighbouring occupier is, in all the circumstances of the case, *plus quam tolerabile*, or more than reasonably tolerable.[4] In the reported cases such injury has arisen in a variety of ways, for example, from the poisoning of trees by acidic gas[5]; from damaging the fabric of a building by gas and water vapour[6]; from damaging the structure of a building by nearby construction work[7]; from the noise of constructing scaffolding[8]; from flooding occasioned by a burst sewer[9]; and from interference with a water course, either by pollution, obstruction or augmentation.[10] The law of nuisance has been said "without exception to provide a remedy for any relevant damage suffered by a neighbouring occupier as the result of any type of use of adjoining subjects by the occupier thereof."[11] The damage need not amount to physical injury to persons or property. Serious disturbance or substantial interference with comfort may arise from noise[12] or from fumes which are not considered injurious to health.[13] However, discomfort or annoyance which is not material but which may be regarded as "sentimental, speculative, trivial discomfort or personal annoyance" will not give rise to a cause of action.[14]

### Fault as the Basis for Nuisance

**8.2.3**    It is now clear that under the law of Scotland liability for nuisance is based on *culpa* or fault.[15] Fault may result from a positive act or from an omission. Fault may therefore arise where the nuisance is a consequence of a deliberate act or is caused by negligence. Where the act is malicious, liability may be based on the doctrine *in aemulationem vicini*.[16] In general, however, liability may arise from a positive act which is not intended to damage neighbouring land and such an act need not be shown to be a non-natural, unusual or unreasonable use of land.[17]

Certain recent cases may be read as suggesting that a use of land **8.2.4** must be unreasonable before liability arises.[18] The arguments in these cases were, however, concerned with the rights of a lower proprietor in relation to the water sent down to him from an upper tenement of land, where it was said that the lower proprietor must show an overstretching without necessity, or an undue pressing of the upper proprietor's rights, or the servitude being made intolerable, before damages could be recovered. In effect this was to say no more than that the lower proprietor was bound to receive the water from the upper tenement unless the upper proprietor could be shown to be at fault.[19]

As far as nuisance generally is concerned, in *Watt* v. *Jamieson* it **8.2.5** was said: "The balance in all such cases has to be held between the freedom of a proprietor to use his property as he pleases and the duty on a proprietor not to inflict material loss or inconvenience on adjoining proprietors or adjoining property; and in every case the answer depends on questions of fact and of degree."[20] Nevertheless, the principle of locality, "that a certain amount of inconvenience, annoyance, disturbance and even damage must be accepted as the price the pursuer pays for staying where he does,"[21] for example, in a city tenement, may preclude a person from obtaining protection against a material addition to a previously existing discomfort.[22] It is not the law, however, that the public interest in a use or development beneficial to the community can overrule the protection afforded to the citizen by the law of nuisance.[23]

The case which established fault as the basis for liability in **8.2.6** nuisance was *RHM Bakeries (Scotland) Ltd.* v. *Strathclyde Regional Council.*[24] In this case bakery premises were flooded as a consequence of the collapse of a sewer, which was under the operation and control of the defenders. The House of Lords was asked to consider whether the local authority were liable at common law for the damage caused to the bakery by flooding, even if it occurred without fault on their part, or whether they were only liable if they were to some extent at fault.[25] The conclusion reached by the House of Lords was that liability depended upon *culpa*, and the pursuer's averments were irrelevant for failing to include any reference to fault on the part of the defenders.[26] A possible exception to this general rule was considered in respect of diverting the flow of a natural stream in the way which arose in *Caledonian Railway Co.* v. *Greenock Corporation.*[27]

**Onus of Proof**

**8.2.7**    The onus of proof of nuisance lies on the pursuer.[28] In some circumstances, however, it may not be necessary for the pursuer to aver the precise nature of the fault committed by the defender which caused the accident.[29] As Lord Fraser said in *RHM Bakeries (Scotland) Ltd.* v. *Strathclyde Regional Council*:

"It would be quite unreasonable to place such a burden on a pursuer, who in many cases will have no knowledge, and no means of obtaining knowledge, of the defender's fault. As a general rule it would, in my opinion, be relevant for a pursuer to make averments to the effect that his property has been damaged by a flood caused by an event on the defender's land, such as the collapse of a sewer which it was the defender's duty to maintain, that properly maintained sewers do not collapse, and that the collapse is evidence that the defender had failed in his duty to maintain the sewer. The onus will then be on the defender to explain the event in some way consistent with the absence of fault on his part. As a general rule the defences available will be limited to proving that the event was caused either by the action of a third party for whom he was not responsible . . . or by a damnum fatale."

**8.2.8**    Lord Fraser's approach to this issue is of only limited applicability, but it is not yet clear where its limits lie. In *Logan* v. *Wang (U.K.) Ltd.*[30] discussed further below, the pursuer's claim in nuisance was dismissed for lack of specification of fault in the pleadings.

**8.2.9**    As a result of the decision in *RHM Bakeries*, Whitty has argued that probably the most important single issue in the modern Scots law of nuisance is: "what types of delictual conduct on the part of the defender are actionable by reference to the test of *plus quam tolerabile*, and which categories are actionable by reference to the ordinary principles of negligence."[31] In theory this point is one of considerable weight. In practice, however, it is highly likely that where a pursuer has incurred such substantial harm as to contemplate raising proceedings based on negligence, that harm will be far beyond anything which the defender could argue was less than *plus quam tolerabile*. In cases based on negligence the harm to the pursuer will probably be apparent and consideration of what is reasonably tolerable will not arise. In cases where the intentional,

non-negligent use of the defender's land incidentally harms neighbouring land, the test of *plus quam tolerabile* will still have to be
applied.

## Causation

Associated with the onus of proof is the question of causation. **8.2.10**
Difficulties of causation are particularly likely to arise where the state
of scientific knowledge about a particular issue is insufficient or
controversial. This is not a problem solely of the twentieth century. In
*Shotts Iron Co.* v. *Inglis*, Lord O'Hagan, in considering damage
allegedly caused to the respondent's plantations by acidic gas, said:

> "The controversy is as to the cause of that damage. The
> appellants say it had its origins in overcrowding and over-
> shading, bad drainage and wet soil, the evil effects of the
> roots of old trees and the injudicious planting of new ones,
> the influence of weather, and other things. The respondent
> asserts that it was produced by the process of calcination,
> instituted by the appellants at three several places in the
> neighbourhood of his property, and blighting his trees to a
> considerable distance with sulphur fumes, which were fatal,
> wherever they were present, to the health and verdure of the
> woods. We have to determine to which of these causes the
> mischief, which was admittedly accomplished somehow,
> may justly be ascribed."[32]

In the same case Lord Chancellor Selborne said: "It is unfor- **8.2.11**
tunately much too common, in cases of this kind, for scientific
witnesses to differ from each other on points as to which it might
have been expected, *a priori*, that there would be no room for such
controversy; and, when these differences do exist, Judges or juries
must (as in all other cases) decide as well as they can between
them."[33] In this case evidence was taken from, among others, a
Professor of Chemistry from Glasgow University and one from
Cambridge. On the other hand, in *Logan* v. *Wang (UK) Ltd.*[34] the
pursuer was not able to establish any causal link between three
alleged incidents of pollution and the damage averred.

## Difficulties in Establishing Liability

The difficulties of establishing fault and of proving causation are **8.2.12**
illustrated by a comparison between *Young* v. *Bankier*[35] and *Logan* v.
*Wang (UK) Ltd.*[36] In *Young* a coal mining company were sued by the

proprietors of a distillery. The distillery depended upon pure, soft burn water to make their product. The colliery were pumping into the burn water from their mine, which, although pure, was hard and much less suitable for distilling. The distillery were granted interdict against the colliery on the grounds that the water from the mine was being artificially conveyed to the burn, and the upper proprietor of the burn was permitted to send down only such a flow of natural water as was due to gravitation. The lower proprietor could not object to receiving the natural flow due to gravitation but could object to receiving foreign water brought to his neighbour's land by artificial means, whether conveyed from a distant stream or pumped from the mine. The lower proprietor could also object if the flow due to gravitation had been unduly and unreasonably increased by operations which were *in aemulationem vicini, i.e.* malicious.

**8.2.13** Several law lords also made the *obiter* comment that an upper riparian proprietor should not alter the chemical properties nor diminish the volume of the water flowing to a lower riparian proprietor. In *Duke of Buccleuch* v. *Cowan* it was said that the upper proprietor of a private river must not render the water unfit for the primary purposes of washing, bleaching, cooking within certain limits, and watering cattle.[37] Drinking was not included as a primary purpose.

**8.2.14** In *Logan* v. *Wang (UK) Ltd.* the lower proprietor of a burn, who was a farmer, sought to interdict the upper proprietors of the burn both from increasing the rate of flow and from polluting the burn with chemicals. The upper proprietors occupied sites on which buildings, roads and car parks had been constructed. It was argued that this increased the rate of flow through surface drainage and caused flooding of the lower proprietor's land. The lower proprietor also alleged that the burn was polluted and that his cows and his land had been adversely affected by this pollution.

**8.2.15** The farmer's claim failed both in respect of the flooding and the pollution. As far as the flooding was concerned the upper proprietors were not obliged to keep their land undeveloped. The lower proprietor had failed to aver that the actions of the upper proprietors were an undue pressing of their rights without necessity and were unreasonable, in the sense referred to at para. 8.2.4, above. On the question of pollution the claim failed for lack of specification of fault on the part of the upper proprietors. Tests for pollution had only been carried out on three occasions, separated by substantial intervals, and these tests did not give rise to any general inference of pollution. No causal link was established between the alleged incidents of pollution and the damage averred. The alleged pollution could not be attributed to any one of the defenders so as to justify interim interdict.

The *Logan* case illustrates the limitations of nuisance as a practical **8.2.16** remedy for alleged environmental damage. Despite the *RHM Bakeries* case it may be necessary to aver fault with some degree of specificity. The existence of pollution must be proved to be material. A causal link must be established between the activities of the alleged polluter, the pollution itself, and the alleged damage.

One hypothetical example of the practical limitations of the law of **8.2.17** nuisance might be seen where land had been contaminated by toxic chemicals, such as airborne dioxins. Where pollution was present and was shown to be the cause of harm, there might be more than one possible source of the contamination. In the case of airborne dioxins, their presence could be accounted for from a variety of sources, from car exhausts to incinerator chimneys, at varying distances from the contaminated site. The presence of a particular chemical in minute quantities might be measurable, but a dispute might arise as to the level of contamination at which such a chemical was to be regarded as harmful to users of the land. A particular source of harm, for example from radioactivity, might have a naturally occurring level, varying from area to area, which might have to be disregarded in assessing harm. Even if the alleged polluter was proved to have caused the pollution, damage would still have to be shown to have been attributable to the pollution, rather than accounted for by some other reason.[38] Furthermore the damage caused must not be too remote, in the sense that the damage must be a reasonably foreseeable consequence of the polluter's conduct.[39]

### Classes of Person Liable for Nuisance

Where a remedy for nuisance is sought the question will naturally **8.2.18** arise as to the nature of the interests in neighbouring land which may be held liable—be they, for example, owner, tenant or occupier. In *Gourock Ropework Co. Ltd.* v. *Greenock Corporation*[40] liability was said to depend upon foreseeability. The question was whether a particular interest ought to have foreseen the damage to neighbouring land. In that case the owners of the land were not liable for the blockage of a water course, which had been blocked by the actions of independent contractors in occupation of the site. It was said that the owners would only be liable if they had created or caused the actual nuisance, or if they had knowledge, or means of knowledge, that the nuisance was likely to be committed by other persons.[41]

**8.2.19** In *RHM Bakeries (Scotland) Ltd.* v. *Strathclyde Regional Council*, Lord Fraser suggested that a defender might be interdicted "from using some artificial work on his land, even although he had no personal responsibility for putting it there in the first place and had not begun to use it, if there was reason to believe that he was likely to use it in the future."[42] In *Noble's Trs.* v. *Economic Forestry (Scotland) Ltd.*, landowners were not liable for the actions of independent contractors where the operations carried out were not inherently dangerous nor likely to be conducted in a way which would require particular precautions to be taken against damage to others.[43]

**8.2.20** In *Webster* v. *Lord Advocate* it was argued on behalf of the Secretary of State as the effective proprietor that he had no responsibility for the actions of his licensees.[44] However, he remained in possession and control of the site and made no effort to monitor the licensees' contractual obligation not to create a nuisance. Declarator was granted against him as against the licensees. A lease will normally contain appropriate provisions prohibiting any activity constituting a nuisance and addressing the respective liabilities of the landlord and the tenant for any nuisance which may arise. It may also be envisaged that where a lender acting on a security over property enters into control of that property the lender will become liable for any continuing or subsequent nuisance.

**8.2.21** In some circumstances the activities of a particular polluter may not be harmful until weighed cumulatively with the activities of others. In *Duke of Buccleuch* v. *Cowan*[45] the pursuers sought to interdict a number of paper mills from polluting a river. It was not necessary for the pursuers to prove that each mill by itself would pollute the river but only that the river was polluted by the mills belonging to the defenders generally and that each defender materially contributed to the production of the nuisance.[46]

**8.2.22** In *Logan* v. *Wang (UK) Ltd.* action was also taken against the water authority for having allegedly given negligent advice to the developers of the site in question relating to drainage and the discharge of effluent.[47] The court accepted that the water authority could be subject to a duty of care on such a basis, although negligence was not established in this case.

A further question is the extent of geographical proximity required **8.2.23** between two proprietors for liability in nuisance to arise. Although the standard definition of nuisance refers to liability for damaging the property of a neighbour, airborne pollution may be carried for considerable distances.[48] There seems little reason why such pollution should not be actionable.

## Time at which Liability for Nuisance Arises

In *Gourock Ropework Co. Ltd.* v. *Greenock Corporation*[49] the **8.2.24** owners of the site argued that liability for causing a nuisance had to be allocated according to who was in control and occupation of the site creating the nuisance at the time when the nuisance occurred. This argument was accepted by the court but is, of course, of less relevance to a continuing nuisance, which may persist through changes of owner or occupier. After a person has ceased to be the owner or occupier of a site it is not appropriate to seek interdict against him[50] but liability in damages may still arise out of his period of ownership or occupation.[51]

It is competent to seek interdict against an anticipated nuisance. In **8.2.25** *Fleming* v. *Hislop*,[52] Lord Halsbury said: "A large quantity of gunpowder, say, has been held to be a nuisance if stored up in a place unfit for the purpose, so that its explosion would do mischief."

## Availability of a Remedy for a Pre-existing Nuisance

Where a nuisance is of a continuing nature a question may arise as **8.2.26** to whether the pursuer came to the nuisance and, if so, whether that restricts the pursuer's right to a remedy. In *Webster* v. *Lord Advocate*[53] the pursuer challenged activities connected with the Edinburgh Military Tattoo. The Tattoo had taken place since 1950 but the pursuer had only been in occupation of her property since 1977. Counsel on both sides were agreed that the pursuer was entitled to seek interdict because her house and those in its vicinity in Ramsay Gardens were built and occupied before the nuisance began. Furthermore, the Lord Ordinary also referred to Lord Halsbury's words in *Fleming* v. *Hislop*: "It is clear that whether the man went to the nuisance or the nuisance came to the man, the rights are the same."[54] The right of a man to complain of a nuisance was not diminished because the nuisance existed before he went to it.

Nevertheless the character of the locality must be taken into account, as referred to at para. 8.2.5 above.[55]

**Prescription of a Claim for Nuisance**

**8.2.27**    The defender in an action of nuisance may be able to put forward a defence based on prescription. In *Webster* v. *Lord Advocate* the defenders argued that under s.8 of the Prescription and Limitation (Scotland) Act 1973 a right relating to property was extinguished where that right had subsisted for a continuous period of 20 years unexercised or unenforced. The court acknowledged that this argument might be sound in law but inappropriate to the circumstances of the pursuer's claim, insofar as it related to the noise of constructing the Tattoo stands. In 1975 there had been a significant change in the nature and quality of the construction work and it was against this noise nuisance that the pursuer's claim was upheld. Even to the extent that a nuisance is regarded as an obligation relating to land and as a continuing act the application of the law of prescription contains considerable uncertainty.[56]

**Public Interest in Activity Causing a Nuisance**

**8.2.28**    A further defence which is sometimes advanced by the perpetrator of a nuisance is that there is a public interest in the continuation of the activity causing the nuisance and this outweighs the interest of the pursuer in abating the nuisance.[57] In *Webster* v. *Lord Advocate* it was argued that the public interest in the continuance of the Tattoo, including the interest of the citizens and ratepayers of Edinburgh and of visitors from all over the world, outweighed any interest which neighbouring occupiers might have in its cessation. This argument was decisively rejected by the court in relation to the final determination of the action, although its relevance was acknowledged to any question as to the balance of convenience in granting interim interdict. It was said that "[i]nterest cannot overrule law."[58] In *Young* an argument founded on the community interest in the development of natural resources by mining was also rejected, Lord Shand implying that any protection in nuisance to be afforded to a particular activity was a matter for the legislature.[59]

## Defence of Statutory Authorisation for Nuisance

Where a particular activity has been authorised by the legislature in **8.2.29**
a statute the question arises whether the body carrying out the
activity may be liable in nuisance or whether the statutory authorisation provides a defence. The classic statement of the law on this
question was made by Lord Blackburn in *Geddis* v. *Bann Reservoir
Proprietors*[60]:

> "For I take it, without citing cases, that it is now thoroughly
> well established that no action will lie for doing that which the
> legislature has authorised, if it be done without negligence,
> although it does occasion damage to anyone; but an action
> does lie for doing that which the legislature has authorised, if
> it be done negligently. And I think that if by a reasonable
> exercise of the powers, either given by statute to the promo-
> ters, or which they have at common law, the damage could
> be prevented it is, within this rule, 'negligence' not to make
> reasonable use of their powers."

Since this statement was made a considerable case-law has **8.2.30**
developed on the liability of public authorities or other bodies in
nuisance for the exercise of their statutory powers and duties. In
*Allen* v. *Gulf Oil Refining Ltd.*, Lord Wilberforce said that in this
context negligence had "a special sense as to require the under-
taker, as a condition of obtaining immunity from action, to carry out
the work and conduct the operation with all reasonable regard and
care for the interests of other persons."[61] Liability will depend on
whether the body in question is exercising a statutory duty or a
statutory power and may also depend on whether the statute contains a "nuisance clause," which preserves liability under the law of
nuisance, or an "exoneration clause" restricting liability.[62]

## Title to Sue for Nuisance

It is fundamental to the law of nuisance to identify the classes of **8.2.31**
person who may seek a remedy in this area of law. In most of the
reported cases the interest which has sought protection is that of the
owner, although there is no reason why title to sue should not also
extend to tenants or licensees.[63] Where a nuisance affects the use
and enjoyment of a public place a member of the public with a
sufficient interest may raise proceedings as an *actio popularis*.[64]

## Distinctions between the Law of Scotland and England

**8.2.32**   As Lord Fraser pointed out in *RHM Bakeries (Scotland) Ltd.* v. *Strathclyde Regional Council*: "There are observations in several reported cases to the effect that the law of nuisance is the same in Scotland as it is in England, apart from the distinction between public and private nuisance, which is recognised in England but not in Scotland."[65] The decision in that case firmly established a further distinction between the law of Scotland and the law of England. As Lord Fraser went on to say: "The doubt about whether *culpa* is the essential basis in Scots law for the liability of the proprietor of land to a neighbour arises from the fact that the English decision in *Rylands* v. *Fletcher* has sometimes been referred to as if it were authoritative in Scotland. In my opinion, with all respect to eminent judges who have referred to it in that way, it has no place in Scots law, and the suggestion that it has, is a heresy which ought to be extirpated."[66]

**8.2.33**   In *Rylands* v. *Fletcher*[67] the House of Lords applied a rule of strict liability to the duties owed by a landowner to his neighbours where the landowner in the course of a non-natural use of the land collects or brings on to it anything likely to do mischief if it escapes. The practical importance of the rule in *Rylands* v. *Fletcher* is currently regarded as limited by an acceptance that many modern uses, including industrial uses, are not non-natural uses, particularly where planning permission has been granted.[68] This point is not without controversy, however, and has been tested in recent cases.[69]

## Conclusion

**8.2.34**   There is nothing new in the idea that the environment may be harmed by pollution. Developing technology, though, means that nowadays new forms of pollution arise, sometimes in unforeseen circumstances, or with uncertain or unforeseen consequences. This may in turn lead to difficult questions of proof, causation and remoteness of damage. Such questions are predominantly factual rather than legal, but they raise doubts about the suitability of existing law and procedure for resolving environmental disputes.[70]

**8.2.35**   In particular one may ask whether it is appropriate to rely for protection from some of the more insidious forms of environmental damage on proceedings brought by one person against another. Long term environmental damage is of concern to the community, not merely to a particular proprietor. The activities of a particular polluter may have consequences which are so remote, geographically or temporally, as to be difficult to accommodate within existing forms of liability, particularly in terms of the foreseeability of harm.

The existence of a law of nuisance is of little value if it places **8.2.36** overwhelming obstacles on the path to redress. It may be thought just that where a society recognises that there is an acceptable cost for technological progress, that society as a whole should be prepared to take responsibility for compensating the victims of progress, especially where liability may be difficult to establish in the existing state of scientific knowledge. That is not to say that a remedy should not also be available where a particular person has suffered a specific harm. On the other hand, it would be short-sighted if, owing to the indifference or ignorance of the community, individuals were obliged to shoulder the responsibility of establishing harm from a previously unproven source.

## Civil Liability under Statute

Various statutory provisions impose civil liability towards third parties **8.3.1** for environmental harm. Among the most important of these are certain provisions of the Environmental Protection Act 1990 relating to waste. Other enactments which impose civil liability include the Nuclear Installations Act 1965, and the Merchant Shipping (Oil Pollution) Act 1971.[71]

### Civil Liability for Waste

Under s.73 of the Environmental Protection Act 1990 limited civil **8.3.2** liability may arise for damage caused by waste.[72] Section 33 of the Act creates an offence of treating, keeping or disposing of controlled waste except in accordance with a waste management licence. Commission of this offence, or a related offence under s.63, will give rise to civil liability under s.73. Liability for damage is incurred by any person who committed the relevant offence by depositing waste on land, or knowingly caused or knowingly permitted it to be deposited. It will be a defence to show that the damage was due wholly to the fault of the person who suffered it, or was suffered by a person who voluntarily accepted the risk of the damage being caused. These defences are without prejudice to other grounds of liability. "Controlled waste" is defined in s.75(4) to mean "household, industrial and commercial waste or any such waste."[73]

**8.3.3**   In addition to incurring a potential liability to third parties for the keeping of waste an owner of land may be held liable for the cost of cleaning up land, under s.61 of the 1990 Act, even where the owner did not cause the contamination.[74]

**8.3.4**   A draft directive has been prepared by the European Commission on "Civil liability for damage caused by waste."[75] The directive covers civil liability for waste generated in the course of an "occupational activity," excluding nuclear waste and oil leaked from ships. The directive would impose strict liability on producers of waste for damage to persons and property and for impairment of the environment. Impairment of the environment is defined as any significant physical, chemical or biological deterioration of the environment insofar as this is not considered to be within the meaning of damage to property. Liability for damage caused by waste may be incurred from the time the waste arises, although liability by the producer of the waste ends upon lawful transfer of the waste to an authorised disposal site or installation. The operator of the disposal site is then the "deemed producer" of the waste, as is an importer of waste to the Community. A person who has actual control of the waste may be a deemed producer if he is unable to identify the original producer and it is possible that the definition of a deemed producer might be extended in the future to include a carrier of waste.

**8.3.5**   Under the draft directive there is a 30-year time limit proposed for taking action from the date on which the incident giving rise to liability occurred. A claim by a pursuer will be time-barred after three years from the date on which the pursuer had, or should have had, knowledge of the damage or injury and of the identity of the then producer. The pursuer will be required to prove damage or impairment and show on the balance of probabilities a causal relationship between the waste and the damage. A defender will be able to put forward defences of *force majeure* or contributory negligence. Compulsory public liability insurance is proposed for producers of waste.

### Statutory Nuisances

**8.3.6**   It has long been recognised that the common law may be inadequate for a purpose such as protecting the public at large. The common law is mainly concerned with protecting rights of particular persons, rather than with protecting the public as a whole, although the *actio popularis* provides a measure of public protection exercised by a concerned individual. Often, however, it is not enough to rely on an individual response to prevent harm. Instead the community may respond in an organised way to prevent harm or limit damage by regulation or other forms of control, or by taking responsibility for particular functions. The law of statutory nuisances is a long established attempt to protect the community from certain specific forms of pollution.

**8.3.7** The Public Health (Scotland) Act 1897 is an early example of the regulation of nuisance by local authorities. The statutory nuisances covered by the Act include (1) dangerous premises; (2) streets, ditches, gutters, watercourses, privies, cess-pools, etc., in a harmful state; (3) contaminated wells or other water supply; (4) buildings containing badly kept animals; (5) refuse deposits within 50 yards of a public road; (6) works or trades injurious to public health; (7) overcrowded houses; (8) schools or other premises contaminated either by effluvia or fumes, gases and dust; (9) fumes, gases and vapours from dwelling-houses; and (10) dust from trades, businesses or manufacturing.[76] The test usually stated in the statute to determine whether a site or activity constitutes a statutory nuisance is whether it may be said to be "a nuisance or injurious or dangerous to health." The interaction between this test and the common law test is not entirely clear, but the 1897 Act has been said to apply to such nuisances as may reasonably be connected with public health.[77]

**8.3.8** Under the 1897 Act a local authority (islands or district council) has a duty to inspect its district from time to time to see if any statutory nuisances exist (s.17). Information about the existence of a nuisance must be given to the authority by the officers of the authority or by the police (s.19). Any member of the public may also provide such information. The authority has power to obtain access to and investigate an alleged nuisance (s.18). Where it is satisfied as to the existence of the nuisance the local authority may serve a notice requiring the removal of the nuisance (s.20). The notice is served on the author of the nuisance, or on the owner or occupier of the premises where the nuisance is taking place. The notice will give a time limit for removal of the nuisance and may also require measures to prevent its recurrence. The local authority may be able itself to take action to remove the nuisance (s.20(3)).

**8.3.9**    Non-observance of the notice may lead to the authority bringing proceedings in the sheriff court (ss.21 and 22). The sheriff may order the removal of the nuisance or interdict its recurrence (s.23). Non-compliance with an order of the sheriff is a criminal offence punishable by a fine (s.24).[78] Common law rights of action are preserved (s.170).

**8.3.10**    Specific statutory nuisances arise under a variety of other enactments, for example, the Clean Air Act 1956, s.16(1).[79] Noise nuisances may be dealt with by a local authority under the Control of Pollution Act 1974, s.58, by the service of a notice on the person responsible for the noise.[80] It is an offence to contravene the notice without reasonable excuse. Where the noise is caused in the course of trade or business it is a defence to establish that the best possible means were used to prevent or control it. These statutory nuisances are not superseded in Scotland by the Environment Protection Act 1990.

*Yes they are now – 1995 EPA Sch 17.*

## Further Reading

S. Ball and S. Bell,   *Environmental Law*, Chap. 8 (1991, Blackstone Press Ltd.).

D. Hughes,   *Environmental Law* (2nd ed.), Chap. 2 (London, 1992, Butterworths).

F. Lyall,   *Air, Noise, Water and Waste: A Summary of the Law in Scotland*, Chap. 1 (Glasgow, 1982, The Planning Exchange).

N. Whitty,   *The Stair Memorial Encyclopaedia of the Laws of Scotland*, vol. 14, "Nuisance" (Edinburgh, 1988, Butterworths/Law Society of Scotland).

NOTES

[1] *Watt* v. *Jamieson*, 1954 S.C. 56 at 57; *Lord Advocate* v. *Reo Stakis Organisation Ltd.*, 1981 S.C. 104.
[2] 1985 S.L.T. 214.
[3] *Watt* v. *Jamieson, op. cit.* at 58; *Lord Advocate* v. *Reo Stakis Organisation Ltd., op. cit.* at 108; *Webster* v. *Lord Advocate*, 1984 S.L.T. 13.
[4] *Watt* v. *Jamieson, op. cit.* at 58; *Lord Advocate* v. *Reo Stakis Organisation Ltd., op. cit.* at 108.
[5] *Shotts Iron Co.* v. *Inglis* (1882) 9 R.(H.L.) 78.
[6] *Watt* v. *Jamieson, op. cit.*

# Notes

[7] *Lord Advocate* v. *Reo Stakis Organisation Ltd., op. cit.*

[8] *Webster* v. *Lord Advocate, op. cit.*

[9] *RHM Bakeries (Scotland) Ltd.* v. *Strathclyde Regional Council, op. cit.*

[10] *Duke of Buccleuch* v. *Cowan* (1866) 5 M. 214; *Young* v. *Bankier Distillery Co.* (1893) 20 R.(H.L.) 76; *Caledonian Railway Co.* v. *Greenock Corporation,* 1917 2 S.L.T. 67; *Gourock Ropework Co.* v. *Greenock Corporation,* 1966 S.L.T. 125; but see *Noble's Trustees* v. *Economic Forestry (Scotland) Ltd.,* 1988 S.L.T. 662 and *Logan* v. *Wang (UK) Ltd.,* 1991 S.L.T. 580, both discussed further below, paras. 8.2.4, 8.2.14–16.

[11] *Lord Advocate* v. *Reo Stakis Organisation Ltd., op. cit.*

[12] *Webster* v. *Lord Advocate, op. cit.*

[13] *Fleming* v. *Hislop* (1886) 13 R.(H.L.) 43.

[14] *Fleming, op. cit.* at 45 and 47.

[15] See *RHM Bakeries (Scotland) Ltd.* v. *Strathclyde Regional Council,* 1985 S.L.T. 214; and also *Noble's Trs.* v. *Economic Forestry (Scotland) Ltd.,* 1988 S.L.T. 662; *Borders Regional Council* v. *Roxburgh District Council,* 1989 S.L.T. 837; and *Logan* v. *Wang (UK) Ltd.,* 1991 S.L.T. 580.

[16] *Young* v. *Bankier Distillery Co., op. cit.* at 77; *Campbell* v. *Muir,* 1908 S.C. 387.

[17] *Watt* v. *Jamieson,* 1954 S.C. 56 at 58; *Lord Advocate* v. *Reo Stakis Organisation Ltd.,* 1981 S.C. 104 at 108.

[18] *Noble's Trs.* v. *Economic Forestry (Scotland) Ltd.,* 1988 S.L.T. 662; *Logan* v. *Wang (UK) Ltd.,* 1991 S.L.T. 580.

[19] See para. 3.2.1.

[20] *Watt* v. *Jamieson, op. cit.* at 58.

[21] *Ibid.*

[22] *Ibid.*; and see *Webster* v. *Lord Advocate,* 1984 S.L.T. 13 at 15.

[23] *Shotts Iron Co.* v. *Inglis* (1882) 9 R.(H.L.) 78 at 88; *Fleming* v. *Hislop* (1886) 13 R.(H.L.) 43 at 49; *Young* v. *Bankier Distillery Co.* (1893) 20 R.(H.L.) 76 at 81; *Webster* v. *Lord Advocate,* 1984 S.L.T. 13 at 15; and see "Public Interest in Activity Causing a Nuisance," para. 8.2.28, *infra.*

[24] 1985 S.L.T. 214.

[25] *per* Lord Fraser at 215.

[26] *Ibid.,* 219.

[27] 1917 2 S.L.T. 67; *ibid.* at 217–218.

[28] *Webster* v. *Lord Advocate,* 1984 S.L.T. 13 at 15.

[29] *RHM Bakeries (Scotland) Ltd.* v. *Strathclyde Regional Council, op. cit., per* Lord Fraser at 219.

[30] 1991 S.L.T. 580, discussed further below: see paras. 8.2.4, 8.2.14–8.2.16. See also *Argyll & Clyde Health Board* v. *Strathclyde Regional Council,* 1988 S.L.T. 381.

[31] *Stair Memorial Encyclopaedia,* vol. 14, para. 2087.

[32] *Shotts Iron Co.* v. *Inglis* (1882) 9 R.(H.L.) 78 at 85.

[33] *Ibid.* at 79.

34 1991 S.L.T. 580.
35 (1893) 20 R.(H.L.) 76.
36 1991 S.L.T. 580.
37 (1866) 5 M. 214 at 217 and 226; see para. 3.2.1.
38 For further discussion of these points see C. Pugh and M. Day, "Toxic Torts" (1991) 141 N.L.J. 1549, 1596 at 1596–1597.
39 *Overseas Tankship (UK) Ltd.* v. *Miller Steamship Co. Pty. (The Wagon Mound) (No. 2)* [1967] 1 A.C. 617.
40 1966 S.L.T. 125.
41 See also *Sedleigh-Denfield* v. *O'Callaghan* [1940] A.C. 880; *Noble's Trs.* v. *Economic Forestry (Scotland) Ltd.*, 1988 S.L.T. 662; and *Borders Regional Council* v. *Roxburgh District Council*, 1989 S.L.T. 837.
42 *RHM Bakeries (Scotland) Ltd.* v. *Strathclyde Regional Council*, 1985 S.L.T. 214 at 218–219.
43 *Noble's Trs.* v. *Economic Forestry (Scotland) Ltd.*, above; *Borders Regional Council* v. *Roxburgh District Council*, 1989 S.L.T. 837; *GA Estates Ltd.* v. *Caviapen Trs. Ltd.*, Outer House, August 30, 1991, 1991 G.W.D. 32–1933.
44 1984 S.L.T. 13 at 16.
45 (1866) 5 M. 214.
46 *Ibid.* at 216, 228, 232–233, 235–236.
47 1991 S.L.T. 580; see also *Scott-Whitehead* v. *National Coal Board* (1987) 53 P.&C.R. 263.
48 See n. 3, *supra*.
49 *Gourock Ropework Co.* v. *Greenock Corporation*, 1966 S.L.T. 125.
50 *Bankier Distillery Co.* v. *Young's Collieries Ltd.* (1899) 2 F. 89.
51 N. R. Whitty, *The Laws of Scotland*, Vol. 14, paras. 2143 and 2145.
52 (1866) 13 R.(H.L.) 43 at 48.
53 1984 S.L.T. 13.
54 (1866) 13 R.(H.L.) 43 at 49.
55 *Webster* v. *Lord Advocate*, 1984 S.L.T. 13 at 15.
56 On this issue see N. R. Whitty, *Stair Memorial Encyclopaedia*, vol. 14, paras. 2123–2126.
57 *Cf.* para. 7.2.3.
58 *Webster* v. *Lord Advocate*, 1984 S.L.T. 13 at 14–15; *Duke of Buccleuch* v. *Cowan* (1866) 5 M. 214 *per* Lord Cowan at 229; *RHM Bakeries (Scotland) Ltd.* v. *Strathclyde Regional Council*, 1985 S.L.T. 214 *per* Lord Fraser at 219.
59 *Young* v. *Bankier Distillery Co.* (1893) 20 R.(H.L.) 76 at 81.
60 *Geddis* v. *Bann Reservoir Proprietors* (1878) 3 App. Cas. 430 at 455–456.
61 *Allen* v. *Gulf Oil Refining Co.* [1981] A.C. 1001 at 1011.
62 The leading case is now *Department of Transport* v. *North West Water Authority* [1984] A.C. 336, in which these matters were considered. See also *Gillingham B.C.* v. *Medway (Chatham) Dock Co. Ltd.* [1992] J.P.L.

458, noted (1991) 3 L.M.E.L.R. 196; and N. R. Whitty, *op. cit.*, paras. 2110–2122.

[63] *Mull Shellfish Ltd.* v. *Golden Sea Produce Ltd.* Second Division, August 2, 1991, noted at 1991 G.W.D. 32–1936 and (1991) 3 L.M.E.L.R. 203; See also N. R. Whitty, paras. 2133–2134; and also G. Kondilinye, "Standing to sue in private nuisance" (1989) 9 Legal Studies 284.

[64] See *Torrie* v. *Duke of Atholl* (1853) 1 Macq. 65; and Whitty, para. 2160.

[65] *RHM Bakeries (Scotland) Ltd.*, 1985 S.L.T. 214 at 217.

[66] *Ibid.*

[67] (1868) L.R. 3 H.L. 330.

[68] *Rickards* v. *Lothian* [1913] A.C. 263; *Read* v. *Lyons* [1947] A.C. 156; *British Celanese* v. *A. J. Hunt (Capacitors) Ltd.* [1969] 1 W.L.R. 959. For a decision in which the *Rylands* principle was applied see *Halsey* v. *Esso Petroleum Co. Ltd.* [1961] 1 W.L.R. 683.

[69] *Cambridge Water Co.* v. *Eastern Counties Leather plc.*, *The Times*, October 23, 1991, noted (1991) 6 L.M.E.L.R. 198.

[70] For a forthright view see C. G. Weeramantry, *The Slumbering Sentinels*, Penguin, Victoria, Australia, 1983.

[71] See paras. 10.2.23 *et seq.*

[72] See para. 4.3.16.

[73] See para. 4.3.16; for the basis of liability for waste prior to the coming into force of the Environmental Protection Act 1990, see the Control of Pollution Act 1974, s.88.

[74] See paras. 4.7.1 *et seq.*

[75] The original draft was published in Official Journal No. C 251/3, 4.10.89; a revised draft was published in Official Journal No. C 192/6, 23.7.91.

[76] Public Health (Scotland) Act 1897, s.16, as amended by Environmental Protection Act 1990, s.83.

[77] See *Renfrew County Council* v. *Wordrop's Trs.*, 1927 S.L.T. (Sh.Ct.) 68.

[78] As amended by the Control of Pollution Act 1974, Sched. 2, para. 2.

[79] As amended by the Clean Air Act 1968, Sched. 1, para. 5 and the Control of Pollution Act 1989, s.1.; see para. 2.7.1.

[80] See paras. 7.3.1 *et seq.*

# 9. Nature Conservation

**9.1.1** The law which is specifically designed for the purposes of nature conservation falls into two categories. Some of the law aims to protect particular birds, animals and plants from direct harm, making it an offence for people to kill or otherwise injure them. However, no matter how good and effective such laws may be, they cannot secure the survival of any species in the wild if it does not have the right habitat in which to live. Consequently other parts of the law aim to secure the continued existence of the range of natural[1] habitats necessary for species to survive in the wild. In most cases it has been the loss of habitat rather than any deliberate intervention by mankind which has caused the greatest harm to animal and plant life in this country, and which continues to pose the greatest threat to the range and diversity of our wildlife.

**9.1.2** The law is to be found in a range of statutes. The most important is the Wildlife and Countryside Act 1981, which provides the most important rules for the protection of birds, animals and plants, and some habitat. In addition to the 1981 Act, a range of individual statutes deal with particular species, *e.g.* seals and deer, or with activities which have an impact on wildlife, *e.g.* shooting and fishing. The range of habitat designations are based on a large variety of statutory sources, including some legislation from the European Community. The law in this field is thus very fragmented.

**9.1.3** Much of the responsibility for nature conservation matters lies with Scottish Natural Heritage (SNH), a new body formed in 1992 to exercise the functions previously undertaken by the Nature Conservancy Council (and its short-lived successor the Nature Conservancy Council for Scotland) and the Countryside Commission for Scotland.[2] It is responsible for the designation and management of nature reserves, for the designation of sites of special scientific interest, for some other forms of habitat protection, and for licensing activities otherwise unlawful under the laws protecting individual species.

164

Species Protection

The Wildlife and Countryside Act 1981 contains most of the general **9.2.1** provisions in this area. A feature of the Act is the use of Schedules in which individual species are listed in categories which are entitled to greater or lesser protection than that provided by the general rules. In several places the Act also allows greater freedom of action to "authorised persons," defined as the owner or occupier of the land concerned, or a person authorised by the owner or occupier, by the local authority (either tier) or in some cases by Scottish Natural Heritage or a district salmon fisheries board (s.27). In most cases the Act also allows licences to be granted to permit otherwise prohibited acts, the licensing authority most commonly being Scottish Natural Heritage or the Secretary of State (s.16).

## A. Birds

1. *General*

Under the Wildlife and Countryside Act 1981, it is an offence **9.2.2** intentionally to kill, injure or take any wild bird, to take, damage or destroy the nest of a wild bird while it is being built or in use, or to take or destroy the egg of a wild bird (s.1(1)). The definition of "wild bird" excludes poultry and game birds (s.27(1)) and birds shown to have been bred in captivity are also excluded (s.1(6)). Defences are provided for a range of circumstances, the onus frequently lying on the accused to establish them (s.4). Most generally no offence is committed by acts which are the incidental result of a lawful operation and which could not reasonably have been avoided. Authorised persons have a defence for actions shown to have been necessary for preserving public health, public safety or air safety, for preventing the spread of disease or for preventing serious damage to livestock, crops, growing timber or fisheries. Statutory measures for agricultural pest control and animal health are permitted, as is mercy killing and the taking of injured birds to tend them and the taking of some seabirds' eggs for human consumption (s.16(2)). Many methods of killing or taking birds are proscribed, including the use of poison, bird-lime, traps and snares (s.5); criminal liability extends to the setting of such devices in circumstances likely to cause harm, and to those who knowingly cause or permit their use.[3]

**9.2.3**    Possession of any wild bird, alive or dead, or of its eggs or anything derived from the bird, is an offence of strict liability (s.1(2)). It is a defence for the person in possession to establish that the bird was bred in captivity, or had come into his possession as the result of natural means or of conduct lawful under the 1981 Act or its predecessors (s.1(3), (6)). The keeping of many species of bird is controlled by a registration and marking scheme (s.7). It is an offence to sell, offer for sale or possess for sale wild birds or their eggs (s.6). Exceptions are allowed for controlled sales of live birds listed in Part I of Sched. 3, and dead birds in Parts II and III of the same Schedule.

### 2. *Protected Species*

**9.2.4**    More than 100 species of bird, listed in Sched. 1 to the 1981 Act, enjoy enhanced protection, *e.g.* ospreys and kingfishers. It is an offence to disturb any of these while it is building its nest or is at or near its nest containing eggs or dependent young, or to disturb the dependent young of such birds (s.1(5)). The defences available to authorised persons do not apply in relation to these protected species (s.4(3)), and the penalties in the event of a conviction for harming or possessing such birds are significantly greater (ss.1(4),21).

### 3. *Birds which can be Hunted*

**9.2.5**    Game birds fall outwith the protection of the 1981 Act, but a number of other species may also be hunted, *e.g.* greylag geese. These are listed in Part I of Sched. 2 to the Act, and outside the close seasons laid down in the Act it is not an offence to kill or take such birds, or to injure them in the attempt to kill them (s.2). The Secretary of State can alter the close seasons and make orders protecting the birds during periods of temporary hardship.

**9.2.6**    For game birds, namely grouse (red and black), partridges, pheasant, ptarmigan, snipe, and probably capercailzie, close seasons are prescribed, and as well as the permission of the person with the right to take game, licences are required for the killing and taking of game birds and for their sale.[4] A range of offences exists to punish those trespassing on land to take game or found in unlawful possession of it.[5]

4. *Pests*

Authorised persons are permitted to kill or take birds from the pest **9.2.7**
species listed in Part II of Sched. 2 to the 1981 Act, *e.g.* herring gulls
and starlings, and to destroy, damage or take their eggs and nests
(s.2(2)).

**B. Animals**

1. *General*

A number of animals—mammals, reptiles, fish, insects and inverte- **9.2.8**
brates—are given protection under the Wildlife and Countryside Act
1981. These are listed in Sched. 5 to the Act, and it is an offence
intentionally to kill, injure or take a wild animal of these species (s.9).
Damage, disturbance or obstruction of a place used by the animal
for shelter or protection is also an offence, as is disturbance of the
animal in such a place, unless the animal is found sheltering in a
dwelling-house. As with birds, a number of defences exist (s.10),
covering the incidental results of lawful operations, mercy killing and
the tending of injured animals, and action authorised for pest control
and animal health purposes. Authorised persons may also take
action to prevent serious damage to livestock or crops, but a licence
from SNH must be sought if the need for such action becomes
apparent beforehand. Possession and sale of these animals, alive or
dead, or of anything derived from them, is a strict liability offence,
subject to similar defences to those available in relation to the
possession of birds and eggs (s.9).

A lesser degree of protection is given to the species listed in **9.2.9**
Sched. 6 to the Act. The law prohibits the killing or taking of them by
particular methods, including the use of traps, snares, poisons, gas,
nets, automatic weapons, or dazzling devices (s.11).

2. *Bats*

All the species of bat likely to occur in Scotland are listed in **9.2.10**
Scheds. 5 and 6 to the 1981 Act, but they are further protected by
limits to the defences which normally cover the disturbance of
creatures found in dwelling-houses and the killing or injuring of
animals incidentally to a lawful operation (s.10(5)). For bats, it is only

action taken in the living areas of a house which is protected (therefore disturbing bats found in the loft of a house is unlawful), and SNH must be notified and given an opportunity to advise on any intended action which is likely to affect bats (*e.g.* timber treatment of a known roosting place).

### 3. *Badgers*

**9.2.11**  As well as being protected under Scheds. 5 and 6 to the 1981 Act, badgers are the subject of special legislation.[6] This largely repeats the prohibitions on killing, injuring, possessing and disturbing badgers, with special emphasis on prohibiting disturbance of their setts, but the onus of proof is reversed for some offences, so that an accused found in suspicious circumstances must prove that he was not attempting an unlawful act. Only firearms of the specified size and power can be used to kill badgers. There are special provisions for the licensing of activities affecting badgers and special sanctions in cases where dogs have been used to harm badgers.

### 4. *Deer*

**9.2.12**  Close seasons are laid down for the four species of deer in Scotland,[7] but killing or taking during the close season is lawful if authorised by the Red Deer Commission or carried out by the occupier of agricultural land or enclosed woodland in order to avoid serious damage to crops, pasture, trees or foodstuffs.[8] In most circumstances a game licence is required before deer can be killed,[9] as well as permission of the landowner or other person owning the right to take deer. Licences are not required for action authorised by the Red Deer Commission,[10] nor for action taken by the occupier of enclosed land.[11] The only lawful method of killing a deer is by shooting with a firearm and ammunition of the prescribed form,[12] and, with some exceptions, the killing of deer at night is unlawful.[13]

**9.2.13**  The control of deer is under the supervision of the Red Deer Commission.[14] The Commission can authorise the killing of deer where they are causing damage to crops, forestry or farm animals (*e.g.* by serious overgrazing), the scope of such authorisation being wider for red or sika deer than for the other species.[15] More general schemes can be introduced by the Commission for the control of red and sika deer in a locality, and the owners and occupiers of land affected must comply with its requirements.[16]

## 5. *Seals*

Seals are protected under the Conservation of Seals Act 1970. This **9.2.14** prohibits the use of poison or certain classes of firearms and ammunition to kill seals (s.1), and the taking or killing of seals outside the close seasons laid down for the two species of seal found off Scotland, close seasons which can be extended by ministerial order (ss.2, 3). Defences are available for mercy killing, taking an injured seal in order to tend it, or harm done as the incidental result of a lawful action. It is also lawful for the person in possession of a fishing net or tackle (or someone authorised by him) to kill or injure a seal in the vicinity in order to prevent damage to the equipment or to fish caught in it (s.9). Licences can be granted for the taking or killing of seals (s.10).

## 6. *Whales*

All species of whales, dolphins and porpoises are protected under **9.2.15** the 1981 Act, and it is an offence to catch any species in British coastal waters.[17] In Scotland it is also a specific offence to drive ashore any of the smaller species of whale commonly known as bottlenose or pilot whales.[18]

## 7. *Fish*

The regulation of fishing in Scotland, especially salmon fishing, has **9.2.16** been subject to detailed legal regulation for centuries. The ownership of fishing rights, the permitted times and methods of fishing, and the powers of district salmon fishery boards are all the subject of much legislation, augmented by byelaws for individual rivers.[19] Here it is possible to mention only a few of the most general provisions.

It is an offence to obstruct the passage of salmon smolt or fry, or of **9.2.17** mature salmon to the spawning grounds during the close season, or to injure any spawn, spawning bed or shallow where spawn might be, except as the incidental result of cleaning any lade or dam or of exercising proprietary rights over the bed of a watercourse.[20] The use of poison to kill fish is strictly prohibited, as is the use of explosive and electrical devices,[21] and the permitted methods of fishing are legally prescribed.[22] In addition, a few species of fish are protected under Sched. 5 to the Wildlife and Countryside Act 1981.

**9.2.18**  The taking of shellfish is subject to legal control, specifying minimum sizes and close seasons and prohibiting the landing or sale of crustaceans at vulnerable stages in their life cycle.[23] Marine fishing is the subject of an immense volume of regulatory legislation, at national and European level.[23a] Under the Sea Fisheries (Wildlife Conservation) Act 1992 the Secretary of State in the exercise of his functions in relation to fisheries is under a duty to have regard to the conservation of marine flora and fauna.

## C. Plants

**9.2.19**  Under s.13 of the Wildlife and Countryside Act 1981, it is a criminal offence for anyone other than an authorised person intentionally to uproot any wild plant; this is defined as any plant growing wild and ordinarily found growing in a wild state in Great Britain. Almost 100 species of plant, listed in Sched. 8 to the 1981 Act, are given additional protection, in that it is an offence for anyone intentionally to pick, uproot or destroy any of them. The sale of these listed plants, or of anything derived from them, possession with a view to sale and advertisement of any sort are also offences. In all cases though, there is a defence for action which is the incidental result of a lawful operation and which could not reasonably have been avoided.

## HABITAT PROTECTION

**9.3.1**  Each of the following designations of land has been created for a different purpose and is governed by its own statutory provisions. They do not form an integrated system. The precise effect of each designation will often depend on the byelaws made for a particular site, or on the terms of management agreements made by the conservation authorities with those with an interest in the land. In addition to any direct consequences, the presence of a formal designation may affect other features of the law, *e.g.* indicating that an environmental assessment should take place before permission is given for afforestation projects or other forms of development.[24]

**9.3.2**  In many of the designated areas management agreements can be used to further the objectives of nature conservation. Under such agreements, the owners and occupiers of land receive payments from the conservation authorities in return for agreeing to manage their land in particular ways, either refraining from activities detrimental to the conservation value of the land, or undertaking positive action to maintain or improve its value. The payments represent compensation for profit foregone or for expenses incurred, and can involve large sums.[25] Agreements are normally registrable in the Register of Sasines or Land Register, and once registered bind the successors in title to the original parties.[26] SNH enjoys a general power to enter management agreements to secure the conservation and enhancement of, or to foster the understanding or enjoyment of, the natural heritage in Scotland.[27]

## A. Nature Reserves

Nature reserves are land managed for the purpose of providing opportunities for the study and preservation of the flora and fauna of Scotland and of geological and physiographical features of special interest.[28] Where the management of land as a nature reserve is considered expedient in the national interest, a reserve can be declared by SNH, which can lease or purchase the land or enter management agreements with those holding an interest in it.[29] A power of compulsory purchase exists where agreements cannot be entered on reasonable terms or where their terms are broken.[30] Land managed as a nature reserve by other bodies can also be brought within the statutory scheme.[31] **9.3.3**

Once a reserve has been declared, SNH can make byelaws for it, including restrictions on access and prohibitions on any form of disturbance of the wildlife and natural features of the site.[32] Byelaws must be confirmed by the Secretary of State and cannot interfere with the rights of the owner or occupier (management agreements must be used if they are to be restricted) or of statutory undertakers. Compensation is available where the byelaws interfere with the exercise of rights vested in other people. **9.3.4**

Local nature reserves can be created and managed in the same way by general or district planning authorities, where this is considered expedient in the interests of the locality.[33] **9.3.5**

## B. Marine Nature Reserves

Areas of the sea can be designated as marine nature reserves where it is considered expedient that they should be managed by SNH for the purpose of conserving their flora, fauna and geological **9.3.6** or physiographical features of special interest.[34] The standard restriction is to areas landward of the baselines used for measuring territorial waters and seaward of these baselines for up to three nautical miles, but special orders can extend the reserves to any part of British territorial waters.

**9.3.7** Marine nature reserves are designated by the Secretary of State on the application of SNH. The application and the proposed byelaws for the reserve must be advertised and notified to a range of public bodies likely to be affected, and objections and representations must be heard before the Secretary of State decides whether to make the designation, any designation being similarly advertised and notified.

**9.3.8** Once a reserve has been created, byelaws can be made by SNH, subject to the Secretary of State's confirmation, to restrict access to the reserve and to protect the wildlife therein.[35] However, the scope of the byelaws is restricted in many ways. Byelaws cannot restrict the right of passage of vessels other than pleasure boats, and cannot prohibit pleasure boats from all of the reserve for the whole year. They cannot prohibit the discharge of any substance from a vessel,[36] nor can they interfere with the exercise of the statutory functions of the listed public bodies, which include local authorities, harbour boards, river purification boards and district fisheries boards.

## C. Sites of Special Scientific Interest

**9.3.9** Under the Wildlife and Countryside Act 1981, there is a duty on SNH to designate as a Site of Special Scientific Interest (SSSI) land which is of special interest by reason of its flora, fauna or geological or physiographical features (s.28).[37] Every owner and occupier of the site, and the planning authorities, must be notified, the notification containing the reasons why the site is of special importance and a list of the operations likely to damage its special features (potentially damaging operations). The notification takes effect at once, but lapses after nine months unless confirmed by SNH after a consideration of any objections or representations made by those affected.

**9.3.10** Where an objection relates to the grounds justifying the designation, the case must be referred to the special advisory committee created by the Natural Heritage (Scotland) Act 1991 (s.12). Existing designations must also be referred to this committee if the owner or occupier makes representations that any of the grounds justifying designation are no longer valid. If such representations were made at the time of designation, a case can be referred to the committee at once, otherwise it is only after 10 years from designation or the last consideration by the committee that cases can be referred. The final decision, however, remains with SNH.

If the owner or occupier wishes to carry out any of the potentially **9.3.11** damaging operations which have been notified, written notice must be given to SNH; failure to do so is an offence.[38] It is a further offence to proceed with the operation within four months of this notice, unless the operation is authorised by consent from SNH, by an express grant of planning permission, or by the terms of a management agreement. Emergency operations are permitted provided that SNH is given full details as soon as practicable. The four-month delay (which can be extended by agreement) is to allow SNH to consider and negotiate a management agreement or the making of a Nature Conservation Order to secure the future of the site, and it is only through such further action that a potentially damaging operation can be prevented for more than the four-month period.

Where a planning application relates to an SSSI, the planning **9.3.12** authority will have to consult with SNH before reaching its decision, and an environmental assessment may be required. For SSSIs on agricultural land, if a farm capital grant is refused because of SNH's objections, a management agreement must be offered.[39]

## D. Nature Conservation Orders

Nature Conservation Orders can be made by the Secretary of State **9.3.13** in order to strengthen the protection given to a particular site.[40] He can take this step for the purposes of securing the survival in Great Britain of any kind of animal or plant, of complying with international obligations, or of conserving the wildlife or features of a site of national importance. Orders take effect at once, but after public advertisement and notification to owners, occupiers and the planning authorities, the Secretary of State must consider whether to confirm the order, taking heed of any representations made and holding a local inquiry if necessary.

The effect of an Order is much the same as for ordinary SSSIs, but **9.3.14** with some modifications. It is a criminal offence for any person, not just the owner or occupier, to carry out any of the potentially damaging operations notified without informing SNH and waiting for the prescribed period or gaining relevant consent. The period of delay here is three months, but this is automatically extended to 12 if SNH offers to acquire the person's interest in the land or to enter a management agreement. There is also a power of compulsory purchase for SNH if an agreement is not possible on reasonable terms. In the event of an offence being committed, the penalties are greater than for ordinary SSSIs and the court has the power to order the offender to take restorative action.[41]

**9.3.15** Compensation is available for the loss in value of an agricultural unit covered by an Order, and for loss incurred (including abortive expenditure) when the three-month delay is extended as a result of an offer to acquire the land or enter a management agreement.[42]

### E. Natural Heritage Areas

**9.3.16** This new designation of land applies to areas which are of outstanding value to the natural heritage of Scotland and where special protection measures are considered appropriate.[43] Areas are to be recommended by SNH to the Secretary of State, who must advertise the proposal and listen to any representations before deciding whether to make a designation order. The legal effects of designation are minimal: planning authorities must maintain a list of Natural Heritage Areas in their district and must pay special attention to the desirability of preserving or enhancing their character in the exercise of powers under the Town and Country Planning (Scotland) Act 1972.

**9.3.17** It is intended, however, that an overall management statement should be produced for each Natural Heritage Area by SNH, acting in co-operation with the public bodies and private interests involved in the area. This statement will then provide the basis for an integrated approach to the management of the areas, with co-ordination between the various government departments and other public bodies involved augmented by the use of existing powers to enter management agreements and to offer advice and assistance in order to involve the private sector. Further legal measures, such as the designation of SSSIs or the making of directions removing permitted development status from some operations might also be appropriate, but the emphasis should be on voluntary co-operation.

### F. National Scenic Areas

**9.3.18** National Scenic Areas are areas which were designated by the Secretary of State after consultation with the Countryside Commission for Scotland as being areas of outstanding natural beauty in a national context where special protection measures are appropriate.[44] No new National Scenic Areas can be created.[45] Within these areas, planning authorities must pay special attention to the desirability of preserving or enhancing the character or appearance of the areas. To this end the Secretary of State has made directions under the General Development Order to require express permission for some forms of development normally enjoying permitted development status, and consultation with SNH (as successor to the Countryside Commission) when considering some categories of application for planning permission.

### G. Special Protection Areas

Under the European Directive on the Conservation of Wild Birds,[46] **9.3.19** Member States of the Community are obliged to take measures to protect wild birds and their habitat. Special protection areas have to be identified and appropriate steps taken to avoid the pollution or deterioration of these habitats and the disturbance of birds there. Only in exceptional circumstances is it permissible for a State to allow development or other operations detrimentally affecting such an area.[47] In Scotland such areas are designated by the Secretary of State and notified to the Commission of the Community. The areas should already be designated as SSSIs or covered by a Nature Conservation Order, and the significance of the European designation lies in the fact that when considering applications for planning permission and the like, the interests of nature conservation should be given overriding weight, and not merely taken into account alongside competing economic or recreational concerns.

### H. Limestone Pavement Orders

Areas of limestone pavement, *i.e.* areas of limestone wholly or **9.3.20** partly exposed on the surface of the ground and fissured by natural erosion, can be protected where they are of special interest by reason of their flora, fauna or geological or physiographical features.[48] SNH is under a duty to notify the relevant planning authority of any area meeting this test, and it is then up to the planning authority or the Secretary of State to make an order where the character or appearance of the land would be likely to be adversely affected by the removal or disturbance of the limestone. It is a criminal offence to remove or disturb limestone on designated land without reasonable excuse, *e.g.* an express grant of planning permission.

## I. Areas of Special Protection

**9.3.21**    These areas are designed to provide additional protection for birds. They can be designated by the Secretary of State by means of statutory instrument, but only if there are no objections from the owners and occupiers of the land affected. The orders designating areas can make it a criminal offence to kill or disturb any bird in the area, to damage any egg or nest, or to enter the area or part of it during all or part of the year. These restrictions do not affect the exercise of any vested right, and the owner or occupier continues to have the rights of an authorised person under the general law protecting birds.[49]

## J. Environmentally Sensitive Areas

**9.3.22**    Environmentally Sensitive Areas can be created in areas where it is particularly desirable to achieve any of the following objectives and the maintenance or adoption of particular agricultural methods is likely to facilitate this: the conservation and enhancement of the natural beauty of the area, the conservation of the flora, fauna or geological or physiographical features of special interest, the protection of buildings or other subjects of archaeological, architectural or historical interest.[50] Areas are designated by means of statutory instruments made by the Secretary of State after consultations with SNH.

**9.3.23**    Within Environmentally Sensitive Areas, any person with an interest in agricultural land can make an agreement with the Secretary of State that the land will be farmed in accordance with the agreement. The designation order may set out the rates of payment and other terms to apply to all agreements in the area. The owner of the land must be informed if anyone with a lesser interest seeks to enter such an agreement, and the Secretary of State is obliged to keep under review the effects of the agreements on the area as a whole.

## K. Ramsar Sites

**9.3.24**    The United Kingdom is a party to the Convention on Wetlands of International Importance especially as Waterfowl Habitat (the Ramsar

Convention) signed in 1971, under which special protection is to be given to wetlands of international significance in terms of ecology, botany, zoology, limnology, or hydrology, especially in relation to birds. Wetlands are designated by the Secretary of State for inclusion in the List of Wetlands of International Importance maintained under the Convention. Sites in Scotland should already be protected as SSSIs or under Nature Conservation Orders, but the obligations to promote the conservation of wetlands and to avoid as far as possible the loss of any wetland resource should strengthen the interests of nature conservation on such sites against proposals for development etc.

## L. World Heritage Sites

The World Heritage Convention was signed in 1972 under the **9.3.25** auspices of UNESCO to provide international recognition of and assistance for the protection of monuments, buildings and sites which are the natural and man-made treasures of the world. Sites which are of outstanding universal value can be added to the World Heritage List, and the protection, conservation, preservation and transmission to future generations of the natural heritage in their territory is an obligation on all parties, to be carried out by active and effective measures. Only sites which already enjoy full legal protec-tion, *e.g.* as nature reserves, are likely to be accepted for the List, and once adopted must be fully protected and conserved.

*Further Reading*

G.W.S. Barry and P. Birnie: "Fisheries," *Stair Memorial Encyclopaedia of the Laws of Scotland*, vol. 11 (Edinburgh, 1990, Butterworths/Law Society of Scotland).

J.F. Garner and B.L. Jones: *Countryside Law* (2nd ed.) (London, 1991, Shaw & Sons).

S. Lyster: *International Wildlife Law* (Cambridge, 1985, Grotius).

C. Parkes and J. Thornley: *Fair Game* (London, 1989, Pelham Books).

S. Scott Robinson: *The Law of Game, Salmon and Freshwater Fisheries in Scotland* (Edinburgh, 1990, Butterworths/Law Society of Scotland).

S. Scott Robinson: "Game," *Stair Memorial Encyclopaedia of the Laws of Scotland*, vol. 11 (Edinburgh, 1990, Butterworths/Law Society of Scotland).

NOTES

[1] Or rather, semi-natural, as virtually all of Scotland's landscape shows signs of human intervention at some stage in history.
[2] Natural Heritage (Scotland) Act 1991, Part I.
[3] Wildlife and Countryside (Amendment) Act 1991, s.1.
[4] Game (Scotland) Act 1772, Game Licences Act 1860.
[5] *e.g.* Night Poaching Acts 1828 and 1844; Game (Scotland) Act 1832.
[6] Badgers Act 1973 (as significantly amended by Wildlife and Countryside Act 1981, Sched.7; Wildlife and Countryside (Amendment) Act 1985, s.1; Badgers Act (1991); Badgers (Further Protection) Act 1991.
[7] Deer (Scotland) Act 1959, s.21(1); Deer (Close Seasons) (Scotland) Order 1984, S.I. 1984, No. 76.
[8] Deer (Scotland) Act 1959, ss.6(3), 33(3) (as amended by Deer (Amendment) (Scotland) Act 1967, s.2).
[9] Game Licences Act 1860, s.4.
[10] Deer (Scotland) Act 1959, s.14.
[11] Game Licences Act 1860, s.5.
[12] Deer (Scotland) Act 1959, s.23(2); Deer (Firearms) (Scotland) Order 1985, S.I. 1985 No. 1168.
[13] *Ibid.*, ss.23(1), 33(4A) (as amended by Deer (Amendment) (Scotland) Act 1982, s.13).
[14] Deer (Scotland) Act 1959, Part I.
[15] *Ibid.*, ss.6, 6A (as amended by Deer (Amendment) (Scotland) Act 1982, ss.3, 4).
[16] Deer (Scotland) Act 1959, ss. 8–11.
[17] Whaling Industry (Regulation) Act 1934, ss.1, 2 (as amended by the Fisheries Act 1981, s.35).
[18] Fisheries Act 1981, s.36.
[19] See Scott-Robinson, *The Law of Game, Salmon and Freshwater Fishing in Scotland* (Edinburgh, 1990, Butterworths/Law Society of Scotland).
[20] Salmon Fisheries (Scotland) Act 1868, s.19.
[21] Salmon and Freshwater Fisheries (Protection) (Scotland) Act 1951, s.4.
[22] Salmon and Freshwater Fisheries (Protection) (Scotland) Act 1951, s.2 (as amended by Salmon Act 1986, s.21).
[23] Sea Fisheries (Shellfish) Act 1967, Sea Fish (Conservation) Act 1967, Oyster Fisheries (Scotland) Act 1840, Mussel Fisheries (Scotland) Act 1847.

## Notes

[23a] See paras. 10.3.1 *et seq.*
[24] See paras. 6.4.17 *et seq.*
[25] See, *e.g. Cameron* v. *Nature Conservancy Council*, 1991 S.L.T. (Lands Tr.) 81.
[26] *e.g.* Countryside Act 1968, s.15.
[27] Countryside (Scotland) Act 1967, s.49A (added by Countryside (Scotland) Act 1981, s.9, amended by Natural Heritage (Scotland) Act 1991, Sched. 10).
[28] National Parks and Access to the Countryside Act 1949, s.15.
[29] *Ibid.*, s.16.
[30] *Ibid.*, ss.17–18.
[31] Wildlife and Countryside Act 1981, s.35.
[32] National Parks and Access to the Countryside Act 1949, s.20.
[33] *Ibid.*, s.21.
[34] Wildlife and Countryside Act 1981, s.36 (as amended by Territorial Sea Act 1987, s.3 and Sched.).
[35] *Ibid.*, s.37.
[36] See paras. 10.3.1 *et seq.*
[37] As amended by Wildlife and Countryside (Amendment) Act 1985, s.2; Wildlife and Countryside (Service of Notices) Act 1985, s.1.
[38] Wildlife and Countryside Act 1981, s.28.
[39] *Ibid.*, s.32.
[40] *Ibid.*, s.29.
[41] *Ibid.*, s.31.
[42] *Ibid.*, s.30.
[43] Natural Heritage (Scotland) Act 1991, s.6.
[44] Town and Country Planning (Scotland) Act 1972, s.262C (added by Housing and Planning Act 1986, Sched.11).
[45] Natural Heritage (Scotland) Act 1991, s.6(8).
[46] Directive 79/409/EEC (as amended).
[47] *Commission of the European Communities* v. *Germany* (case 57/89); see (1991) 34 SPLP 81.
[48] Wildlife and Countryside Act 1981, s.34.
[49] Wildlife and Countryside Act 1981, s.3.
[50] Agriculture Act 1986, s.18; following Art.19 of EEC Regulation 797/85 on improving the efficiency of agricultural structures.

# 10. Marine Issues

**10.1.1** Conservation of the marine environment has long been recognised as an issue that must be tackled on an international scale, and this is reflected in the number of international conventions which form the basis for much of the national legislation referred to in the following brief outline. The European dimension is also increasingly important. Space dictates that this outline concentrates on the national legislation, but it is as well to bear in mind from the outset that national legislation cannot be looked at in isolation.

**10.1.2** Space also dictates that this chapter is directed to issues of practical importance, rather than consideration of broader policy questions, *e.g.* whether there should be a single planning regime for controlled waters. It addresses firstly the question of pollution, that is unintentional pollution, and considers firstly prevention, secondly intervention where imminent crisis looms and finally compensation where efforts of prevention and intervention have failed. It then moves on to consider regulation of commercial activity, which in many cases produces controlled pollution. The emphasis is therefore on the commercial user: nature conservation as such, *e.g.* creation of marine nature reserves, is considered elsewhere.[1]

POLLUTION

## Prevention

*Oil Pollution*

**10.2.1** The first international effort to reduce the pollution of the sea by oil was the International Convention for the Prevention of Pollution of the Sea by Oil 1954 (OILPOL), implemented in the United Kingdom by the

Prevention of Oil Pollution Act 1971. OILPOL was superseded by the International Convention for the Prevention of Pollution from Ships 1973 (MARPOL) which is a comprehensive Convention dealing with pollution prevention. Annex I to MARPOL and the 1978 Protocol (referred to as MARPOL 1973/78) were implemented in the United Kingdom by the Merchant Shipping (Prevention of Oil Pollution) Order 1983[2] and the Merchant Shipping (Prevention of Oil Pollution) Regulations 1983 and 1985.[3]

The Regulations apply to all ships registered in the United Kingdom, **10.2.2** subject to certain exceptions and contain very detailed requirements as to construction, equipment and operation of vessels. In addition there are extensive powers of enforcement including powers of inspection, detention, denial of entry to United Kingdom ports or offshore terminals and service of an Improvement Notice and a Prohibition Notice, under which a vessel may be detained from going to sea until the matters complained of are remedied. If a ship discharges or is otherwise in contravention of the regulations, the owner and master of the vessel will each be found guilty of an offence and liable to potentially substantial fines. The court imposing a fine may order the whole or a part of the fine to be paid to a person who has incurred expense in removing any pollution or making good any damage resulting from the offence,[4] and the vessel may be detained until the case has been heard (when it may be sold to defray unpaid expenses, compensation and penalties) or a bond is put up.[4a]

## Other Pollution

Annex II to MARPOL is concerned with the control of pollution by **10.2.3** noxious liquid substances in bulk. This has been incorporated into United Kingdom law by the Merchant Shipping (Control of Pollution by Noxious Liquid Substances in Bulk) Regulations 1987[5] and the Merchant Shipping (Control of Pollution by Noxious Liquid Substances in Bulk) (Amendment) Regulations 1990.[6] This essentially creates a parallel regime under which the discharge of chemicals from tank cleaning or deballasting operations may be carried out.

Annex III lays down regulations for the prevention of pollution by **10.2.4** harmful substances carried by sea in packaged forms, or in freight containers, portable tanks or road and rail tank wagons (*i.e.* otherwise than in bulk). This has been implemented by the Merchant Shipping

(Prevention and Control of Pollution) Order 1990,[7] and the Merchant Shipping (Dangerous Goods and Marine Pollutants) Regulations 1990.[8]

**10.2.5**   Annex IV regulates sewage but is not yet in force. Meanwhile the discharge of sewage effluent from ships within the territorial waters is exempt from the requirement to obtain Discharge Consents under the Control of Pollution Act 1974.[9]

**10.2.6**   Annex V deals with garbage—for which see the Merchant Shipping (Prevention of Pollution by Garbage) Order 1988,[10] the Merchant Shipping (Prevention of Pollution by Garbage) Regulations 1988[11] and the Merchant Shipping (Reception Facilities for Garbage) Regulations 1988.[12] It is illegal for any vessel, including pleasure craft and oil platforms and drilling rigs, to throw anything at all overboard within three miles of the nearest land and in all inland waters and within 12 miles to throw overboard plastic, or (if not ground to less than 1") paper, glass or food. Moreover the North Sea is now a "Special Area" and there is a complete ban on dumping of all refuse, with the exception of food—and that not within 12 miles of land.

**Intervention**

*Salvage Generally*

**10.2.7**   The right to claim salvage has traditionally depended on success. This principle of "no cure, no pay" is well known and, until recently, was absolute. There has been increasing public awareness of possible environmental damage from escape of pollutant cargo and of the necessity to encourage investment in larger, more sophisticated but costly tugs necessary to conduct salvage operations. Moreover, shipowners have a direct financial interest in preventing oil pollution, since they will have to pay for damage done by the escaped cargo and the cost of cleaning up and/or prevention of damage. The cumulative effect of these pressures has been reflected in the New Salvage Convention (International Salvage Convention 1989) on the one hand, and amendments to the Lloyds Open Form (LOF) under which most professional salvage services are rendered, on the other.

*New Salvage Convention*

**10.2.8**   The New Salvage Convention[13] reflected those increasing public pressures already referred to, and a decade's experience of LOF 80, and introduced significant changes.

*Pollution*

In the Convention, "salvage operations" means any act or activity **10.2.9**
undertaken to assist a vessel *or any other property* in danger in
navigable or in any other waters whatsoever (Art. 1(a)).

"Property" is defined as "any property not permanently and inten- **10.2.10**
tionally attached to the shore line and including freight at risk" (Art.
1(c)). Article 3 specifically excludes "fixed or floating platforms . . .
or . . . mobile offshore drilling units when such platforms or units are
on location engaged in the exploration, exploitation or production of
seabed mineral resources" but that would not appear to exclude
salvage where platforms or units are in transit. It might also include,
depending upon how these were moored, fish farm cages.

One of the criteria to be taken into account in the fixing of the **10.2.11**
reward for such salvages is a new element, defined as "the skill and
efforts of the salvors in preserving or minimising damage to the
environment." "Damage to the environment" means "substantial
physical damage to human health or to marine life or resources in
coastal or inland waters or areas adjacent thereto, caused by
pollution, contamination, fire, explosion or similar major incidents"
(Art. 1(e)).

Where the new Salvage Convention departs radically from the 1910 **10.2.12**
Convention, is in the introduction of special compensation where
efforts have been made to prevent damage to the environment.
Article 14(1) reflects the original LOF 80 safety net and provides: "If
the salvor has carried out salvage operations in respect of a vessel
which by itself or its cargo threaten damage to the environment and
has failed to earn a reward under Article 13 at least equivalent to the
special compensation assessable in accordance with this Article, he
shall be entitled to special compensation from the owner of that
vessel equivalent to his expenses as herein defined." Under Article
14(1) there is therefore no requirement that the salvor should actually
achieve any success in salving the vessel itself. Special compensation cases only apply, however, where it is a vessel or its cargo which
threatens damage to the environment: the extended definition of
salvable property does not apply. Moreover, the threatened damage
must be "substantial." This is not defined in the Convention, and it is
not clear whether this means that the damage must be extensive, or
merely that it may have a significant effect, *e.g.* on rare marine flora
and fauna.

While Article 14(1) provides for special compensation where there is **10.2.13**
no success, Article 14(2) provides for enhanced special compensation

if the salvage operation has actually "prevented or minimised damage to the environment."

**10.2.14**   Article 14 is a departure from the established basis of general average in so far as contributions are concerned. However, Article 14(6) preserves any right of recourse on the part of the owner of the vessel. While this does not preserve an ability to recover in general average, it would enable the shipowner to recover by way of damages from the cargo owner if the potentially damaging incident occurred through the cargo owner's fault—*e.g.* the cargo owner failed, in breach of the contract of carriage, to state with complete accuracy the precise nature of a dangerous cargo, or packed it in an inappropriate manner.

*Lloyds Open Form 90 (LOF 90)*

**10.2.15**   The New Convention will only come into force after it has been ratified by 15 States, and it may be some time before it either comes into force or is enacted into United Kingdom legislation. The industry has therefore responded relatively quickly, and the new LOF 90, published in September 1990 has specifically adopted the Special Compensation Provisions of the New Convention and extended the equivalent provisions of LOF 80.

**10.2.16**   By Clause 1(a)(ii) a contractor expressly undertakes an obligation to use his best endeavours "while performing the salvage services to prevent or minimise damage to the environment." That is a significant extension of the equivalent provision of LOF 80 which related only to the escape of oil.

**10.2.17**   Articles 1((a) to (e)), 8, part of Article 13 and Article 14 of the Convention are specifically incorporated. By the incorporation of Article 1, the definitions of salvage operations, vessel, property, damage to the equipment and payment are included, thus extending the classes of property capable of being salved (see above) at least so as to create a contractual claim for salvage although it is not certain whether this can create a maritime lien valid against third parties. By incorporating Article 13, with one minor exception, and the whole of Article 14, this means in practical terms that where services are rendered under LOF 90, the salvor would qualify not only for payment under the safety net provisions previously available under LOF 80, but also the enhanced special compensation payable under Article 14(2).

Article 8 incorporates duties of the salvor and of the owner and **10.2.18**
master. The salvor owes a duty to the owner of the vessel *inter alia* to
exercise due care to prevent or minimise damage to the environment.
Similarly, the owner and master of the vessel or the owner of other
property in danger owes a duty to the salvor to co-operate fully with
him during the course of the salvage operation. If the salvor has been
negligent and has thereby failed to prevent or minimise damage to
the environment, he may be deprived of the whole or part of any
special compensation due (Art. 14(5)). In addition, Article 14(6)
preserves the owner's right of recourse and that may include a right
against salvors: there is no absolute protection for salvors, although
they are entitled to limit their liability in the ordinary way. There is also
the possibility that the imposition of a duty to minimise damage to the
environment exposes the salvor as a third party, or possibly even as
a potential defender, in any action at the instance of persons who
have suffered pollution damage.

*Government Intervention*

When the *Torrey Canyon* ran aground, the Government eventually **10.2.19**
ordered the wreck to be bombed so as to destroy the remaining oil
by fire and avoid serious pollution to the coast. There was considerable doubt as to the United Kingdom's right to take such measures,
since the vessel was outside United Kingdom territorial waters, and
this led eventually to the International Convention Relating to Intervention on the High Seas of Oil Pollution Casualties 1969. Article 1 allows
parties to: "take such measures on the high seas as may be
necessary to prevent, mitigate or eliminate grave and imminent
danger to their coastline or related interests from pollution or threat of
pollution of the seas by oil following upon a maritime casualty."

Power to intervene was extended by a 1973 Protocol to a long list **10.2.20**
of dangerous or noxious chemicals other than oil, and the 1969
Convention and 1973 Protocol have been enacted into United
Kingdom law by the Prevention of Oil Pollution Act 1971 and the
Merchant Shipping (Prevention of Pollution) (Intervention) Order
1980.[14]

There is no right to compensation from the Government for damage **10.2.21**
or loss caused by the exercise of the intervention powers unless the
action taken was not reasonably necessary to prevent pollution or
was disproportionate: however, the shipowner would usually be
insured against intervention damage.

*European Community*

**10.2.22**  More than 25 directives or decisions have been adopted covering both fresh water and sea water, aimed at controlling dangerous substances and at setting minimum quality standards. Of particular importance are the directives on the quality of bathing water,[15] on water supporting fish life[16] and on shellfish waters.[17]

## Liability and Compensation for Pollution Damage

*Oil Pollution*

**10.2.23**  The *Torrey Canyon* incident exposed other deficiencies in the existing law including difficulties in proving fault or negligence, not to mention the stark fact that many shipowners were unable to pay the full amount of potential damages. The incident was a major stimulus to the development of a parallel regime, the first at governmental level, the second at industry level.

*Liability for Oil Pollution*

**10.2.24**  The first response on a governmental level was the International Convention on Civil Liability for Oil Pollution Damage 1969 (CLC). The provisions of the CLC were implemented in the United Kingdom by the Merchant Shipping (Oil Pollution) Act 1971 which imposes strict liability on the owner of a vessel. Where, as a result of any occurrence taking place while a ship is carrying a cargo of persistent oil in bulk, any persistent oil carried by the ship (whether as part of the cargo or otherwise) is discharged or escapes from the ship, the owner is liable:

> (a) for any damage caused in the area of the United Kingdom by contamination resulting from the discharge or escape; and
>
> (b) for the cost of any measures reasonably taken after the discharge or escape begins for the purpose of preventing or reducing any such damage in the area of the United Kingdom; and
>
> (c) for any damage caused in the area of the United Kingdom by any measures so taken (s.1).

**10.2.25**  Section 10 requires tankers carrying 2,000 tonnes or more of persistent oil in bulk as cargo to be insured against liability for pollution, and to have a certificate demonstrating this on board. There is a right of direct action against the insurer (s.12(1)) though in any proceedings brought against the insurer it is a defence (in addition to any defence affecting the owner's liability) for the insurer to prove that the discharge or escape was due to the wilful misconduct of the owner himself (s.12(2)). The owner is entitled in the absence of actual fault or privity to limit his liability to an amount assessed in special drawing rights of the International Monetary Fund (SDRs): the insurer may limit his liability irrespective of whether or not the discharge or escape occurred without the owner's actual fault or privity (s.12(3)).

*Compensation for Oil Pollution*

Even at the 1969 Diplomatic Conference, it was felt the financial **10.2.26** limit set by the CLC might be inadequate. Under the auspices of the International Marine Organisation (IMO) the International Convention on the Establishment of an International Fund for Compensation for Oil Pollution Damage 1971 (the Fund Convention) set up the International Oil Pollution Compensation Fund (the Fund). The Fund is financed by the governments of signatory countries, who impose a levy on oil imports in their countries which, in turn, is paid by the importing oil company. The Fund pays compensation in respect of pollution damage in a contracting state if a person has been unable to obtain full and adequate compensation under the CLC because no liability for damage arises under the CLC, or because the owner is financially incapable of meeting his obligations, or the damage exceeds the shipowner's liability as limited under the CLC. The maximum available for the Fund is still limited.

Practical experience of the CLC and Fund Convention in operation **10.2.27** demonstrated a need for their amendment. In May 1984 a Diplomatic Conference was held at IMO to revise the Conventions, and the resulting Protocols (the 1984 Protocols) will introduce revisions. Firstly, tankers in ballast will be within the scope of the regime. Secondly, the CLC will not be limited to actual spillage, but will apply to liability for preventative measures. Thirdly, the test for breaking the owner's right to limit liability will change from "actual fault or privity" in line with the new Limitation Convention (see below). Finally, the maximum limit of liability for the shipowner and maximum compensation available from the Fund will be radically increased. IMO have proposed revisions (the 1984 Protocols) but these have not been ratified and are unlikely to be so in their present form. It is possible that revised protocols may be agreed in the near future, subject to less stringent ratification requirements.

*The Industry Response to Oil Pollution*

**10.2.28**   At the time of the 1969 Conference, there was widespread concern in the tanker and oil industries about the length of time it would take for the CLC and Fund Convention to enter into force. Industry therefore evolved two voluntary schemes to ensure acceptable compensation in the interim. TOVALOP (Tanker Owners' Voluntary Agreement Concerning Liability for Oil Pollution) which came into effect in October 1969, is an agreement entered into by tanker owners and bare boat charterers under which the parties undertake to pay compensation for oil pollution even though they might not otherwise be legally liable. CRISTAL (the Contract Regarding an Interim Supplement to Tanker Liability for Oil Pollution) came into force in 1971. Parties include cargo owners, charterers and oil traders and the compensation is intended to be supplementary to TOVALOP.

**10.2.29**   Since February 20, 1987, TOVALOP has been augmented by a TOVALOP Supplement which applies in cases in which CRISTAL is involved. Where CRISTAL is not involved, the pre-1987 TOVALOP Conditions apply (now termed the Standing Agreement). Under TOVALOP where a participating tanker spills *or threatens to spill* persistent oil, the owner or bare boat charterer will be liable for reasonable costs in responding to the incident, including attempts to prevent or minimise pollution damage. They will also be responsible for pollution damage which includes direct loss, and proven economic loss.

*Other Pollution*

**10.2.30**   There may well be cases of pollution, or the threat of pollution, from vessels not covered by the CLC and Fund Convention, or TOVALOP and CRISTAL. This would include oil escaping from dry cargo vessels, damage caused by non-persistent oil (*e.g.* gasoline, fish or vegetable oil), discharge of chemicals, or discharge of poisonous or toxic substances, and the lack of a coherent liability and compensation regime is a matter of serious concern. This is under consideration but it is fair to say it will be some considerable time before any equivalents of the CLC and Fund Convention are introduced.[17a]

**10.2.31** Where the pollution was caused by an incident within United Kingdom territorial or internal waters, the ordinary United Kingdom courts will have jurisdiction. It may be possible to frame an action in nuisance but, in general, claims would be framed in delict.[18] That may present problems in relation to liability and also recovery, since the operators may be entitled to limit their liability in terms of the Merchant Shipping Act 1979.

**10.2.32** The duty on salvors to minimise damage to the environment and the incentive of adequate salvage rewards, may conceivably therefore be of even greater practical importance to the public in cases where there is the possibility of damage from a chemical tanker than where there is threatened oil pollution. If there is oil pollution, claimants may be more or less assured that they will make full recovery: as present, where there is pollution from other sources, it may be more difficult to recover and will certainly be far more time-consuming and expensive.

COMMERCIAL ACTIVITY

## Fishing

*Quotas*

**10.3.1** The decline in fish stocks has been of concern to commercial fishermen and independent conservationists alike and commercial fishing is now subject to stringent quotas and effort limitation measures in an effort to halt the decline. After bilateral consultation with Norway, Sweden, Denmark and the Faroes, the EEC Fisheries Council sets quotas (Total Allowable Catches) for Member States in the United Kingdom's case after application of the Hague Preference which favours partners of the Community particularly dependent on fishing.[19] There are different TACs for individual species—*e.g.* present TACs for cod and haddock ("pressure stock" species) are low while a TAC for nethrops was introduced only in 1992.

**10.3.2** Member States allocate a TAC amongst individual fishermen by the issue of licences.[20] In the United Kingdom these are issued by Local

Fisheries Offices and every vessel over 10 metres[20a] is now required to hold a licence for relevant species/areas. Although licences are issued to named fishermen/companies, a licence must be attached to a vessel, except with consent of the Fisheries Office. Any transfer of a licence must therefore be in conjunction with the sale of at least a share in the vessel. With the introduction of licences, attempts were made to restrict ownership of vessels (and therefore issue of licences) to United Kingdom nationals[21] but the European Court has ruled that this is incompatible with Community Law.[22] Companies whose beneficial owners are EEC nationals may therefore own British registered vessels, and participate in United Kingdom TACs, but all United Kingdom registered vessels must (a) fish under licence and (b) may be required to demonstrate that control is exercised from the United Kingdom and that there is a real connection with the United Kingdom.

**10.3.3** Licences are in turn subject to reporting and other conditions, and limitation measures, principally the restriction on vessel operation—in 1991 vessels which had caught more than the qualifying amounts of cod and haddock were required to tie-up for eight consecutive days in each month.[23] From February 1, 1992, those vessels have had to tie-up for 135 days, although fishermen can choose when those days will be and how long periods should be.[24] There is also a "gear option"—vessels using nets with a larger mesh size are not required to observe the 8 day/135 day tie-up.

**10.3.4** Conditions for the issue, transfer and operation of licences are highly technical and complex, and not readily available in textbook form. In general, reference should be made to (i) licences themselves, which must be aboard the vessel at all times; (ii) Scottish Office press releases; (iii) trade journals such as *Scottish Fishing Weekly*; and (iv) Local Fisheries Officers.

*Fishing Methods*

**10.3.5** Certain fishing methods may also be prohibited for conservation reasons.[25] These include prohibition of monofilament gill nets.[26]

**Dumping**

**10.3.6** Dumping of materials is regulated by two relevant international Conventions, the Convention for the Prevention of Marine Pollution by Dumping from Ships and Aircraft, Oslo 1972 (the Oslo Convention) and the Convention on the Prevention of Marine Pollution by Dumping of Waste and other Matter, London 1972 (the London Convention). Those conventions were enacted into United Kingdom law by the Dumping at Sea Act 1974, which has now been replaced by the similar provisions of the Food and Environment Protection Act 1985 which applies to all ships in United Kingdom territorial waters.

**10.3.7** Both Conventions list substances which are supposedly prohibited from dumping (Annex I—the Black List, *e.g.* mercury and cadmium). Others may be dumped with a special permit (Annex II—the Grey List, *e.g.* pesticides and by-products, arsenic, lead, copper and zinc). Dumping of Annex I substances is only permitted if they are present as "trace contaminants" while Annex II substances must not be present in "significant quantities," a term which is defined as 0.1 per cent by weight. In addition, at the second North Sea Conference in 1989, it was agreed that annual loads of various chemical compounds (the Red List) be reduced by 50–70 per cent by 1995. A licence is also required for incineration at sea.

**10.3.8** In deciding whether to issue a licence, the licensing authority (in Scotland, the Secretary of State) must take into account the need to protect the marine environment, human health and to prevent interference with legitimate uses at sea, *e.g.* fishing or leisure activities.[27] Account must also be taken of alternative methods of disposal. There is increasing public concern over the dumping of waste materials at sea, particularly sewage sludge and industrial wastes, and this may lead the licensing authorities to look far more closely at the possibility of alternative disposal on land particularly with the introduction of integrated pollution control under the Environmental Protection Act 1990.[28]

## Discharge Consents

**10.3.9** Under s.31 of the Control of Pollution Act 1974, it is an offence to cause or knowingly permit the entry of "poisonous, noxious or polluting matter" or any solid waste into controlled waters, which waters extend seawards for three nautical miles. The offence is committed when either coastal or inland waters are polluted.[28a] "Poisonous, noxious or polluting matter" includes suspended solids from quarries or chemical discharges, and may include chemicals administered either directly or mixed with fish farm feed, although not necessarily organic waste products.

**10.3.10**    It is also an offence under s.32 to cause or knowingly permit any trade effluent or sewage effluent to be discharged into any controlled waters. A person is not guilty of an offence under either section if the entry or discharge is authorised by a discharge consent granted by the appropriate river purification authority, and is in accordance with the conditions, if any, to which the consent is subject.[29]

**Works within Harbour Areas**

**10.3.11**    In certain designated harbour areas, anyone wishing to operate a fish farm must obtain a works licence from the local harbour authorities. In Orkney and Shetland the Islands Council acts as harbour authority, river purification authority and planning authority. Dredging must normally be authorised under local Harbour or Conservancy Acts and may also require the consent of the Crown Estate Commissioners, while disposal of dredging soil must be licensed under the Food and Environment Protection Act 1985 unless done by harbour authorities in execution of harbour maintenance works and deposit is made on the site of the works. Harbour works may be subject to environmental assessment under the Harbour Works (Assessment of Environmental Effects) (No. 2) Regulations 1989.[30]

**Fish Farming**

**10.3.12**    As the seabed and most of the foreshore are part of the Crown Estate, fish farmers have to apply to the Crown Estate Commission for a lease of the area which the fish farm will occupy. The Environmental Assessment (Salmon Farming in Marine Waters) Regulations 1988[31] which implement the European Community Directive 85/337 require that all applications to the Crown Estate for salmon farming leases must be submitted with a supplementary environmental statement if the proposed development is likely to have significant environmental effects because of its type, scale or location.[32] The special requirement extends to:

> (i) Marine salmon farming using fixed equipment within 2 kilometres of the coast.
> (ii) Projects over a certain size, with a lower threshold in certain sensitive areas.

**10.3.13**    In the current (1992) economic climate there is little demand for new salmon farm sites, but where an existing business is sold, the current practice of the Crown Estate Commission is to require surrender of the existing lease and the grant of a new lease. Following receipt of an application the Crown Estate Commissioners follow consultation procedures agreed with the Scottish Office— consultees will include the general public, planning authorities who are responsible for onshore development, agencies and interested groups including Scottish Natural Heritage.

All drugs used for treatment of fish are, by statutory definition, **10.3.14** veterinary drugs for the purposes of the Medicines Acts 1968 and 1971. The Acts require that all veterinary medicines have a product licence covering sale, supply and manufacture and the Veterinary Products Committee recommend to the licensing authority that grants a licence only if it is satisfied that the product meets the required standards of safety, quality and efficiency. However, s.9(2) of the 1968 Act allows a vet to prescribe any medicine, licensed or unlicensed, for animals under his/her care so long as it is specially prepared to order. This means any product, including unlicensed products, can be prescribed and can be introduced into the sea. There is considerable concern over the use of pesticides, whose environmental impact is, to say the least, uncertain.

Classification as a pesticide or medicine depends upon the **10.3.15** purpose to which the products are put: the same substance can be both medicine and pesticide, *e.g.* dichlorovos (the active ingredient in Nuvan). Pesticides as such are controlled by the Food and Environment Protection Act 1985. The Act contains powers to make regulations governing the maximum residue levels of pesticides in foods; current regulations[33] do not include fish, although this is under active consideration.

All fish farms must be registered with the Scottish Office for **10.3.16** disease control purposes and certain diseases must be notified to the Department. Restrictions may be placed on movement of infected stock and procedures are laid down for treatment and disposal.[34]

## Shellfish

Shellfish are particularly susceptible to the effects of pollution. One **10.3.17** major source is the build-up of nutrients in coastal waters owing to sewage disposal and agricultural run-off. Excessive nutrient input may be evidenced by toxic algae blooms (these also occur naturally) which can cause paralytic and less severe diarrhetic shellfish poisoning (PSB and DSP) if bivalve molluscs, which have accumulated these toxins, are eaten.[34a] Under the powers conferred by s.1 of the Food and Environment Protection Act 1985,[35] the Secretary of State has power to issue Emergency Prohibition Orders, prohibiting the fishing for, taking or removing of bivalve molluscs out of designated areas. Several such Orders have already been made in the course of 1991 covering both the east and west coasts and Orkney. The Secretary of State also has power to prohibit the deposit of shellfish in designated waters.[36]

*Further Reading*

J. H. Bates: *United Kingdom Marine Pollution Law* (London, 1985, Lloyds of London Press) (now slightly out of date, but essential).
G. Brice: *Maritime Law of Salvage* (London, 1983, Sweet & Maxwell).
G. Darling and C. Smith: "LOF 90 and The New Salvage Convention" (London, 1991, Lloyds of London Press).
J. F. Garner: *Garner's Environmental Law* (formerly *Control of Pollution Encyclopaedia*) (London, 1976–, Butterworths).
N. J. J. Gaskell, C. Debattista and R. J. Swatton: *Chorley & Giles, Shipping Law* (8th ed.) (London, 1987, Pitman) (succinct, particularly good on construction, maintenance and equipment of vessels).
W. Howarth: *The Law of Aquaculture* (Oxford, 1990, Fishing News Books) (comprehensive, but treat with some caution for Scotland).
D. W. Steel and F. D. Rose: *Kennedy's Law of Salvage* (5th ed.) (London, 1985, Stevens).
Scottish Office: "Guidance on the Location of Marine Fish Farms" (Consultative Draft, December 1991) (useful bibliography).

NOTES

[1] See paras. 9.3.6 *et seq.*
[2] S.I. 1983 No. 1106, made under powers contained in s.20 of the Merchant Shipping Act 1979.
[3] S.I.s 1983 No. 1398; 1985 No. 2040, made under para. 3 of the 1983 Order.
[4] Prevention of Oil Pollution Act 1971, s.20(2).

# Notes

[4a] With effect from February 1, 1992; Merchant Shipping (Prevention of Oil Pollution) (Amendment) Regulations 1992 (S.I. 1992 No. 98).

[5] S.I. 1987 No. 551.

[6] S.I. 1990 No. 2604.

[7] S.I. 1990 No. 2595.

[8] S.I. 1990 No. 2605.

[9] Control of Pollution Act 1974, s.32(4)(*a*); see also paras. 3.8.12 *et seq.*

[10] S.I. 1988 No. 2252.

[11] S.I. 1988 No. 2292.

[12] S.I. 1988 No. 2293.

[13] Replacing the Brussels Convention of 1910.

[14] S.I. 1980 No. 1093.

[15] Directive 76/160/EEC.

[16] Directive 78/659/EEC.

[17] Directive 79/923/EEC; see generally paras. 11.5.2 *et seq.*

[17a] Draft Convention on Liability and Compensation in connection with the Carriage of Hazardous and Noxious Substances by Sea (HNS).

[18] See generally Chap. 8.

[19] Council Regulation No. 170/83/EEC.

[20] Sea Fish (Conservation) Act 1967.

[20a] From January 1, 1993 it is proposed to extend the regime to vessels under 10 metres (MAFF Circular of March 11, 1992).

[21] Merchant Shipping Act 1988; Merchant Shipping (Registration of Fishing Vessels) Regulations 1988 (S.I. 1988 No. 1926).

[22] *R.* v. *Secretary of State for Transport, ex p. Factortame Ltd. and Others* (No. 3) (221/89) [1991] 3 All E.R. 769.

[23] Sea Fishing (Days in Port) Regulations 1991 (S.I. 1991 No. 139).

[24] Sea Fishing (Days in Port) Regulations 1992 (S.I. 1992 No. 130) and Sea Fishing (Days in Port) (Amendment) Regulations 1992 (S.I. 1992 No. 670).

[25] Council Regulations Nos. 171/83/EEC and 3094/86/EEC.

[26] *Procurator Fiscal, Stranraer* v. *Marshall* (370/88) (*sub nom. Walkingshaw* v. *Marshall*) 1991 S.C.C.R. 397.

[27] Food and Environment Protection Act 1985, s.8(1).

[28] See generally Chaps. 4 and 5.

[28a] *Mackenzie* v. *Tractor Shovels Tairse*, 1992 S.C.C.R. 71.

[29] See generally paras. 3.5.8 *et seq.*

[30] S.I. 1989 No. 424.

[31] S.I. 1988 No. 1218.

[32] See paras. 6.4.17 *et seq.*

[33] Pesticides (Maximum Residue Levels in Food) Regulations 1988 (S.I. 1988 No. 1378).

[34] See Diseases of Fish Acts 1937 and 1983 and Sea Fisheries (Shellfish) Act 1967.

[34a] Scottish Office Consultation Paper of March 11, 1992 on the Urban Waste Treatment Directive (91/271/EEC) and the Nitrates Directive (91/676/EEC).

[35] As amended by Food Safety Act 1990, s.15.

[36] Sea Fisheries (Shellfish) Act 1967.

# 11. European Environmental Law

The European Community in 1992 is both expanding as new coun- **11.1.1**
tries seek to join, and consolidating, as the imminent completion of
the internal market produces closer integration. Its influence on the
activities of its constituent members is increasing and nowhere is this
more apparent than in the field of environmental policy.

The reasons for this developing involvement are several. Firstly, the **11.1.2**
realisation that the increasingly serious problem of environmental
damage cannot be adequately addressed at national level only.
Pollution is an international concern. Secondly, one of the principal
objectives of the Treaty of Rome is the continual improvement in the
quality of life of the citizens of Europe (Preamble and Art. 2) and this
demands the achievement of as clean an environment as possible in
which to live and work. Thirdly, the central objective of the Treaty of
Rome is to establish a single Common Market with no barriers to
trading on an equal footing throughout the Community (Art. 2).
Differences in standards of environmental control could seriously
distort the concept of fair competition and harmonisation of laws in
this field is therefore essential. Lastly, the Community itself has
collectively been responsible for much of the pollution and contamination which has occurred in Europe and it has a responsibility
to its individual citizens to ensure that the efforts of Member States
(upon whose individual laws the implementation of most European
environmental policy depends) are effectively directed, co-ordinated
and enforced.

Accordingly, the existence of an effective Community system of **11.1.3**
laws which will afford the environment a high level of protection while
at the same time promoting the internal market is essential to the
proper functioning of the Community. This was recognised by the
European Commission when, in the Fourth Action Programme on the
Environment (1987–92)[1] it emphasised that "the effective implementation of Community environmental legislation by all Member States
will be of primary importance for the Community."

**Relevance of EC Environmental Law**

**11.1.4** A knowledge of European environmental law and the policy which
has promoted it is essential to any consideration of Scottish environmental issues. This is partly because EC law is now a part of the law
of Scotland so that it is necessary to have an understanding of how
Community rights and obligations are applied through our own laws.
More importantly, it is essential to understand the purpose of the
underlying policy, given that the courts in this country are required to
interpret national law so as to ensure compliance with the Community
policy in question. This "purposive" construction to be given to
national law designed to give effect to directives was established in a
House of Lords case in 1989.[2] That case in fact dealt with employment law but, given the increasing incidence of United Kingdom
legislation enacted specifically to implement EC environmental directives, it is likely that this approach will be adopted in any
environmental decision in the near future. The judgment in a recent
unreported Scottish case contains a quite clear indication that the
courts will indeed adopt this approach.[3]

DEVELOPMENT OF EUROPEAN ENVIRONMENTAL LAW

**11.2.1** As originally enacted the Treaty of Rome made no mention of the
environment and there was no formal environmental policy. In 1972
the United Nations Conference on the Environment at Stockholm
highlighted the global concern at the damage being done to the
world and its ecosystems. Later in the same year the European
Community Summit Meeting in Paris recognised that the continuing
encouragement of economic growth would require improvements in
the quality of life.[4] The Commission was directed to formulate the first
formal statement of Community environmental policy which as well as
addressing the overall aim of preventing, or at least greatly reducing,
pollution, would recognise the need to achieve co-ordination
amongst national governments on such aspects as:
1. The planned use of scarce resources.
2. The problem of trans-frontier pollution.
3. Preventing distortion of competition where the cost of compliance with environmental legislation differs from Member
State to Member State.

4.  The desire to promote similar living conditions throughout the Community.
5.  Recognition that although extremely important *per se*, environmental policy is a critical element of economic development.

Having established a general policy, the Commission, wishing both to **11.2.2** establish a programme of legislation to start the process of controlling further damage to the environment and, at the same time, to have the opportunity of reviewing progress, discussing changes in policy, etc., provided for an Environment Action Programme for the four-year period from 1973 to 1976.[5] This first programme laid down the Commission's plans to cope with pollution of the atmosphere, of water and of land (particularly waste management). In addition, considerable emphasis was placed on the protection of natural habitats and wildlife.

The first programme was designed to focus the original primary **11.2.3** aims of the Community into more identifiable plans to:

1.  Reduce and prevent pollution and nuisances;
2.  Improve the quality of life; and
3.  Take action at Community level.

The first action programme was followed by a second,[6] third[7] and fourth[8] spanning the period 1977 to 1992 and the fifth is in final draft and due to be promulgated very shortly.

The different action programmes had different emphases. The first **11.2.4** two were designed to produce a relatively speedy response to the worst effects of pollution. The third emphasised the concept of the preventative approach while the fourth heralded a major change in the status of the environment in EC law. The fifth seems likely to mark a further development in policy, away from prescriptive legislation towards voluntary action and market-based measures.

The Treaty of Rome in 1957 did not specifically provide for the **11.2.5** environment. The Paris Summit meeting based the environmental policy which it established on the fact that the Preamble to the Treaty committed the signatories to *inter alia* "the constant improvement of the living and working conditions of their peoples." In addition it was rapidly becoming clear that the absence of a "level planning playing field" arising from the differing degrees of environmental regulation pertaining in different Member States could work against the principles of free trade and fair competition. With the rapidly developing importance of the environment as an international issue, this slightly contrived authority for action on the environment was replaced with formal recognition of environmental policy as an established part of the Treaty, in terms of the amendments introduced by the Single European Act in 1987. The Treaty of Rome now has a new "Environment" Title (Title VII) which finally provides environmental policy with a proper legal basis.

**11.2.6** Some reference at this stage would seem appropriate to the problems which have arisen recently regarding the appropriate Article of the Treaty on which to base environmental legislation. Prior to the Single European Act, legislation tended to be based either on Article 100 or Article 235. The former provides "for the approximation of such provisions laid down by law, regulation or administrative action in Member States as directly affect the establishment or functioning of the common market." Thus, harmonisation of national laws to permit free movement of goods or induce fair competition proved to be a relatively satisfactory basis for some aspects of environmental legislation (water quality for example) which had a direct bearing on the economic activity of the Common Market and Article 100 was relied on in the early years to establish the Community environmental policy.

**11.2.7** For aspects without so direct a connection with the functioning of the market, Article 235 had to be used. A catch-all provision, this Article sanctions legislation where it is "necessary to attain in the course of the operation of the common market, one of the objectives of the Community," and where provision of the necessary powers is not made elsewhere in the Treaty. In a judgment in 1985 the European Court of Justice held that environmental protection was indeed an objective of the Treaty.[9]

**11.2.8** As indicated above, the Single European Act amendments introduced new Articles 130R–130T giving formal legislative recognition to environmental policy. Article 130R lays down the basic objectives of Community environmental policy as originally established following the 1972 Paris Summit. Paragraph (2) of the Article establishes the by now well known "Holy Trinity" of environmental principles, namely:

1. Taking preventative action.
2. Tackling pollution at source.
3. Making the polluter pay.

Even more importantly for the wider ambit of Community policy it requires that "environmental protection requirements shall be a component of the Community's other policies."

Articles 130R–130T accordingly provide a clear legal basis for **11.2.9**
legislation where the action proposed is specifically related to the
environment. It is still possible to base legislation on Article 100A
which reflects the original Article 100 of the Treaty in requiring
legislation to have as its objective "the establishment and functioning
of the internal market." The main distinction between the two has
been that under Article 100A, also added by the Single European
Act, proposed legislation can be adopted by a majority vote in the
Council whereas under 130S unanimous agreement is required.
Furthermore, (and it is in this respect that most friction has arisen) the
European Parliament has under Article 100A a considerable impact
on the process of approving legislation whereas under 130S the
Council is required only to consult the Parliament.

The Commission has tended to favour 100A given that it offers the **11.2.10**
Parliament considerable scope for involvement in the process of
legislation and emphasises the importance of Community law over
that of Member States. Conversely, the Council has supported the
basis provided by Article 130S as this gives Member States a greater
degree of control and offers less opportunity for the Parliament and
Commission to interfere.

This friction was brought to a head over the correct basis on which **11.2.11**
legislation was enacted to control pollution caused by waste from the
Titanium Dioxide industry. The significance of the Directive 89/428
was that it sought at one and the same time to protect the environment (for which Article 130R would be appropriate) and to harmonise
laws relating to this industry throughout the EC thus promoting the
internal market (for which Article 100A was designed). The European
Court ruled[10] that while such a dual objective would normally require
two directives to be issued (one under each article), Article 100A
could in fact embrace both aims whereas Article 130R was confined
to legislation with the sole purpose of protecting the environment and,
accordingly, Article 100A was the proper basis for the directive. The
principal result of this case (apart from the need to re-enact the
Titanium Dioxide Directive and other directives which have been
based on Article 130R) is that if the Commission can demonstrate
that the proposed new legislation is at least partly intended to avoid
unfair competition it can be based on Article 100A which, because of
the qualified majority voting requirement, will avoid the vetoing of the
measure by any one Member State.

The confusion surrounding the appropriate basis for the introduc- **11.2.12**
tion of new environmental legislation continued notwithstanding the

outcome of the "Titanium Dioxide" case. To a considerable extent the matter has been resolved by the terms of the Maastricht agreement reached in December 1991. Two aspects in particular should result in a further strengthening of the Community's environmental protection powers:

**11.2.13** Firstly, the restraint on unchecked economic development which the Single European Act applied to the objectives of the Rome Treaty has been tightened by an amendment to Article 130R to the effect that "environmental protection requirements must be integrated into the definition and implementation of other Community policies." In addition, the Community's objectives now require to include the promotion of "sustainable and non-inflationary growth respecting the Environment."

**11.2.14** Secondly, the principle of the adoption of environmental legislation by qualified majority voting has been extended to include all but a few areas of EC policy. Unanimous voting will still be required where there is a direct link to other policies which require unanimity, for example, in respect of fiscal measures (including the carbon tax proposals—see para. 11.5.23), town and country planning and the supply of energy.

**11.2.15** The European Parliament's powers in relation to environmental issues have been further strengthened by these developments. By and large, however, the only remaining area where the Parliament will have an explicit right of veto will be over the Community's Environmental Action Programmes.

[The future of the Maastricht agreement has been put in doubt by the result of the Danish referendum rejecting its ratification—*Editor*.]

INCORPORATION INTO UNITED KINGDOM LAW

**11.2.16** The European Communities Act 1972 provides the legal basis for incorporation of EC law into that of the United Kingdom. Section 2(1) enacts in very wide terms that all rights, powers, liabilities and restrictions under the Treaties and all remedies and procedures provided by them are *without further enactment* to be given legal effect to in the United Kingdom. This means that any rights and liabilities which under EC law have immediate effect in the United Kingdom (*e.g.* regulations and directives with direct effect) have to be recognised by our national courts.

Apart from the few areas of environmental policy enacted by **11.2.17**
regulation[11] the impact of EC environmental legislation on United
Kingdom law is not immediately obvious and yet it has had (and is
increasingly having) a profound influence. Apart from direct compliance with directives through enactment of United Kingdom statutes, implementation is often achieved by means of statutory
instruments or other forms of subordinate legislation or merely by
administrative action on the part of central Government departments
advising the regulatory bodies on action to be taken.

There is no better example of the influence of EC aspects on the **11.2.18**
framing of national environmental policy than the Environmental
Protection Act 1990. Many of the provisions of Part I on, *inter alia*
integrated pollution control have been included to achieve compliance with the Air Framework Directive and the Large Combustion
Plants Directive.[12] Throughout the Act there are requirements for
information to be made publicly available—a direct response to the
Freedom of Environmental Information Directive.[13]

## THE INSTITUTIONS OF THE EUROPEAN COMMUNITY

For many who will read this *Guide*, the Institutions of the EC will be **11.3.1**
familiar territory. For those for whom European Community law was
not an integral part of law studies or general knowledge, a brief
résumé may be of assistance.

### The Commission

The Commission is the starting-off point for all community legisla- **11.3.2**
tion and it is in effect the Community's "civil service." At its head is
the President and there are currently 17 Commissioners who are
appointed by the national governments and who are responsible for
the work of one or more of the 23 Directorates-General, including DG
XI which deals with the environment. The principal functions of the
Commission are, firstly, to initiate legislation arising from proposals
made by the appropriate Commissioner and, secondly, to monitor
and enforce implementation of and compliance with existing legislation by Member States as part of its overall task as guardian of the EC
Treaties.

## The Council of Ministers

**11.3.3**   The Council is made up of one Minister from each of the Member States, headed by a Presidency which rotates every six months. It debates proposals for legislation submitted to it by the Commission and can adopt, amend or reject any proposal put to it. If national differences are likely to emerge at any point in the process of Community law-making then it is within the Council that they will be most sharply focused. The dichotomy between the narrower interests of the Member States and the greater good of the Community is reflected in the requirement that the Council in its deliberations should seek the highest common denominator as between the Community and the Member States. Depending on the basis for action adopted for proposed legislation, voting in the Council requires to be either unanimous or by qualified majority.[14]

## The European Parliament

**11.3.4**   Members of the European Parliament are directly elected by the citizens of each Member State but strictly speaking, the Parliament is not a legislative body. Although its powers of supervision over the Commission were increased by the Single European Act, its main function is as a consultative link in the process and formulation of laws. Its opinion must be sought by the Commission and Council before any proposed legislation can be adopted. The Single European Act by introducing what is known as the "Co-operation Procedure" further increases Parliament's influence over the Council's legislative powers.[15] Parliament now has the right to reject or amend proposals on which the Commission and the Council have adopted a "common position." Accordingly, those matters initially subject to qualified majority voting may thereafter require unanimous approval from Council before they can be adopted. The likelihood of co-operation from Parliament has now, therefore, to be taken into account when considering the facility (or otherwise) with which new environmental proposals can be expected to progress.

## European Court of Justice

**11.3.5**   The Court which is situated in Luxembourg and whose judges are appointed by national governments is the highest authority on matters of Community Law. It seeks to provide independent and consistent interpretation of EC legislation, undistracted by the influence of national courts who must follow its rulings. Decisions of the Court have considerable influence on the development of policy within the Community. One notable example in recent years has been the establishment at the hands of the Court of the doctrine of "direct effect" which will be referred to later.[16]

## The Economic and Social Committee

This is a consultative body whose opinion on proposals for new **11.3.6** legislation is sought by the Commission. Many of its members are technical experts and representatives of different industries, small businesses and general consumers. Particularly for environmental matters where the end results of new controls on industry and commerce are important, it has considerable influence.

IMPLEMENTATION OF ENVIRONMENTAL POLICY

## Legal Instruments

The principal types of instrument used to translate environmental **11.4.1** policy into legislation are the *regulation* and the *directive*. Article 189 of the Treaty of Rome provides also for the use of *decisions, recommendations* and *opinions* but these are seldom seen in the field of environmental policy, although the *decision* (which is binding in its entirety on those to whom it is addressed) has been used, mainly to implement international conventions.

The *regulation* introduces directly applicable law, that is, it requires **11.4.2** no legislation on the part of Member States to implement it and legal rights and responsibilities are created as soon as it is passed. *Directives* on the other hand are binding only in respect of the results to be achieved. National governments have freedom to determine how these results are to be obtained. They have less choice, however, as to the time of implementation, each directive having a set date for compliance.

The *directive* has tended to be the principal instrument for the **11.4.3** translation of environmental policy into law. This is partly because Article 100 (on which the majority of environmental policy has to date been based) specifies the *directive* as the means by which approximation of laws is to be achieved. Furthermore, there are few areas of environmental policy where an immediately binding and *uniform* result can be readily obtained, such is the variety of social, climatic and regulatory backgrounds pertaining throughout the Community.

**11.4.4** The *regulation*, which traditionally has tended to be used for such areas as agricultural policy where immediate implementation is essential, has also been used in the environmental field on one or two occasions. Regulation 3322/88 requires Community-wide action on the part of manufacturers to reduce CFC production by 50 per cent by the year 2000.[17] Another example is Regulation 1210/90 establishing the European Environmental Protection Agency. This will be brought into force once the Member States have agreed amongst themselves where its headquarters are to be situated!

**11.4.5** In the environmental field a "blurring" can be discerned in the distinction between regulations and directives arising out of the use made of the latter. Environmental controls increasingly require emission or discharge standards to be met and many directives are now framed to include details of limits and concentrations as well as provisions for monitoring and analysis to ensure that they will be adhered to. A directive containing such requirements which give the Member States comparatively little flexibility as to their application is much more akin to the *regulation* than a *framework directive* which, by definition, only establishes a broad outline, requiring for its complete implementation one or more subsidiary or *daughter directives*.

**The Doctrine of Direct Effect**

**11.4.6** Until comparatively recently, environmental policy enacted by directive has required national legislation to make available to individual citizens the rights and obligations under the policy it enacts. The European Court of Justice has, however, developed a doctrine resulting in such underlying rights and responsibilities being immediately enforceable before national courts. Hitherto, non-compliance with a directive has not been a matter which an individual citizen has been able to raise—it has been an issue to be resolved between the Commission and the Member State guilty of the infringement. Following the establishment in the last few years of what is known as the doctrine of "direct effect" it is now possible for an individual, or say an environmental pressure group in an action against the government (or a government agency) to rely on provisions of a directive even if they have not been implemented under the national law.

This doctrine, which is entirely judge-made, has been developed **11.4.7** over a number of years and is particularly appropriate to issues of environmental policy so much of which is enacted by directives. The doctrine was relied upon in a recent case in Scotland involving environmental assessment.[18]

There are two aspects which restrict the availability of the doctrine **11.4.8** of direct effect:

1. It cannot be invoked in respect of every provision of a directive. The obligation being relied upon must be "clear and unconditional" and so provisions according a Member State a large degree of discretion will not be accorded direct effect.[19]

2. It is not available as a remedy in cases where the parties to the dispute are both private individuals. One of the parties must be an "emanation of the State" which would, for Scotland, appear to include not only the obvious examples to the Scottish Office itself but also its Environment Department, local authorities, Her Majesty's Industrial Pollution Inspectorate, etc., and public corporations such as British Rail.[20]

## Compliance

A lack of consistent implementation and compliance in all Member **11.4.9** States has somewhat tarnished the image of EC law as an effective self-sufficient legal system. This is particularly so in the case of the environment. The general public's increasing concern with the quality of life itself ensures that delayed implementation and infringements will be accorded maximum publicity. The Commission, although aware of the problem, has not matched its enthusiasm for promoting environmental laws with any determination to enforce them. There has been an increasing number of cases before the European Court of Justice brought by the Commission for failure on the part of a Member State to translate European law into its own national system.[21] What is of much greater importance for the protection of the environment is the failure to ensure that the various technical standards, *e.g.* for air and water quality, are being met.

There are now indications, however, that the Commission intends **11.4.10** to grasp this particular nettle. A directive (91/689) requires Member States to lodge reports detailing standarised data in respect of a series of 30 or more directives and legislation is in place to establish a European Environment Agency to monitor compliance and co-ordinate the collection of data.[22] Furthermore, the Commission has proposed setting up a network of Environmental Inspectorates which it is hoped will ensure a more level playing field in environmental compliance by comparing experience and working practices. The United Kingdom Government has very recently proposed a refine-ment of this proposal in the form of a smaller and, hopefully, more effective Community Audit Inspectorate which would carry out regu-lar checks on the work of the various national enforcement bodies.

**Complaints Procedure**

**11.4.11**   It remains to be seen whether these initiatives produce any improvement in the record of compliance. As indicated above the only way of drawing attention to incomplete or inconsistent enforce-ment has been to persuade the Commission (if it has not already pursued the matter—the Commission is required by terms of Article 155 of the Treaty to ensure that Community law is observed) to commence infringement proceedings against the government of the transgressing Member State. Until recently, lobbying the Commission has been about the only way in which individual citizens can take practical steps to seek redress. However, a very recent case has established that (in some circumstances at least) any EC citizen may himself take his national government to the Court of Justice for non-implementation of EC laws and, indeed, may claim damages from the Member State for non-transportation of the directive into national law.[23]

**11.4.12**   There is an established complaints procedure which can be initiated by an individual, an association or a corporate body. Although a rather cumbersome and lengthy process, complaints will eventually be dealt with. Very few survive to the stage where the Member State is actually brought to Court. It is much more likely that the Commission will, during earlier stages in the complaint, bring pressure to bear on the Member State to comply. Even if the Commission's case is found by the Court to be justified there is no effective sanction that the Court can apply nor is there any redress available to a complainant who considers that the Commission has not fully dealt with his complaint, although there are suggestions that the Court may in future be given powers to impose financial penalties.

SPECIFIC ENVIRONMENTAL LEGISLATION

It is not possible in the space of one chapter to do more than to give **11.5.1**
a very brief outline of some of the specific areas of environmental
control for which there is legislation in force, in draft or still just
anticipated. Emphasis is given to the three principal media of water,
air and land (waste) with more brief comments on noise pollution and
the protection of wildlife and, finally, a brief reference to aspects of
publicity and economic control of environmental issues.

## Water

Control over pollution of water was one of the earliest areas of **11.5.2**
environmental concern, the first proposal in this respect being
introduced in 1973. The 25 or more directives that have since been
passed divide into two principal areas of protection: firstly, general
control over discharges to the aquatic environment and, secondly,
the setting of specific standards for the quality of water according to
its uses (for example bathing water and drinking water) and related
source controls, namely surface water, ground water, etc. In addition, an action programme concerning marine oil pollution has been
established.

The most significant legislation under the first branch is the **11.5.3**
Framework Directive on Substances Discharged into the Aquatic
Environment (76/464). This established a system of prior authorisation
for discharges of dangerous substances on the so called "Black" or
"Grey" lists and gave birth to a series of "daughter" directives setting
limit values on particular individual toxic substances, for example,
mercury, cadmium, dieldrin, hexachlorobenzene, etc. The United
Kingdom Red List (substances prescribed for prior authorisation
under Part I of the Environmental Protection Act 1990) is similar but
not identical to the Black List.[24]

EC policy on the discharge of dangerous substances has pro- **11.5.4**
ceeded along the dual approach of, on the one hand, setting
Community-wide limits for the maximum concentration of substances
that can be released and, on the other, establishing standards based
on the quality of the waters receiving the discharges. This twin-track
basis has given rise to considerable conflict in the past as the United
Kingdom has been the only Member State to support the latter
approach. The hiatus was, to some extent, resolved by the Framework Directive which gives priority to discharge standards but also

acknowledges the need for the receiving water quality test and this compromise has been repeated in some of the more recent derivative directives.

**11.5.5** In addition, measures have been taken to reduce damage to the aquatic environment by controlling the output from specific industries. The best known of these are the directives designed to limit the dumping at sea of ferrous sulphate waste from the Titanium Dioxide industry.[25]

**11.5.6** Of the directives setting quality objectives for different uses of water, those on Bathing Water (76/160) and on Drinking Water (80/778) are two which have attracted considerable attention in recent years as a result of the persistent failure of many of our designated beaches to meet the required standards and of the reporting of the United Kingdom government to the European Court for excessive nitrate and lead levels in drinking water, the affected supply points for the latter being mainly in Scotland.

**11.5.7** As far as future initiatives are concerned, the most important is, without doubt, the Directive on Municipal Waste Water Treatment (91/271). This will require the secondary treatment of most sewage discharges with additional restrictions for outfalls in particularly sensitive areas. Directive 90/415 (requiring standards to be met from 1993 onwards) is a further derivative of the Framework Directive and applies the same twin-track approach to other dangerous substances, *e.g.* trichlorobenzene.

**Air**

**11.5.8** Control over atmospheric emissions is probably the sector of European environmental policy which has received the most publicity. The problems of acid rain, global warming and ozone depletion feature prominently in any research into those aspects of environmental damage giving most cause for concern. Initially the policy was to legislate to protect human health but more recent directives recognise the need to have regard to the wider environment. There are many directives controlling air pollution, several of which interact and overlap but, essentially, they fall into three main groups: those setting quality standards for different products, those dealing with air quality standards for specific gases and those controlling emissions from vehicles and industrial plants.

**11.5.9** In the first of these appear some of the earliest initiatives. A 1975 directive (75/716) fixed the maximum sulphur content of gas oils and one of 1978 (78/611) set limits on the lead content of petrol. A later directive (85/210) was adopted in which the emphasis is on the promotion and availability of unleaded petrol as distinct from preventing the distortion of trade in petrol (and motor vehicles) from differing limits on lead concentration.

Air quality standards for sulphur dioxide and suspended particu- **11.5.10** lates (smoke) were set in 1980 (80/779) and for nitrogen dioxide in 1985 (85/203), the latter considered to be one of the main constituents of acid rain. The concentration of lead in the air is dealt with by a 1982 directive (82/884).

Chlorofluorocarbons (CFCs) are not air pollutants in the traditional **11.5.11** sense in that they are non-toxic and not directly injurious to human health. However, the damage they cause to the upper atmosphere ozone layer now seems incontrovertible. Two Decisions in 1980 (80/372)[26] and 1982 (82/795)[27] limiting the production of CFCs and reducing their use in aerosols were followed by the Community's signing of the Montreal Convention in 1988 (implemented by Regulation 3322/88), imposing a commitment to a 50 per cent reduction in the use of CFCs by the year 2000. This was further strengthened in 1989 by the Council resolving to call for a total ban on most CFCs by the same date.

There has been a series of directives on measures to be taken to **11.5.12** reduce air pollution from motor vehicle engines, both petrol and diesel.[28] As well as the moves to reduce damage caused by lead in petrol (the "clean car" initiatives requiring, for example, all new cars to run on lead free petrol by specified dates) limit values for other exhaust gases such as carbon monoxide, nitrogen oxide and unburnt hydrocarbons have been set and standards for private diesel cars were laid down in 1988.

Alarm over the damage being caused to the forests of Germany **11.5.13** and Scandinavia resulted in the adoption of directives on combating air pollution from industrial plants. The 1984 Framework Directive (84/360) was a more general measure requiring certain categories of plant to have prior authorisation before being able to operate, while that of 1988 (88/609) limits the emission of sulphur dioxide and the nitrogen oxides from large combustion plants. It was the requirement to implement these two directives which was largely responsible for the enactment of Part I of the Environmental Protection Act 1990.

Future developments in EC control over air pollution (or existing **11.5.14** legislation yet to be fully implemented in the United Kingdom) include directives (89/369 and 89/429) on air pollution from municipal waste incinerators and proposals to limit particulate emissions from large diesel engined vehicles.

**Waste**

**11.5.15**  The EC estimates the annual production of waste throughout the Community to be 2,000,000 tonnes, with 150,000 tonnes emanating from industrial sources, 30,000 tonnes of which is of a hazardous nature. A shortage of sites for landfill disposal coupled with increasing concern regarding the movement of hazardous waste within the Community (especially following completion of the internal market) has resulted in an increasing number of legal measures on waste control. EC policy on waste is largely based on three precepts, namely concentration on the recycling of recoverable waste, reduction in the amount of waste produced and the proper management and disposal (including transport) of non-recoverable waste.

**11.5.16**  The waste Framework Directive (75/442) required Member States to take action in respect of household and toxic waste in these general areas, including the preparation of plans for waste disposal and recycling and the licensing of persons handling waste. "Daughter" directives stemming from 75/442 tightened the control over toxic waste (78/319) and polychlorinated biphenyls (PCBs) (76/403). A new Framework Directive (91/156) with a compliance date of April 1, 1993 which will replace much of 75/442 redefines and strengthens many of the earlier measures and lays particular emphasis on Member States (and thus the Community at large) achieving self-sufficiency in the disposal of waste.

**11.5.17**  The increasing problem of the trans-frontier shipment of hazardous waste and its effective disposal has prompted several directives following the outline directive in 1978 on toxic waste (78/319) which made no provision for the transport of waste between Member (and Non Member) States. This was rectified by the 1984 Directive (84/631) which established a system of monitoring and control based on the consignment note procedure and introduced requirements for labelling and packaging of waste. The directive was later adapted and amended on several occasions and it is now likely to be replaced by a new proposed directive which will redefine hazardous waste and set up a licensing system for recycling plants.

Other measures related to the issue of waste reduction and its safe **11.5.18**
disposal include:
1. A directive (91/157) restricting the marketing of batteries.
   This will come into force between September 1992 and
   January 1994 and will also require national plans to be drawn
   up for the collection and recycling of waste batteries.
2. A proposed directive on landfill of waste setting design
   standards and establishing controls over monitoring of landfill
   gas and providing for aftercare and restoration.
3. A draft proposal for a directive on packaging to replace the
   ill-fated 1985 Directive on Beverage Containers which,
   largely as a result of the Danish Bottle Case[29] was accepted
   as being virtually unworkable.
4. A draft directive has been prepared on civil liability for
   damage caused by waste.[30] The draft which has now been
   amended several times would impose strict, joint and several, liability on producers of waste for damage to persons
   and property and "impairment to the environment."[31] At the
   time of writing, progress with the directive has come to a halt.
   It may be withdrawn and, in addition, the Commission is now
   considering various radical new measures which would
   include civil liability for general environmental damage.

**Noise Pollution**

Pollution from noise (both in the workplace and from different vehicles **11.5.19**
and appliances) is not an area of environmental control that springs as
readily to mind as, say, that of air or water pollution and yet is one which
will be of increasing concern. The concept of harm to man's senses is
an important expansion to the traditional definition of environmental
pollution. To date, the Commission has tackled the problem of noise
pollution from the standpoint of the levels of noise emitted by different
products, attempting to ensure that free circulation of goods is not
inhibited by varying standards applied in different Member States.
Accordingly, maximum noise levels for aircraft, four-wheeled vehicles
(including tractors), motor cycles, lawnmowers and even household
appliances have been laid down by a series of directives.[32] It may well
be that the Commission will progress to considering the problem of
general noise quality as an integral component of environmental
protection. The Directive on the Protection of Workers from the Risk of

Noise in the Workplace (86/188) could perhaps be regarded as a move in that direction although based on the Community's social, rather than strictly environmental programme.

## Protection of Wildlife and Countryside

**11.5.20**    In contrast to the preceding section, this is an area of EC endeavour which has attracted much public interest and support and one where European environmental policy is closely linked to action at the international level. Fauna, particularly migratory wild birds and marine mammals such as whales, seals, etc., are no respecters of national boundaries and several important treaties and directives have been issued with a view to regulating numbers, protecting habitats and prohibiting trade in those species most at risk of extinction.

**11.5.21**    The Directive on Conservation of Wild Birds (79/409) is one of the most important landmarks in the development of this aspect of EC environmental policy. It was enacted as a direct result of public outcry at the indiscriminate killing and capturing (in several of the Community's Member States) of migrating wild birds and it lays down rules not only for the overall protection of many species but also regulates methods of hunting and the preservation of habitats. The Commission's determination to enforce this measure has been demonstrated on several occasions, one notable Scottish example being the priority accorded to the protection of wild geese at Duich Moss in Islay over the competing interests of the whisky industry.

## Publicity and Economic Control

**11.5.22**    If market forces are to play their part along with legislative regulation in implementing the environmental policy of the European Community, it is essential that the public be given comprehensive access to information on environmental matters to enable informed choices to be made including, for example, the initiating of action to bring to heel regulatory agencies who are deemed to have been lax in enforcement. The Freedom of Environmental Information Directive 90/313 and the proposed Regulation on Environmental Auditing are both designed to meet this objective at the individual and industry level while the Regulation (1210/90) setting up the European Environmental Agency is intended to allow the dissemination and exchange of environmental knowledge between Member States.

## Conclusion

In the longer term, the Commission has also been considering the **11.5.23** use of economic and fiscal measures as a method of achieving some degree of harmony between economic growth and environmental protection. Pollution taxes on carbon dioxide and other gases, deposit refund schemes and tradeable emission permits are all areas which may expect considerable future attention from the Community.

## CONCLUSION

As this short review has hopefully shown, European Community **11.6.1** environmental law is of considerable scope, diversity and importance for the future of the Community. Its effectiveness is subject to the same shortcomings in terms of compliance and enforcement as are found with our own national system. Nevertheless, there is no denying that its development as a system of laws separate from but interacting with those of its Member States has resulted in considerable achievements in the field of environmental protection and it will continue to be a critical element in the functioning and future refinement of the new internal market.

For those with an interest in or actively practising environmental **11.6.2** law in Scotland, knowledge of European environmental law and policy is essential. This is not merely because it is part of and prevails over our national law and requires to be brought into the equation when interpreting "local" provisions. More importantly, as the full measure of damage to planet Earth becomes clear, as environmental issues assume increasing importance internationally and as the costs of responding to environmental liability mount, commerce and industry will require to include environmental aspects in their longer term strategic planning. Given the political importance of the European Community in the world order and the willingness of the Commission (unhindered by electoral considerations) to propose radical solutions, it is to Brussels that lawyers (who in the environmental field will have to become increasingly anticipative in their advice) will look for the majority of new environmental legal initiatives.

### Further Reading

S. Ball and S. Bell: *Environmental Law*, Chapter 4 (London, 1990, Blackstone).

N. Haigh: *EEC Environmental Policy and Britain* (2nd revised ed.) (London, 1990, Longman).

S. P. Johnson & G. Corcelle: *The Environmental Policy of the European Communities* (London, 1989, Graham & Trotman).

L. Krämer: *EEC Treaty and Environmental Protection* (London, 1990, Sweet & Maxwell).

NOTES

1 O.J. 87/C 328.
2 *Litster* v. *Forth Dry Dock & Engineering Company Limited*, 1989 S.L.T. 540.
3 *Kincardine & Deeside District Council* v. *Forestry Commissioners*, 1991 S.C.L.R. 729; see commentary by C. T. Reid and J. B. Hunter in 1991 S.L.T. (News) 274.
4 Meeting of Heads of State and of Government of the Enlarged Community (Paris, October 1972) (Cmnd. 15109).
5 O.J. 73/C 112.
6 O.J. 77/C 139.
7 O.J. 83/C 46.
8 O.J. 87/C 328.
9 *Procureur de la République* v. *Association de défense des brûleurs d'huiles usagées* (240/83) [1985] E.C.R. 531.
10 *EC Commission* v. *EC Council* (300/89) ECJ, June 11, 1991 (*The Times*, August 21, 1991)
11 See paras. 11.4.2, 11.4.4.
12 See para. 11.5.13.
13 Directive 90/313; see para. 11.5.22.
14 See paras. 11.2.9–11.2.14.
15 EEC Treaty, Art. 149(2) (as added by Single European Act).
16 See paras. 11.4.6 *et seq.*
17 See also para. 11.5.11.
18 *Kincardine and Deeside District Council* v. *Forestry Commissioners* (see Note 2 above).
19 *Becker* v. *Finanzamt Münster—Innenstadt* (8/81) [1982] E.C.R. 53.
20 *Marshall* v. *Southampton and South-West Hampshire Area Health Authority (Teaching)* (152/84) [1986] E.C.R. 723, [1986] Q.B. 401; *Foster* v. *British Gas* (188/89) [1991] Q.B. 405.
21 There are many examples involving most of the Community Member States. A representative sample includes: *Commission* v. *Germany* (361/88) (ECJ, May 30, 1991) for failure to implement Directive 80/779 on air quality values for sulphur dioxide; *Commission* v. *United Kingdom* (Case 56/90) (pending) for failure to implement Directive 76/160 concerning

bathing water quality; *Commission* v. *Spain* (Case 355/90) (pending) for failure to implement Directive 79/409 concerning conservation of wild birds.

[22] Council Regulation 1210/90/EEC.

[23] *Francovich and Others* v. *Italian Republic* (6/90, 9/90) E.C.J. November 9, 1991.

[24] See para. 5.3.2.

[25] 78/176; 83/29; 82/883 and 89/428. Following the annulment of 89/428 by the European Court of Justice a new draft directive has very recently been issued (O.J. 91/C 317/06).

[26] Council Decision 80/372 concerning chlorofluorocarbons in the environment (March 26, 1980) O.J. 80/L 90/45.

[27] Council Decision 82/795 on the consolidation of precautionary measures concerning fluorocarbons in the environment (November 15, 1982) O.J. 82/L 329/29.

[28] See paras. 2.9.1 *et seq.*

[29] *Commission* v. *Denmark* (302/86) [1988] E.C.R. 4607.

[30] Initial proposal O.J. 89/C 251/3, revised O.J. 91/C 192/6.

[31] See para. 8.3.4.

[32] 89/629 (Aircraft); 74/151 (Tractors); 84/538 (Lawnmowers) and 86/594 (Household Appliances) (see para. 7.4.16).

# Index

# Index